MOTHER OF THE BUDDHAS
Meditation on the Prajnaparamita Sutra

LEX HIXON

D1287739

MOTHER OF THE BUDDHAS
Meditation on the Prajnaparamita Sutra

LEX HIXON

A publication supported by
THE KERN FOUNDATION

Quest Books
Theosophical Publishing House

Wheaton, Illinois ◆ Chennai (Madras), India

Quest Books
Theosophical Publishing House
PO Box 270
Wheaton, Illinois 60187-0270

www.questbooks.com

Cover image: Prajnaparamita, The Goddess of Transcendental
Wisdom, c. 1300 East Java, from Candi Singasri, andestite.
Museum Nasional, Jakarta.

Library of Congress Cataloging-in-Publication Data

Hixon, Lex.
Mother of the Buddhas: meditation on the Prajnaparamita Sutra/
Lex Hixon.
    p.   cm.
Includes Astasahasrika in English.
Includes index.
ISBN 978-0-8356-0689-9
1. Tripitaka. Sutrapitaka. Prajnaparamita. Astasahasrika-Paraphrases,
English. I. Tripitaka. Sutrapitaka. Prajnaparamita. Astasahasrika.
English. II. Title.
BQ1912.E5H59 1993
294.3'85—dc20   92-56485
                                                   CIP

Printed in the United States of America

For Vajra Holder
Ngawang Gyaltan Jigme Chöki Wangchuk

CONTENTS

PART III
PRACTICE

FOREWORD

THE *Great 25,000 Verse Prajnaparamita Sutra,* one of the longer versions of the main text that Lex Hixon has put before us as *Mother of the Buddhas,* begins with an extraordinary event. The Buddha performs a miracle that creates a cosmic setting for the teaching of transcendent wisdom, or Prajnaparamita. It is essential to quote it at sufficient length to transmit a flash of this visionary happening.

Thus I once heard. The Lord dwelt on the Vulture Peak at Rajagriha with a large gathering. He sat down cross-legged on His lion throne, and entered the "King Samadhi," the samadhi which contains, encompasses, combines all samadhis. His whole body became radiant. The thousand-spoked wheels on the soles of his feet shone forth sixty hundred thousand trillions of billions of light rays, as did every other part of his superhuman body. These light rays illumined and lit up our vast billion-world universe, lighting up worlds in the East, South, West, North, Southeast, Southwest, Northwest, Northeast, Zenith and Nadir. And all the beings lit up and illuminated by these dazzling light rays became focused upon the unexcelled, true and perfect enlightenment.

Thereupon on that occasion the Lord put out his tongue. With it he covered this entire billion-world universe, and it shone forth many hundreds of thousands of billions of trillions of light rays. Each one of these light rays turned into thousand-petaled golden lotuses, made of the finest jewel substance. On these lotuses were Buddha-emanations giving teachings, this very teaching of the truth of the six transcendent Perfections. And the beings who heard these true teachings became all the more focused on unexcelled, true, perfect enlightenment.

Thereupon the Lord, seated there on His lion throne, entered the samadhi "Lion Play." With His miraculous power, He shook this vast billion-world universe in six ways. It became soft and pliable and all beings came to be at ease. The hells, the underworlds, and the animal realms were abolished and became empty, and all places of horrible rebirth disappeared. And all beings deceasing from these states, with joy and jubilation, were reborn among men, and also among the six kinds of gods of the desire realms throughout this billion-world universe, beings born blind saw forms, the deaf heard sounds, the insane regained their consciousness, the distracted became concentrated, the hungry were fed, the thirsty were satisfied, the sick were healed, and the cripples were made whole.

The passage continues with a vision of the Buddha's Body of Glory, given to the beings in all the worlds of the universes. They were enraptured with such beauty, all of them beholding the others beholding the Buddha in his glory, and yet each one feeling as if the Buddha were present just before him or her, as if he were there solely to give the blessing and the teaching to him or her personally.

The Buddha manifests this extraordinary environment in order to teach the transcendent wisdom, both the Sutra and the Enlightenment it accesses, known as the Mother of all Buddhas. It is important for us to envision this setting to develop a state of inspiration and focus to make most practical use of the teachings of the text.

The *Prajnaparamita* is considered the originating text of the Mahayana, the Universal, or Messianic vehicle of Buddhism. Western and Buddhist scholars agree that it began to emerge into prominence in India from about 100 years B.C.E. (Before the Common Era), about

400 years after the Final Nirvana of Shakyamuni Buddha in around 483 B.C.E. Western scholars consider that it was composed by the Indian Buddhists of that era, yet attributed to Shakyamuni Buddha as deriving from his mystical inspiration. Traditional Mahayana Buddhist scholars consider that the Sutra actually records the messianic teachings of the Buddha himself, though these texts were taken away from the human realm by Gods and Dragons and recovered only after four centuries. This temporary hiding of the teaching is believed to have been prophesied by the Buddha himself. He considered that the developing societies of his time in India needed four hundred years of preparation and purification by the monastic education and renunciative ethic he taught more openly, as recorded in the Pali Suttas foundational in the Monastic, or Individual vehicle of Buddhism. A people still rough and violent might otherwise have misappropriated the messianic intensity of the Transcendent Wisdom and other universalist Sutras, using it to legitimate crusades and other campaigns of conquest. Only a people with deeds tamed by the ethic of nonviolence, minds focused by the discipline of meditation and intellects cultivated by the education in critical wisdom could be safely entrusted with the profound liberation of the teaching of voidness and the magnificent energization of the vision of the jeweline Buddhaverse. Or as Western scholars might prefer to put it, the Indian Buddhists of 100 B.C.E. were tired of monastic restraint and purity and longed for a social gospel of love and compassion, to go along with their burgeoning, universalizing civilization.

There was a young bodhisattva, or messianic hero, Priyadarshana, who dwelt in the city of Vaishali in the Licchavi kingdom during the Buddha's time. He was a student of the great lay sage Vimalakirti, and he attained a high level of wisdom during Vimalakirti's famous session on nonduality, as recounted in the *Holy Teaching of Vimalakirti Sutra*. The Buddha subsequently predicted that this young man would be reborn in South India four hundred years later and would be recognized by the word *naga* (dragon) in his name.

Sure enough, a great master known as Nagarjuna emerged in South
India in the first century B.C.E., passing away at the ripe old age of
six hundred plus in the fifth century C.E. (Western scholars date him
in the second century C.E. and attribute Nagarjuna's deeds of other
eras to other masters with the same name.) The legend goes that
Nagarjuna was approached by *nagas* (dragons) in human form after
one of his lectures at the monastery of Nalanda. They invited him
to their undersea kingdom to see some texts they thought would
be of great interest to him. He went with them magically under the
sea and discovered a vast treasure trove of the Mahayana Sutras—
not only the many versions of the *Prajnaparamita* but also the
Inconceivable Liberation, the *Jewel Heap*, the *Lotus*, and the *Pure Land*
Sutras. Nagarjuna spent fifty earth years studying these texts, and
then he brought them back into human society and promulgated
them throughout India.

He later wrote under his own authorship the masterwork *Wisdom:
The Root Verses of the Central Way*, in which he elaborated a systematic program of critical meditations that lead the practitioner
into the understanding and samadhi of emptiness and relativity. He
wrote other philosophical, meditational and ethical works over the
next centuries, until going away with the *nagas* a second time, this
time to the "Northern Continent," Uttarakuru (maybe what we now
call *America*). There he discovered other treasured teachings and
taught the local populations many spiritual and practical things.
When he returned to India for the last time, he taught the Unexcelled Yoga Tantras, especially the *Esoteric Communion*, founding
the seminal "Noble" tradition of the practice of perfection stage yoga.
His Tantric great adept persona is also essentially included in the
semi-esoteric "direct mind transmission" tradition known as Ch'an
and Zen in East Asia. Overall, Nagarjuna is associated with the angelic
bodhisattva Manjushri, the archetype of transcendent wisdom, and
is considered the pioneer of the wisdom teachings in the human
realm.

The original *Prajnaparamita* is the text called the *Great Mother: the Prajnaparamita of 100,000 Lines.* It purports to record the full audience given by Shakyamuni Buddha on Vulture Peak with the greatest explicitness and completeness, though even it falls short of a full record, which would have run to many hundreds of thousands, perhaps millions of lines. Over the centuries various abridged versions have emerged, including the very short *One Letter Sutra*, (the letter *A*), the short *Heart Sutra*, the concise *Diamond-cutting Sutra*, the *8,000 Line*, the *18,000* or *20,000 Line*, and the *25,000 Line Sutras*, from a total of eighteen Sutras. These are all considered the same Sutra, differing only in length and detail, never in basic import. Among them, the *8,000 Line* version, on which Lex Hixon's meditations are based, is very highly regarded in all Mahayana traditions, although traditional Buddhist scholars do not consider it the oldest or "Ur" text, as some modern scholars do.

These perfect wisdom texts served as the foundation for a systematic curriculum developed over many centuries in the Mahayana Buddhist monastic universities, among the earliest universities on this planet. This curriculum involved three phases. There was first a phase of memorization of the basic *Prajnaparamita* texts, as well as of the systematic updated interpretations that made the text live anew for succeeding generations. The second phase required formal debating practice with masters and other student-practitioners. The ideas of the *Perfect Wisdom* are not merely dogmas that became effective by being grasped and held with rigid conviction. They are liberating thoughtways that launch the understanding beyond its constricting cultural and even instinctual preconditioning. To serve as such, they must be deeply and critically investigated. They must help one to doubt every familiar supposed known thing, to open ever deeper realms of knowledge. Before one's internal debate of critical inquiry can become intense, it is necessary to debate publicly with others, to learn to move around in the public mind revealed in open discourse. Finally, the third phase requires concentrated meditation, an intensely disciplined focus on the new avenues of understanding opened up by the critical uncovering of freedom from intrinsic realities, intrinsic objectivities and intrinsic identities in self and things, in relatives and absolutes, in bondages and liberations. With the successful completion of this third phase, the scholar-practitioner in this ancient curriculum would graduate, sometimes, as in the case of the immortal Shantideva (seventh century), literally floating out of the monastery to continue his bodhisattva career of working for the liberation of all beings and the transformation of the entire universe.

This ancient curriculum opened the minds of millions of practitioners for a thousand years in India. Around 1000 C.E., it was transferred to the Tibetan monastic universities and six hundred years later to the Mongolian institutions, wherein it has flourished until the present day. The recent destruction of Mongolian and Tibetan civilizations by Russian and Chinese communist invasions has severely restricted the number of practitioners who have access to the curriculum. About fifteen thousand Tibetan monks in monastic universities rebuilt in India and the Himalayan countries are the last practitioners of this transformative spiritual curriculum of Prajnaparamita education.

In East Asia, it seems clear that Prajnaparamita served as the basis of the Ch'an and Zen traditions. Some might think this controversial, since Ch'an tends to refer to itself as the "Sutra-less tradition," in contrast with the T'ien T'ai school based on the *Lotus Sutra*, the Hua Yen school based on the *Garland Sutra*, and the Pure Land school based on the *Land of Bliss Sutra*. But the *Prajnaparamita Sutra* refers to itself as the "teaching that is no teaching," its understanding as the "understanding by way of nonunderstanding," its attainment as "attained by not attaining," and so on and on. The bottom line is that perfect wisdom is the direct teaching of the highest enlightenment of all the Buddhas, radical, uncompromising, emphasizing absolute reality over relative reality, the definitive meaning-teaching over all interpretable meaning-teachings. The Ch'an tradition claims

Nagarjuna and Aryadeva, among other illustrious central way masters, as patriarchs of their direct mind-to-mind transmission, the tradition that "piles up snow in a silver bowl," the transmission of the "truth that has never been spoken." The famous Sixth patriarch of Ch'an in China, Hui Neng, recalled his own perfect wisdom upon a single hearing of the *Diamond-cutting* version of the *Prajnaparamita*.

So the *Sutra* is also a natural foundation for the mainstream East Asian enlightenment curriculum of profound study of the puzzling sayings and doings of past masters of perfect wisdom, hair-raising intellectual combat with the spiritual master to deepen doubt and refine critical insight, and prolonged, life-devoted concentrative meditation. Nowadays Ch'an or Zen has become an important part of American Buddhist discipline. It is time that a live practitioner's version of Prajnaparamita should be available to go along with it.

All versions of these *Perfect Wisdom Sutras* are considered holy "matrices" or indices for the attainment of perfect wisdom. They make possible the truly meaningful use of a human lifetime, in devoting it to evolutionary education in perfect wisdom. This transcendent learning can lead one to the security that there will never be another lifetime lost in egocentric delusion and suffering, that there will be no loss of the human exaltation, and that the future continuity will be an infinite expanse of freedom, happiness, love and artful creativity in sharing liberation with numberless associates. The *Perfect Wisdom Sutras* are thus revered as accomplishing the impossible, expressing the inexpressible, and making trans-verbal enlightened reality accessible to the verbally cultivated mind. They constantly deconstruct themselves as they go along, proclaiming that their teaching is not a teaching at all, that there is no attainment, no attainer, no understanding, no understander, but, importantly, no nonattainer, nor nonunderstander either.

Prajnaparamita thus leaves immense room for creative reinterpretation. Indeed, it demands constant reinterpretation for the sake of new generations. It is a mother overflowing with kindness, opening her arms to all her innumerable children. And she is a very exacting mother, fiercely determined that no harm befall her children from any sort of error or misunderstanding. It is a serious fault to mistake the "teachingless teaching" for mere meaningless verbiage without coherent logic, as merely rubbing in a message of nihilism *ad nauseam.* This error is not condoned by the caring mother, since it injures the spirits of her children and can ruin their many lives. It blocks their evolution by crippling their intelligence. It dulls the razor's edge of wisdom's sword that must cut away confusion and free the practitioner's genius from entrapment in habitual misperceptions.

Most English versions of *Prajnaparamita* up to now have been marred by such basic preconceptions of nihilism on the part of their translators. Some of them have been great linguistic scholars, well versed in many languages and painstaking in their critical perusal of the various editions in various languages. The late Edward Conze, an eminent scholar and translator, is most notable for his erudition and for his heroic efforts of a lifetime in working on the *Prajnaparamita.* It is his work that provided the linguistic basis for Lex Hixon's meditations below. Yet Conze did not himself practice the yoga of transcending wisdom, and he was somewhat skeptical about its "mystical" message. Only late in his life did he encounter the great Japanese scholar and meditation master, D. T. Suzuki, who helped him change his attitude to one of greater reverence to the *Great Mother of All the Buddhas.* But this was too late to transform his whole oeuvre of translation. He never found the liberating logic of what might superficially appear to be meaningless paradoxes or irreconcilable contradictions. His translations thus resemble cookbooks full of recipes translated with a dictionary by someone who has no idea what the foods and spices are, who has never cooked or never eaten such a meal. I have assigned his translations to classes of students, decade after decade, with the invariable result that they feel confused, mystified, and shut out of the real message of the text. Once

I translate it for them in lectures, they become more appreciative. Mr. Conze's works have value mainly as pioneer studies. *Prajnaparamita* still cries out for a completely revised presentation.

When I read Lex Hixon's *Mother of the Buddhas,* I was amazed to discover in his eloquent meditations a beginning for the real translation of the *Prajnaparamita.* He has relied on past translations, without systematically consulting Sanskrit or Tibetan texts. He does not pretend to be presenting an exercise in erudition. Hixon does, however, bring an essential scholarly understanding. From his own studies and practice of the perfect wisdom curriculum, he possesses an effective lever of understanding with which to pry away the rock that has been blocking the treasure cave of the text of perfect wisdom. He has studied and understood the revelatory teaching of voidness-relativity left to us in the writings of the great Tibetan genius, Tsong Khapa Lo Sang Drakpa (1357-1419). Tsong Khapa reinterpreted and revitalized the perfect wisdom insight so masterfully, he came to be regarded by millions of followers over centuries as a living incarnation of the bodhisattva Manjushri. The essence of his insight was that voidness does not mean nothingness, but rather that all things lack intrinsic reality, intrinsic objectivity, intrinsic identity or intrinsic referentiality. Lacking such static essence or substance does not make them not exist—it makes them thoroughly relative. Once they are so thoroughly relative, there is no limit to their being creatively reshaped by enlightened love. So the *via negativa* of the *Prajnaparamita* does not annihilate things; it frees them from entrapment in negativity, opening them up to a creative relativity.

This insight enabled Hixon not to fall for the simplistic misinterpretation of critical wisdom as nihilistic dialectics. Hixon has approached the text with reverence, as a scholarly intellectual and a spiritual practitioner. He has allowed the Mother of Buddhas herself to speak through him. And she has done so, with eloquence and beauty. In the earlier versions, where the Sutra was thought to be reducing the world to a chaotic rubble, the exemplary story of the passionate bodhisattva Sadaprarudita, "Ever-Weeping," seemed completely out of place. The bodhisattva encountered Perfect Wisdom and felt the great relief of freedom from subjective and objective self-habits. His joy and gratitude knew no bounds, and the story relates how he went to great lengths to requite the kindness of his teacher and express his adoration of the Great Mother of All Enlightened Ones. Once we know that his profuse tears of joy and love well up from the wisdom teaching, from his realization that voidness frees all things from being pinned down and frozen into static and inadequate forms by our habitual misconceptions and misperceptions, the ecstatic behavior of the bodhisattva becomes quite natural, though no less astonishing.

Lex Hixon must be a modern incarnation of Sadaprarudita, though he usually expresses his ecstatic vision not by weeping but in a cheerful mode. He spends his time revitalizing the classics of world religions, meditating on them to make them alive and relevant to the rest of us, rather than building a stupa or an organization. He shares the same sense of gratitude expressed by the bodhisattva Sadaprarudita toward the teachings he has received. And he has a genius for sharing his appreciation with a heartfelt eloquence that makes us look again at what we thought we already knew. I am grateful to him for these inspired meditations on a text that remains foundational in my own intellectual and spiritual architecture. I pray to Mother Prajnaparamita that these pages may shine her golden light on countless others, too.

Robert A. F. Thurman
Jay Tsong Khapa Professor
of Indo-Tibetan Studies,
Columbia University

Woodstock, New York
October, 1992

PART I

INTRODUCTION TO PRAJNAPARAMITA

MAHAYANA: THE GENTLE REVOLUTION

*M*AHAYANA is the compassionate and liberating illumination of our conventional universe through subjectless, objectless knowing. *Mother of the Buddhas* presents forty selections from the root scripture of Mahayana Buddhism, the *Prajnaparamita Sutra in 8,000 Lines*. This precious Sutra revealing the Bodhisattva Way has created spiritual cultures in India, Tibet, China, Mongolia, Korea and Japan, just as the Bible and the Quran have in Europe, Africa, the Middle East, Southeast Asia and the Americas.

Buddhism, Christianity and Islam are inherently expanding traditions, presenting Sutra, Bible and Quran to the entire globe. They are not culture-specific, yet neither do they sacrifice their integrity as they spread. Their teaching energy is generous and embracing, regardless of the historical distortions which inevitably arise. These three great traditions have become global presences, remaining very much alive and active in what we call the modern world—a realm which is not confined to the West but which is now springing up everywhere on the planet as the conjunction of technological advancement and democratic aspiration.

Through spiritually refined and scholarly Buddhist teachers, who arrived both as visitors and immigrants to North America, first from

3

Japan, and then from Tibet, Mongolia, Korea and China, Mahayana Buddhism has taken root in North American culture. A new generation of authentic Western Buddhist scholars, practitioners and teachers is now emerging. Mahayana has expanded into Canada, Europe and, more recently, Central and South America.

The Dalai Lama, exiled spiritual and temporal leader of Tibet, is the first Buddhist monk to receive the Nobel Prize for Peace. This planetary honor was conferred upon him in 1989 for upholding the Mahayana principles elucidated in this book. Practitioners of Mahayana Buddhism like the Dalai Lama spontaneously display a brilliant artfulness of compassionate action in order to awaken human beings, and indeed all living beings, into harmonious, loving interdependence or community.

The *Prajnaparamita Sutra* clearly describes the mature practitioner of Mahayana, the diamond being or *bodhisattva:*

> The bodhisattva will always maintain a motherly mind, consecrated to the constant protection, education and maturing of conscious beings, inviting and guiding them along the path of all-embracing love. This Mahayana mind never succumbs to fear, anxiety or depression and is never overwhelmed by the strange adventures of awareness in the three realms of relativity—mundane form, sublime form and formlessness.

To sustain this wonderful courage and compassion, the bodhisattva drinks the mother's milk of transcendent insight from the *Prajnaparamita Sutra*, for *Prajnaparamita is mother, creator, native ground and tender wet-nurse in omniscience for every past, present and future Buddha or Awakened One.* All conscious beings, including ourselves, are these future Buddhas, still evolving toward omniscience.

In Buddhist thought, *omniscience* refers not to some fantastic omnicomputation but to the subjectless, objectless knowing so cherished and revered by the Mahayana. This knowing is called *wisdom* or *transcendent insight into emptiness.* Such panoramic knowing unveils Reality, which is neither an entity nor a separate region, and which is without any substantial foundation. As the Sutra reveals:

> The unthinkably deep realization of the bodhisattva is to abide without abode, to dwell where no objective or subjective structures can dwell— without any underlying physical or metaphysical foundation. This spontaneous and foundationless dwelling in isolation from every abstract world view is of infinitely greater value than any religious teaching or contemplative experience.

Mother of the Buddhas is not a new translation of the *Prajnaparamita Sutra in 8,000 Lines* but a contemplative expansion of forty selected passages. The Sutra encourages not only the study, chanting and ceremonial veneration of its powerful text but also the commentarial expansion of its implications. My experience of expanding upon passages from this ancient scripture has convinced me that the Sutra is spiritually alive. Glimpses of the astonishing Buddhist world view and of the subtle refinements of Buddhist contemplative practice are constantly offered by the Sutra, which consists of delightful yet rigorous conversations between Lord Buddha and his illumined disciples Shariputra, Subhuti and Ananda, as well as Shakra, king of the heavenly realms and aspirant to Perfect Wisdom.

These timeless conversations about enlightenment, loosely gathered together as the *Prajnaparamita Sutra in 8,000 Lines,* are dramatized and clarified in the present rendition but have not been essentially changed. My version makes no claim to spiritual or scholarly authority. My special gratitude extends to two Western Buddhist scholars—Edward Conze, a pioneer in opening up these astonishing Prajnaparamita texts to the English-speaking reader, and Alex Wayman, whose translations of Tsongkhapa sensitized my view of voidness, or emptiness of self-existence.

I have selected these particular discourses and conversations from the Sutra in order to present the fullest spectrum of Buddhist teaching.

This volume can serve as a stimulating introduction to the Buddhist universe for students of religion and other thinkers, as well as a challenging study for contemplative practitioners, not just from Buddhism but from all sacred traditions. I offer this book to the bodhisattvas of all traditions whom I have encountered personally, glimpsing through their kindness the flash of nondual wisdom.

Although the *Prajnaparamita Sutra* provides essentially a religious rather than a philosophical, psychological or literary experience, I believe it will attract not only students of religion, meditation and esoteric knowledge but also thinkers who are secular or nontraditional, who practice humanism through art, science and social action. Mahayana teachings present important guidance to every seeker of truth, to every honest investigator of the nature of the universe and the mind. Mahayana Buddhism also proposes a model for any society or institution which purports to be truly humane.

Spiritual Lineage of Prajnaparamita

Emerging somewhat mysteriously around the first century of the Common Era, the revelatory Prajnaparamita literature signals a gentle revolution in Buddhist thinking, a vast maturing in the Buddhist mind and heart after five hundred years of intensive meditation and realization which followed the passing of the founder, Shakyamuni Buddha. The shockingly radical yet tenderly compassionate nature of the *Prajnaparamita Sutra in 8,000 Lines* is still evident to modern sensibilities. These teachings are fresh as a dew-covered flower—even now, after some two thousand years. This fact seems no less miraculous than the various flower rains and other cosmopoetic events described in the ancient text.

The *Prajnaparamita Sutra,* first and foremost, is revelation. Its heightened poetic and heart-melting devotional atmosphere, illuminated by free dialectical play among enlightened minds, far transcends the spheres of metaphysics and contemplative science as they had been understood and practiced by early Buddhist adepts. The unexpected, shocking and revolutionary nature of Perfect Wisdom is confirmed by the Sutra, which reports that some Buddhist practitioners actually walked out of assemblies where the Prajnaparamita teachings were being presented.

At the same time, one must note the extraordinary continuity between the many creative periods of Buddhist manifestation during its 2,500 years of recorded history. The Mahayana is a vast reservoir in which the uncompromising insight of early Theravada Buddhism is preserved and which contains in seed form the brilliant explosiveness of Deity Yoga and the radically nondualistic Mahamudra later expressed by Tantric Buddhism. The inner affinity between the *Prajnaparamita Sutra* and the later approaches of Mahamudra and Zen is particularly striking.

The greatest master of the Buddhist dialectical philosophy of enlightenment was Nagarjuna, who lived in India during the early centuries of the Common Era. He rooted his thought precisely here, in the rich soil of the *Prajnaparamita Sutra in 8,000 Lines*. His spiritual successors throughout the following centuries provided the spinal column for the most profound schools of Buddhist realizational philosophy—the contemplative existentialism that springs from the direct experience of Reality. Diverse lines of interpretation flow from Nagarjuna's *Mulamadhyamikakarika*, his exposition of the functioning of Perfect Wisdom, but these philosophical differences, significant as they are, do not arise in the *Prajnaparamita Sutra*, which is more primordial and multivalent than any philosophical system, no matter how intellectually brilliant or spiritually illuminated it may be.

The *Prajnaparamita Sutra* is revelation, not exposition. To immerse oneself in this Sutra is to swim in an ocean which is sometimes awesomely calm and other times filled with thunderous waves. These are the Sutra's two principle themes: its stillness is transcendent insight and its turbulence, a flood of overwhelming compassion. Wandering through the realmless realm of Prajnaparamita, we remain always surprised, even awestruck. Tears of joy gather in our eyes and other profound emotions stir the depth of our being.

Yet delightful companionship with Lord Buddha and his disciples, which this Sutra provides, does not release us from interpersonal, philosophical and meditational responsibilities. We must emerge from the ecstatic experience of the Sutra into more focused forms of service, study and practice. But we can never forget, even for an instant, the source of our nourishment and inspiration—the holy Sutra, the living body, speech and mind of the Buddha and the direct presence of Perfect Wisdom, Mother of the Buddhas. The *Prajnaparamita Sutra* is not just an external, historical text. It is a manifestation of the universal Buddha nature that courses through us as we contemplate this potent verbal icon of Awakened Enlightenment.

One of the more recent Chariots of Dharma who has valiantly and creatively carried on the line of Nagarjuna and his successors is Lama Tsongkhapa, a monastic yogi and teacher who lived in Tibet during the fourteenth century. Among the disciples of this master philosopher and meditational adept was the First Dalai Lama. Now that global civilization is enjoying the warm companionship of the Fourteenth Dalai Lama, we can sense more clearly the amazing transmission of Lama Tsongkhapa—six hundred years of reliable spiritual guidance, streaming like a fountain of nectar through thousands of fully evolved practitioners. Under this tutelage, men and women continue to reach the highest level of human possibility—gnostic awakening fused with selfless love.

Lama Tsongkhapa attained enlightenment at the age of forty, after engaging in intensive contemplative practice and scriptural study since childhood under some sixty great philosophical and meditational masters. The consummating insight occurred as he was reading a commentary by one of the principle successors in the line of Nagarjuna. The final truth was startling, the Lama tells us candidly in his auto-

biography, because it was precisely the opposite of what he had con-
cluded on the basis of his lifetime of study and contemplation.

What was this key reversal in Tsongkhapa's comprehension of Prajnaparamita? This question can be discussed adequately by advanced
scholars who are also masters of meditation. As beginners on the path,
we can sense only its general contours. Tsongkhapa's revelation
reestablished the primary role of loving compassion on all levels of
Buddhist practice and, by extension, the primary role of the relative
existence of suffering beings. All living beings suffer, teaches the Buddha. Sentient beings are, therefore, the inspirers and recipients of heartfelt compassion and are, in this sense, benefactors or even mothers
of the bodhisattvas who vow to liberate them from suffering. Blissfully
awakened bodhisattvas come forth from the ranks of sentient beings
who are immersed in the terrible dream of suffering.

At issue here is the root principle of Mahayana. The relative truth
of existence is that it is an expanse of suffering beings, a condition
which is the motivation for the precious Mahayana commitment to
universal conscious awakening. This relative truth of suffering must
not be swallowed up, even subtly, by the absolute truth that Reality
is an inherently selfless expanse, an infinite, empty space, intrinsically
peaceful and blissful. Relative truth and absolute truth must remain
in subtle balance or even in perfect unison.

Our personal responsibility for the physical well-being and spiritual
evolution of all life forms must not only be taken seriously but placed
consistently at the forefront of Buddhist practice. Paradoxically, the
more radically the teaching of Perfect Wisdom removes from our
view the slightest physical or metaphysical basis, the slightest substantial self or world, the more intensely we fall in love with living beings,
regarding them all without exception as most precious, most beloved,
most intimately connected to our existence. As the Tibetan commen-
tators always stress, all sentient beings are to be regarded as our
mothers.

Philosophically, this paradox means that we must uphold, protect and even exalt the coherent functioning of relative structures, beings and events, no matter how insubstantial they are from the standpoint of absolute truth. Our own reincarnational careers as continuous mind streams and the moral imperative of universal compassion upon which these careers eventually come to be founded are not some form of illusory existence. The relative is a full partner in mystic union with the absolute. In fact, because it is the proper sphere of compassionate action, the relative becomes more prominent, more spiritually charged, than the absolute. This is what startled Lama Tsongkhapa in his final realization.

The fusion of absolute and relative into a totally enlightened compassion, free from the bifurcation of experience into subject and object, is what mystically gives birth to Mother Prajnaparamita's children, *who clearly and blissfully perceive the emptiness, insubstantiality and transparency of all apparent self-existence, while continuing to abide in the very depths of loving concern—continuously contemplating the unthinkable depth of Reality without disappearing into those infinite deeps, remaining active instead in the destiny of all lives.* This exaltation of relativity, this adamantine concern for relative existence, implies that compassion, far from being an external or secondary adjunct to transcendent insight, must itself become the primary expression of unitive awareness. Such gnostic Great Compassion permits one to embrace the absolute, which is transparent openness, and the relative, which is the harmonious functioning of all possible structures, at the very same time and with the very same passionate gesture of heart and mind. Selfless love for all beings thus itself becomes the radical wisdom of nonduality. This love-wisdom, or *bliss-emptiness* as it is termed in the Tantric or Vajrayana tradition, leaves the relative existence of living beings as the primary, irreducible and ineluctable fact. This ineffable awakening, this fusion of relative truth and absolute truth, enjoyed by Tsongkhapa at the pivotal age of forty, is really impossible to characterize, but the *Prajnaparamita Sutra* constantly adumbrates it:

Whatever high realms of meditative attainment may be mastered, this compassionate mind stream does not focus or abide there, during this life or future lifetimes, but remains so concentrated on suffering beings in the sensory realm of desire that its voluntary rebirth will not occur in any of the refined realms of sublime form or within blissful formlessness.

Images of Lama Tsongkhapa depict him wearing a golden, pointed scholar's hat, sitting between two lotuses that blossom at his shoulders —one bearing the flaming sword of Manjushri, a representation of the wisdom mind of the Buddhas, the other supporting the radiant text of the *Prajnaparamita Sutra in 8,000 Lines,* representing the compassionate expression of Perfect Wisdom. This traditional iconography underlines the central importance of the particular version of the *Prajnaparamita Sutra* which we are exploring here.

The third section of this book, entitled *Practice,* presents short, vivid texts which will aid the reader in entering Mahayana experientially: the Heart Sutra, a very brief condensation of the *Prajnaparamita,* chanted in Buddhist gatherings; a poem by Lama Tsongkhapa on mind training; a poem by Tilopa, the great Indian sage, on Mahamudra; and prayers from the Buddhist oral tradition coming through the present Dalai Lama.

An authentic glimpse of the riches of the *Prajnaparamita Sutra* allows readers to participate in the luminous minds of Nagarjuna, Tilopa, Tsongkhapa and countless other Buddhist masters from the past and present. According to the Sutra itself, by sincerely studying even a single verse, we participate in the sanctifying body, speech and mind of all past, present and future Buddhas who embody truth throughout boundless oceans of inhabited worlds. Even more astounding, it is revealed that our study and comprehension of the *Prajnaparamita Sutra,* however limited, subtly transmits the energy of enlightenment to all conscious beings. Thus our approach to the Mother of the Buddhas is charged with a deep sense of awe and responsibility.

THE UNIVERSE ACCORDING TO
MOTHER PRAJNAPARAMITA

*M*Y intention here is to present, in condensed form, a picture
of the universe as seen through the eyes of Mother Prajnaparamita, the Wisdom Goddess, using the words of these contemporary meditations. Such an overview will help readers maintain their
sense of coherence and not become discouraged by the richness and
density of the text. Readers who experience affinity with these forty
selections in *Mother of the Buddhas* are invited to set forth on an ecstatic
pilgrimage within the complete *Prajnaparamita Sutra in 8,000 Lines,*
only a small portion of which has been expanded into this volume.

The Nature of What Is

The pervasive theme, or themelessness, of Prajnaparamita is signaled
by the phrase: *the depth of unthinkability.* The nature of What Is—
termed *Reality, pure presence,* or *truth* by the Sutra—can never be
described, thought about or indicated in any way.

The following terms are, therefore, used in these meditations to
describe all relative structures as well as to refer to the Perfection of
Wisdom, Mother Prajnaparamita herself: *unfindable, unthinkable,
indescribable, indecipherable, indefinable, ungraspable, unformulatable,
inconceivable, incomparable, unlocatable, unisolatable, unapproachable,*

unchangeable, unreachable, uncalibratable, unframable, uncorrelatable, uncharacterizable, insubstantial, nonperspectival, non-self-existing, foundationless, baseless, traceless, nameless, pathless, goalless, abodeless, stainless, measureless, connectionless, relationless.

These privative terms are always linked with the compassionate warning of Prajnaparamita to her beloved spiritual children never to *thematize, analyze, review, formulate, represent, project, perceive, isolate, define, grasp, crystalize, reify, concretize, objectify, conceptualize* or *personalize* What Is, simply because Reality remains *great, profound, ineffable, limitless, boundless, boundaryless, frontierless, divisionless, identityless, infinite, transparent, harmoniously functioning, open, free, elusive, deep, pure, empty, sublime, calmly quiet, at peace* and *blissfully awakened.* These terms indicate that Reality is not a void or an absence but is simply more real and more fulfilling than any conceptual or perceptual capacity can convey.

Such is the *Prajnaparamita Sutra*'s reliable report on the ineffable nature of What Is. Since the central teaching of the Sutra is a Reality which, by definition, cannot be grasped, it may sound like an exalted yet terribly boring text. Yet quite the reverse is true. The Sutra makes this fundamental and universal ineffability, this elusiveness of truth, come delightfully alive—in the realm of transmundane experience, in the struggles and temptations of the spiritual path and in the daily context of the natural world. It allows us to experience boundlessness and unthinkability, vast cosmopoetic vision and joyous altruistic love. Its scintillating and palpable aliveness indicates that the Sutra is not composed of mere words or abstract ideas but of living spiritual energy, which it refers to as *transferable meritorious energy that can be dedicated and consecrated to the conscious enlightenment of all living beings.*

As we read and participate with our whole being in the esoteric wisdom passages and the heartfelt compassion passages skillfully interwoven in the Sutra, we come alive with the infinitely intelligent life of Mother Prajnaparamita, experiencing new birth from her mysterious womb of Perfect Wisdom. Precisely this transmission of energy *empowers all Buddhas from the beginningless past, the open future and the endless dimensions of the present to express Buddha nature, the total awakeness of omniscience.*

We can sense this current of universal blessing as it flows through our mind stream, which is not our limited personal memory but a moral and spiritual continuity extending over countless lifetimes. Each being's unique, distinct and identifiable mind stream flows uninterruptedly through different cosmic aeons, on habitable planets in *billion-world systems as numerous as the grains of sand in the Ganges River.* A mind stream manifests through physical bodies which have been evolved by interdependent biological and spiritual processes. The same mind stream can manifest as well on subtle and heavenly planes of being, nonphysical in nature.

Astonishingly enough, what we perceive around us as conscious beings, whether incarnated as tiny insects or as advanced contemplatives, are the visible manifestations of unique mind streams that are beginningless and that are evolving interdependently toward omniscience. If we are able to experience this intuitively, our narrow, habitual world will tremble, as the universe *quakes in all six dimensions* whenever Lord Buddha discourses.

However, the core of Prajnaparamita, no matter how extensive or visionary its cosmology or cosmopoetry, remains crystal clear:

The Reality to which all names refer is utterly ungraspable and inconceivable, possessing absolutely no physical or metaphysical self-existence.

The question, How can one engage intellectually with such an antiquated, non-Western world view?, does not really arise. Why? Because this revolutionary teaching of Perfect Wisdom does not present a doctrinal world view that demands either intellectual assent or a leap of faith. In fact, the Prajnaparamita is not a world view at all, but a *viewless view* which transmits the energy of supreme awakening, the *total awakeness of universal Buddhahood.* To participate intimately in this illuminating energy, we must avoid the tendency to objectify or freeze it into words and concepts. As the Sutra proclaims: *Perfect Wisdom is never limited to any of its verbal or nonverbal expressions. Prajnaparamita is sheer limitlessness.*

The Compassionate Wisdom of the Bodhisattva

Once opened by the *Prajnaparamita Sutra* to the inexhaustibly rich mystery of What Is, the eyes of our intuition cannot be closed again. Every line of this timeless text gives us wider access to an indivisible panorama, until we spontaneously come to regard What Is as a *coherently and harmoniously functioning transparency or openness, like empty space, which does not come or go, which does not increase or decrease.* The response that the Sutra subtly generates in our awareness is not step-by-step reasoning but existential intuition, ineffable and direct.

Yet there is no irrationality here. The coherently functional nature of the universe is stressed by the Sutra, because our involvement in the relative world sustains what is essential to enlightenment: *compassionate engagement with the evolutionary careers of all living beings.* Thus sensitive, loving concern and compassionate action become the arena for the most radical, transcendent wisdom. As the Sutra reveals:

> The absolute absence of the substantial creation of any forms is not different from the transparent, harmonious and coherent functioning of all forms. Absolute openness and relative functioning are not divided, not two alternative dimensions, but are utter simplicity. If one labels and hence experiences this simplicity as material forms and personal consciousness, one is foolishly numbering and labeling that which has no multiplicity or identity.

To know this *ontologically transparent functioning,* to perceive it accurately and to reason about it appropriately, makes possible the essential vow of the bodhisattva, *the being of enlightenment who is*

completely committed to the healing, liberation and full awakening
of all that lives and who displays an astonishing array of liberative skills.

The Sutra's teachings on wisdom constantly point out that Reality
does not contain the slightest possibility for *self-satisfaction, self-*
aggrandizement, self-elevation, self-involvement, self-service, self-con-
sciousness, self-perpetuation or even for *self-liberation* or *self-realization.*
This total interdiction of *egocentricity* or *substantial, independent self-*
existence includes even the self-conscious sense of being a bodhisattva:

> The bodhisattva's mind is not frightened by the total absence of any
> recognizable, definable or findable being called a bodhisattva.

Thus the Sutra refers even to its own teaching as a *nonteaching,*
which has never been displayed to any separate students by any separate
teachers. As the brilliant Subhuti, the central speaker in this Sutra
and its most uncompromising dialectician, affirms: *There is absolutely*
nothing to understand. Subhuti even insists that no Buddhas can be
found, nor any principle of Buddha nature, nor any Prajnaparamita,
proclaiming: *Even if there were some reality more exalted than Final*
Nirvana, that too would be a magic display, a dream display. He goes
on to suggest:

> Those conscious beings who are mature enough to receive the radical
> teaching of Perfect Wisdom always regard themselves simply as a brilliant
> display of magical power without any substantial self-existence. There
> should be no residual tendency to hear and grasp as some independent
> reality the words of the wisdom teaching, nor to isolate and reify their
> meaning, nor to experience as a separate reality what they are indicating.

These and other purposely shocking statements made by Subhuti
are balanced by the more mellow approach of his brother disciple,
Shariputra, who teaches us to be *authentically established in truth by*
being free from any personal claim to truth, to be perfectly stationed
without the slightest physical or metaphysical ground upon which to
stand. Shariputra, whose depth of realization is kept subtly hidden,

often poses key questions to his brother Subhuti, *whom Lord Buddha has rightfully called the foremost among those who dwell in the inconceivable peace of Perfect Wisdom.* Shariputra's approach is an exquisite balance of the pure *via negativa* of Subhuti and the cosmo-poetic tone of revelation. He sings beautifully about Prajnaparamita in the selection *Mystic Hymn to the Wisdom Mother:*

> She is worthy of infinite praise. She is utterly unstained, because nothing in this insubstantial world can possibly stain her. She is an ever flowing fountain of incomparable light, and from every conscious being on every plane of being, she removes the faintest trace of illusory darkness.

This and similar passages suggest that the feminine nature of Prajnaparamita is taken seriously by the Sutra. But this *mother, matrix, guide, power and bliss of all Buddhas and their embryonic forms, the bodhisattvas* is not simply tender and nurturing in some stereotypical sense of the feminine. Mother Prajnaparamita expresses her *mystic motherhood* equally and perhaps more centrally as the uncompromising discipline of transcendent insight. A union of inexhaustible tenderness and diamond clarity that is like open space radiates from this Sutra as the *strong feminine voice of Prajnaparamita, heard directly by all the fully Awakened Ones, the humble Lords of Enlightenment.*

The most intimate companion of Lord Buddha is Ananda, *the very heart of love, the most beloved disciple.* He is given the awesome responsibility of insuring for thousands of years the living presence of Prajnaparamita as scriptural manifestation and as initiatory vehicle. In the selection *Great Disciple Receives Transmission,* Lord Buddha proclaims:

> O blessed Ananda, most blissful disciple of Awakened Enlightenment, I now totally entrust and thoroughly transmit to you the scriptural form and the spiritual energy of Prajnaparamita, the teaching which is beyond any expression or explanation but which I have clothed in Sanskrit letters so that over millennia it may be carefully investigated,

profoundly contemplated and openly proclaimed to the whole world, so that it will not be neglected or disappear for thousands of years.

Twice in these forty selections, Ananda asks Lord Buddha to explain his cosmic smile, which shines forth on certain rare occasions, *illuminating the boundless vistas of all world systems, rising up as a luminous wave even to the highest heaven.* In one of these tender instances, recorded in the selection *Goddess of the Ganges,* a feminine wisdom being is the recipient of this enchanting smile from Mother Prajnaparamita through the golden form of *Awakened Enlightenment,* the impersonal term for Lord Buddha. This feminine visitor to Buddha's assembly is then predicted to become the Buddha Golden Flower in a future time called the Great Starlike Aeon. Her transmundane Buddha field, a Pure Land emerging spontaneously from her Enlightenment, will contain a vast spiritual community called the *immeasurable, inconceivable community of Perfect Wisdom.* Shakyamuni's Buddha field, in which we are now residing spiritually, contains countless suffering beings because of his unusually developed compassion. Golden Flower's transcendent realm, by contrast, will contain *no jungles inhabited by carnivores, no lonely highways attacked by brigands, no deserts without springs, no districts decimated by disease or famine.*

The Goddess of the Ganges is profoundly moved by this precise prediction of her eventual enlightenment from Shakyamuni Buddha.

> She miraculously brings forth golden flowers, joyously and reverently scattering them over the perfect embodiment of enlightenment. These magnificent full blossoms, neither substantially self-existent nor nonexistent, do not fall to the floor of the assembly but remain suspended in a golden cloud about the serene figure of the Awakened One.

These blossoms, neither substantially self-existent nor nonexistent and, therefore, subject neither to conventional laws nor routine perception, signal to sympathetic readers of the Sutra that we are deep in the realmless realm of Prajnaparamita. All structures and processes of relativity, all material or mental forms and every mode of awareness by which they may be perceived or conceived, all possible phenomena, beings or events that could be experienced by any form of conscious life express precisely the same ineluctable existential status as this floating cloud of golden blossoms.

This description is what I call *cosmopoetry*. The cosmopoetry of the Sutra always has a cutting edge, which penetrates our unexamined myths about the independently existing natural world and the substantiality of personal or collective history. We cling to various objectifying myths, both consciously and unconsciously. No passage of the Sutra, no matter how visionary or tender its tone, is without this cutting edge of transcendent, selfless insight which liberates us from even the most subtle clinging. Yet beautiful affection, tenderness, loyalty and love remain primary for the bodhisattva. These radiant qualities become stronger as they are purified from the dross of self-interest, self-assertion and even self-awareness by the flame of Perfect Wisdom.

The moral strand of the *Prajnaparamita Sutra* is very emphatic. It is firmly based upon a single radical principle. The authentic practitioners of Mahayana

> never abandon living beings by crossing over entirely into the expanse of the absolute, by rejecting or negating relativity. These bodhisattvas do not become liberated from life, nor do they pursue any form of separate self-realization. They direct an ecstatic flood of love and friendliness toward all, connecting their mind streams as intimately with all beings as with their most cherished family members and beloved friends. This astonishing spiritual feat frees the bodhisattvas from every impure intention of harming, denigrating, abandoning or even merely ignoring others.

This attitude of constant concern and responsiveness, much more rigorous than any specific set of moral codes, the Sutra calls the *true life of responsibility*. It can be lived with equal intensity and effectiveness by monks and nuns, by married or single lay practitioners, by heads of state or by the most humble working persons. The bodhisattva ideal is democratic. It demands only a way of life and a form of livelihood or service that elevates beings rather than deceiving or oppressing them. It is an active compassion, an intensely practical ideal, a praxis:

> Bodhisattvas illuminate for living beings whatever righteous, dignified, excellent and wholesome ways of life can be envisioned and practically manifested in the world.

When speaking about Mara the Tempter, the Sutra suggests that the most extreme temptation of egocentricity is the desire to attain Buddhahood in order to exalt oneself above other living beings. The bodhisattva manifests as a panoramic compassionate awareness that never separates itself from the collective evolutionary career of all conscious beings. As the Sutra hints, *Buddha mind is really the one mind of all beings—fully awakened, fully matured, fully sensitized.* As Buddha mind confirms, speaking through the *Prajnaparamita Sutra:*

> The Tathagata—one who has beautifully disappeared into pure presence and awakened as sheer Reality, transcending all conventional views—knows the minds of living beings as intrinsically infinite and inexhaustible. Just as empty space cannot disintegrate or be destroyed, neither can the infinitely open space of all minds ever be narrowed or extinguished.

Moral purity is understood by the Sutra as selflessness rather than as any particular form of behavior. But transcendent selflessness never exists in a contemplative void, simply for its own sake. The selflessness of Mahayana is always a selflessness for others — a selfless and, therefore, ecstatic love for all beings. *The thought flow and even the physical body of the bodhisattva become perfectly pure, because they manifest solely for the sake of guiding and maturing all conscious beings.*

Once a being has awakened to the Perfection of Wisdom, it becomes a central core which blossoms as five other transcendent, selfless

Perfections—Generosity, Goodness, Patience, Commitment, Meditation. These supreme excellences or *paramitas* are the mysterious energy of Mother Prajnaparamita that manifests spontaneously through the sincere practitioner of Perfect Wisdom. These five subsidiary Perfections do not result from self-effort. They remain radically different from the salutary qualities which their names usually denote. For instance, the Sutra describes the selfless Perfection of Patience as

> patiently accepting the ultimate elusiveness of truth, which always remains beyond any finite or conventional teaching—beyond doctrine, explanation, description or designation.

In the same light, the Sutra elucidates the selfless Perfection of Goodness:

> These blessed mind streams have become perfect in moral action, which is to say that even their slightest movements and intentions care for, guide and spiritually elevate countless beings, orienting them toward omniscience, which is simply the total awakeness of all the Buddhas of past, present and future.

The nature of the Perfection of Generosity is also distinct from any conventional notion of generosity:

> If hungry predators attack me, I will lovingly offer this body as opportunity for the Perfection of Generosity to develop in this mind stream.

The Perfection of Commitment is characterized by the Sutra in this way:

> Bodhisattvas are free from the slightest mental or physical laziness, actively in every instant expressing the illumined energy of compassion by avoiding the false implications of self-existence, including such notions as gain, fame, honor, respect or self-satisfaction of any kind.

The radiant purity of the mind stream which has become an expression of these five currents of the Perfection of Wisdom streaming from the Mother of the Buddhas is not an ethereal or abstract purity, but is experienced in the very concrete, existential mode of selfless love:

> I can never generate the slightest thought of hatred or even irritation toward any of these most precious living beings, even though they may torture or destroy my body during a hundred consecutive lifetimes.

The Sutra regards the ceaseless practice of Prajnaparamita as *inseparable from every breath of every conscious being*. Such radical metaphysical and moral purity, or universal selflessness, is essential for advancement in Prajnaparamita, as the Sutra affirms:

> One cannot even begin to approach the living presence of Mother Prajnaparamita with a mind stream tainted by basically selfish motivation or even by passing thoughts of self-service or self-aggrandizement.

Cosmic Contemplation of Prajnaparamita

The relationship of the authentic practitioner to the *Prajnaparamita Sutra* as a living presence is richly religious. Perfect Wisdom is not simply a philosophical enterprise or a science of contemplation. It is prayerful devotion:

> They study it prayerfully and venerate its visible symbol, the scriptural text, through traditional modes of worship, thereby absorbing its subtle energy more fully and directly, as nourishment is absorbed into the bloodstream.

This worship and communion with Prajnaparamita, Goddess of Perfect Wisdom and Great Mother of all Buddhas, through the sacred medium of scriptural manifestation, has vast implications for generating universal awakening. The Sutra speaks about its own power in what may appear to outsiders as mere hyperbolic language. But this heightened mode of expression is simply the most adequate representation of the spiritual energy which an authentic practitioner actually experiences during prayerful study and ceremonial worship of the living text. In fact, the ecstatic words of the Sutra are not just representations but actual channels of the measureless transformative power called Mother Prajnaparamita:

> The person honoring and venerating the glorious Prajnaparamita, source and Mother of all Buddhas, will generate more power for universal conscious enlightenment than if all the living beings in billion-world systems as numerous as the grains of sand in the Ganges River were to build sacred reliquary stupas and honor them with purity of intention for an entire aeon.

Our cosmological view of space and time is expanded by the *Prajnaparamita Sutra* far beyond the habitual notions and cosmic myths prevalent in any culture, including modern, scientifically oriented cultures. In practicing Prajnaparamita,

> the bodhisattva contemplates other world systems beyond this planetary system—an expanse of inhabited worlds immeasurable in extent, worlds beyond reckoning in number, inconceivable in their essential nature, infinite in the complexity of their life forms and limitless in the subtlety of their civilizations. The bodhisattva contemplates the range of past aeons in each of these world systems as well.

Such expansive contemplation is more than just a science fiction projection of a vast material universe or a neutral intellectual exercise in pushing back the limits of our habitual world. Rather, it confirms a central principle of Prajnaparamita that states: *the limitlessly creative power of ontologically transparent manifestation can never be exhausted.* In other words, no matter how far mind can reach and whatever mind can imagine, the true nature of manifestation is *pure presence:*

> The Awakened Ones always joyously teach and indicate with every word and wordless gesture the absolute inexhaustibility of pure presence.

The vastness of this cosmopoetic vision is not empty or impersonal but is filled with the incandescent nectar of selfless love, tender joy and gratitude.

The bodhisattva contemplates with the greatest intensity of sympathetic joy and gratitude every single seed of goodness planted by conscious beings during beginningless aeons in all these world systems.

The selection *Incomparable and Measureless Joy* leads us through a complete meditation on sympathetic joy. As the Sutra explains, *sympathetic joy is the obverse of the unbearable compassion experienced by the bodhisattva, who contemplates cosmically and ceaselessly the excruciating suffering, obvious and subtle, of all finite forms of consciousness,* including in this contemplation *the hellish consciousness created by living beings on this earthly plane and on subtle planes.* These tidal waves of astonishing joy and unbearable compassion can be embraced only by the oceanic heart of Prajnaparamita, the Perfect Wisdom which *gazes into the limitless expanse of all structures as into the starry nighttime sky* and which *reveals the expanse of manifestations as an infinite profusion of flowers.* The bodhisattva experiences unique ecstasy and exhilaration, feeling *neither discontent nor complacent contentment.* Obsessive thoughts or emotions cannot persist in the total absence of substantial or independent self-existence.

This vastly expanded spatial and temporal world of the bodhisattva is not merely a larger objective container but is a way of seeing *the insubstantial play of universal enlightenment through the transparent constituents of individual awareness.* The fundamental fact remains that *all is simply suchness, pure presence, inextinguishable and indistinguishable simplicity.* As the Sutra says of Mother Prajnaparamita: *She compassionately reveals the world as purified from any false concepts of worldhood or worldliness.* Therefore, the supervast, beginningless cosmos that shines before the intuitive gaze of Prajnaparamita is not a world in any ordinary sense of the term. It is not even a place:

Appearing structures have no actual localization in space or time, because space, time and locality itself are just other appearing structures, neither locatable nor isolatable.

The measureless universe according to Prajnaparamita is *a boundless field of subjectless, objectless awareness where, without trace, Buddhas freely and joyfully roam.*

Meditating on the Perfection of Wisdom is equivalent to meditating on this non-self-existing cosmos which surrounds and includes us, a cosmos in which all relative structures themselves are *like realized sages who have laid down their burdens by recognizing that no burdens were ever imposed upon them in the first place.* The Sutra tirelessly asserts that the immeasurability and unthinkability of the cosmos as a whole is equivalent to the immeasurability and unthinkability of every single detail of existence—every ungraspable form, thought, perception or event—and is equivalent as well to the immeasurability and unthinkability of Mother Prajnaparamita. Lord Buddha clearly indicates in the Sutra that no one should idealize Perfect Wisdom as especially great, sublime or perfect, because every structure or process of relativity expresses the very same inconceivable and boundless perfection.

To engage in the Perfection of Meditation is to concentrate ceaselessly upon the entire subjective and objective cosmic display as miraculous in the sense that it springs forth spontaneously, without relying on any underlying source, basis or ground. What Is is innately none other than Perfect Wisdom. As the Sutra reveals, *all phenomena are Buddha phenomena.*

The enlightened Subhuti repeatedly rejects any finite, systematic technique of meditation on Prajnaparamita, deftly eliminating even the slightest conceptualized approach, because, as this brilliant master of dialectic proclaims: *This is a teaching without any path to its realization.* Because Perfect Wisdom already reigns, Subhuti and the other masters of Prajnaparamita are reluctant to endorse any formal meditation practice to discover or develop it.

The various spiritual paths or contemplative methods that purport to control, escape from, renounce or destroy limiting structures are ultimately useless, because no structure has ever been or could ever be substantially encountered, much less stopped or dismantled.

However, just as one must learn Sanskrit, English or some other language to read and contemplate the *Prajnaparamita Sutra,* so the basic vocabulary and syntax of Buddhist spiritual disciplines must be mastered before a full appreciation of Prajnaparamita can dawn. Some very advanced meditational suggestions are offered in the selection *Astonishing Lion's Roar:*

> Each and every being or event which can be experienced—small or great, particular or general—is boundaryless like the clear blue sky, like the dazzling rainbow colors of Mount Meru, like interpenetrating rays of light from the sun, like sounds which have no sharp edges, like the frontierless expanse of living worlds and conscious beings, like the supreme wakefulness of the Buddha, like the cumulative kindness and insight of all aspiring beings everywhere, like earth, water, fire, air, space and consciousness manifest as transparent currents in a single ocean.

If we regard these lines as a metameditation instruction, we should not imagine some finite process of sitting in a particular position or engaging in certain techniques of concentration. Simply through prayerful study, chanting, joyous contemplation and veneration of the *Prajnaparamita Sutra,* the metameditation of Perfect Wisdom will manifest spontaneously, both in dream and during the waking state.

In the selection *Interpretation of Dreams,* the Sutra advises aspirants how to recognize authentic dreams which indicate the irreversibility of this spontaneous metameditative or transmeditative state, free from any distinction between absolute expanse and relative existence:

> A sure indication that bodhisattvas have attained irreversibility of commitment is when they dream themselves to be Tathagatas surrounded by radiant Buddha assemblies consisting of thousands of millions of

dedicated practitioners, seated in deep meditation together within a circular Dharma hall beneath a high peaked roof.

The Sutra describes many portents of attainment. In the unique selection *Mirror Image of Pure Presence,* which contains Subhuti's non-discursive discourse explaining how he is a mirror image of Lord Buddha, three hundred monks, five hundred nuns, five thousand high heavenly beings and six thousand male and female bodhisattvas are deeply illuminated in various ways. In similar instances, following discourses of the Buddha which express truth perfectly, our particular billion-world universe trembles, flower petals rain from the empty blue sky and heavenly beings scatter fragrant sandalwood powder.

The same auspicious, non-self-existent phenomena manifest after the earthly bodhisattva Dharmodgata delivers a vibrant discourse in the selection *Tathagatas Neither Come Nor Go.* His transmission of truth manifests even more enlightening energy than Subhuti's discourse, which was directed primarily to heavenly beings. The earth has a more powerful spiritual ambiance than even the high heavens, since human birth is the most fruitful and precious among all possible levels of awareness. This assertion is not to be taken as naive anthropocentrism. Life-bearing planets in other solar systems presumably manifest significantly different lines of biological evolution. Somewhere, awakened bodhisattvas may resemble gentle giant spiders. The precious human birth refers not to an outward biological form but to the inward potential for panoramic awareness and selfless compassion.

After Dharmodgata speaks, *sixty-four thousand practitioners open the pure eye of transcendent insight which penetrates and clarifies all structures of relativity without exception.* This image is not farfetched to someone who has attended the Dalai Lama's Kalachakra initiations in India, where more than one hundred thousand participants receive a very definite and intimate transmission of the energy of Mother Prajnaparamita through the powerful lineage of Vajrayana Buddhism.

In fact, the description of the symbolic city and palace of Dharmodgata, found in the selection *Sublime Saga of Sadaprarudita*, reminds one vividly of the Tantric mandala—a circular diagram symbolizing and actually becoming the abode of a Deity—visualized during the Kalachakra empowerment. Meditating on a mandala ignites our intuitive and transformative vision, not only of the external cosmos, but also of the equally vast and complex inner cosmos, the human body, in its subtle dimensions. The *Prajnaparamita Sutra* alludes to *the mystic door which opens into the sublimely awakened human body, experienced as the culmination and consummation of all possible manifestations.*

The description of Dharmodgata's mandala city is multivalent, but one of its spheres of meaning is as an elucidation of the body's awakened and transformed subtle energy system:

> Five hundred symbolic shops, containing every kind of precious creation, are arranged beautifully and geometrically around the twelve-mile square center of the mandala city, as in a richly colored painting. These exquisite places of display or offering are joined internally by transparent, symmetrical passages and corridors, some designed for animal-drawn vehicles, others for palanquins and still others for pedestrians, so the transactional flow of the symbolic city remains perfectly harmonious.

All such esoteric maps, however, are to be studied with the liberated attitude of Prajnaparamita that *one simply cannot describe what it is that enlightenment experiences.*

Struggles and Triumphs of the Path

The *Prajnaparamita Sutra* maintains an intense honesty about the difficulty, struggle and danger of the spiritual path. Long passages describe the deceitful activity of Mara, the principle of negative egocentricity. The Sutra does not present a modern psychological analysis of unconscious complexes. Mara is described as a non-self-existing yet extremely dangerous presence, operating at large in an insubstantial universe, subtly distorting conceptions and perceptions, able even to generate misleading objective events or sequences of such events:

> The polymorphous Mara may approach the vulnerable practitioner in various guises—during meditative trance, dream or even the waking state. The spiritually polluting influence of Mara can also manifest as a heavenly sounding voice. The psychic energy of Mara names the relatives of its victim through seven generations in order to make the temptation more convincing. Mara can magically or hypnotically project various earthly or heavenly forms, or can act through unsuspecting human beings—monk or nun, mother or father, respected relative or cherished friend.

Lord Jesus rebuked this negative energy when it expressed through his foremost disciple, Peter, using the uncompromising and penetrating words, *Get thee behind me, Satan.* The principle of Mara can even invade, at least momentarily, advanced and loyal disciples. Significantly, both Lord Jesus and Lord Buddha were visited by the power of the Tempter just before their outward manifestations as world teachers. Absolutely no one is exempt from the approach of Mara.

The most terrible delusion purveyed by Mara is spiritual pride, *the disease of self-adulation which seeks personal glory in becoming a Buddha.* The invasions of Mara can be dramatic but also extremely subtle. Mara can manifest almost invisibly as the *pollution of the mental stream by self-oriented and self-serving motivation and behavior.* In the selection *Protective Power of Mantra,* the sovereign of the heavenly realms, King Shakra, receives the supreme antidote against the poison of Mara, *the seed sounds that contain the entirety of Perfect Wisdom,* om gaté gaté paragaté parasamgaté bodhi swaha—*gone, gone, gone beyond, gone beyond even the beyond into full enlightenment, so be it.* Just after the moment of spiritual transmission, as is often the case, Shakra experiences a subtle attack by Mara's delusive forces. Realizing that *not just at this moment but perpetually such forces of negativity are intent on finding a way to invade beginning or advanced practitioners, intent on wounding them spiritually and even destroying them,* the king of the Thirty-Three Heaven uses the mantra he has just received from Lord Buddha, *the all-pervading mantric energy which instantly spreads Prajnaparamita, infusing it profoundly into all minds and hearts.* The effect of this invocation is swift and powerful:

> Immediately Mara the Adversary, who is sheer negative egocentricity, turns away from the luminous Buddha assembly and retreats into peripheral darkness. Mara and his demonic forces will find no way to invade any conscious being who recalls, reveres, chants, communicates, embodies and radiates Perfect Wisdom.

The spiritual power of Prajnaparamita is not some limited form of counter-energy but is the transmission and realization of radical selflessness—not simply personal, but universal selflessness. Mara's only point of entry into King Shakra was the king's natural royal pride. However, any conscious or unconscious self-involvement on the part of Shakra was immediately undercut and dissolved by the transcendent insight generated by the Prajnaparamita mantra.

As King Shakra received the empowerment of Perfect Wisdom directly from Lord Buddha in the radiant Buddha assembly, so we can sense Buddha's vibrant presence and transmission while reading and contemplating the Sutra. When complimented by Lord Buddha on a particularly excellent formulation of Perfect Wisdom, Subhuti responds: *The powerful transmission of the Buddha nature alone speaks through me, O Lord, so my words are never inadequate to Prajnaparamita.* Similarly, Buddha remarks to Shakra, who is not a realized master as Subhuti is: *Listen, O King, to the Buddha nature speaking through you.* So whenever an awakened master or even an aspirant to Perfect Wisdom speaks with authentic inspiration about Prajnaparamita, these words are an actual transmission from Awakened Enlightenment itself.

The speech of the humble Lord of Enlightenment is simple, relaxed, balanced. Shakyamuni Buddha discourses with what the Sutra calls *the wise balance and ease which is free from any sense of doctrinal rigidity.* We can almost hear the beautiful tone of his voice:

> Perfection of Wisdom cannot be expounded and learned, nor isolated and described, nor stated in words, nor reflected upon by means of or in terms of any limited pattern of awareness. This perfect indescribability and unapproachability is a consequence of the fact that all structures of relativity on all levels of experience are inherently indescribable and unapproachable, inconceivably calm and blissful. The same inconceivable peacefulness and innate bliss is manifest in every detail of existence.

Lord Buddha here offers a succinct expression of the advanced teaching in which selfless compassion subtly transmutes into bliss through the realization that *universal enlightenment* is already and always the plain fact. What the bodhisattva vows, with every fiber of his or her integrity, is that all precious and beloved living beings should awaken fully to this naked fact, which then becomes *universal conscious enlightenment.* Thus the bodhisattva is sometimes called *one who upholds the radical understanding of universal enlightenment as present reality* and is at other times referred to as *one who is completely committed to the eventual enlightenment of all beings.* This dialectical relationship between present perfection and future conscious fulfillment is not really a tension. Contrary to popular understanding, the bodhisattva is not a person wholly oriented toward the future but a wisdom being who sees through the non-self-existing veils of past, future and present, for *even the present moment itself possesses no independent self-existence.*

> The bodhisattva never indulges in imagining that full enlightenment can only occur in the distant future, for every single thought flash reveals the absence of limits, separation and distance.

Spiritual awakening is not a process extrinsic to the very principle or nature of awareness, which is already pure presence. The Sutra clarifies: *Can any thought process whatsoever be identified or correlated with this pure presence? No, because its total simplicity is processless.* In its most radical sense, universal conscious enlightenment is not a process at all. Nothing needs to be changed, taken away, gradually refined or even simplified:

> The rare purity of supreme spiritual insight is identical with the natural, spontaneous purity of the countless configurations of forms that present themselves as the universe in all its multidimensionality.

The continuous projecting and veiling, which is generated by the false conception of solid *me-ness* and *my-ness* and which *causes persons to experience Reality as the painful cycle of birth and death,* is like an insubstantial mist that can temporarily obscure the brilliant orb of the sun but can never block its pervasive radiance. The ontologically transparent thread with which the veils of obvious or subtle egocentricity are woven is the conceptual function of affirming and negating:

> The Tathagata knows the ingrained tendencies of countless beings to engage in literal affirmations and negations concerning the ontologically transparent structures of relativity, taking them at face value as solidly self-existing entities. Awakened Enlightenment knows how these kaleidoscopic affirmations and negations arise, like a play of reflected light beams from the constituent processes of personal awareness called form, feeling, impulse, perception and consciousness.

One may wonder how this obscuring network of both dogmatic and instinctive affirmations and negations, which reflects as our habitual sense of separate, individual awareness, can ever be made transparent by any written or spoken teaching, which must inevitably consist of more affirmations and negations. Can logic reach beyond itself? Subhuti offers an important clarification of this fundamental concern simply by refusing to claim solid logical substance for Prajnaparamita, while continuing to extoll the power of its logical functioning:

To reason about uncreated Reality is just to play with words. Yet from this coherent play, lightning bolts flash forth as gnostic intuition— totally insubstantial, not coming into being even for an instant, yet diamond sharp and clear.

Coherent play is an appropriate term for the dialectical passages of *via negativa* which are subtly interwoven by the Sutra with passages of cosmopoetic vision, both of which are gnostic in nature. Logic, and by extension, the entire coherent expanse of valid affirmations and negations, is taken seriously by the Mahayana, without being invested with independent self-existence, precisely as all structures of relativity are taken seriously by bodhisattvas yet never reified or objectified. Commitment to logic is an essential part of the commitment to compassionate action and, therefore, to universal conscious enlightenment. However, relative structures—including logical, linguistic, social and perceptual systems—are never experienced by the bodhisattva to be literally or substantially existent.

The Sutra speaks about the *irrefutable and all-transcending logic of the most revolutionary teaching.* The panoramic compassionate action of the Awakened Ones always includes a logical or dialectical component, although shining forth from prelogical or alogical presence.

The infinitely diverse teachings of truth which the humble Lords of Enlightenment dialectically demonstrate and tenderly transmit to all living beings in this beginningless realm of apparent birth and death— all these subtle teachings flow and shine forth solely from the inexhaustible reservoir, treasury and womb of truth energy, Mother Prajnaparamita.

The practitioner of Perfect Wisdom returns along the compassionately guiding rays—*logos, prajna,* sheer intelligence—into the infinite sun of total awakeness, whereupon the spreading sunlight of innumerable living worlds and conscious beings is directly perceived as the transparent presence of universal enlightenment. As the *Prajnaparamita Sutra* proclaims:

The whole world is the insubstantial play of universal enlightenment through the transparent constituents of individual awareness.
All is simply suchness, or pure presence—inextinguishable and
indistinguishable simplicity.

The favorite traditional illustration for this radical simplicity, which
is referred to in Sanskrit by the term *nonduality,* is open space, empty
space or simply the principle of spaciousness. As the Sutra queries
dialectically:

Can you count, compare, measure, conceive, imagine, perceive or feel
the expanse of open space? Can you approach, reach or attain open
space? Can open space even be described as infinite?

If one seriously contemplates these questions, allowing the cutting
edge of the dialectic to clear away naturally and effortlessly all limiting
conceptualizations and their consequent emotional obscurations, one
can begin to appreciate existentially the central teaching of Prajnaparamita that *all phenomena are Buddha phenomena, or sheer awakeness, essentially like open space.*

Contemplation of the principle of space is always illuminating: *no
possible structures can substantially act upon or grasp one another, because
they are by nature neither active nor passive, just as open space cannot
be designated as active or passive.* As Mother Prajnaparamita promises,
*the bodhisattva will experience the diamond of Perfect Wisdom to be
like brilliant open space, which never decreases or increases, which is
never lost and never found.* The Mother of the Buddhas constantly
elucidates this mystic spaciousness, which is not a doctrine of nihilism
but her most intimate embrace.

No beings or events substantially exist side by side, any more than
open space substantially exists side by side with itself. This impossibility
of any comparison is the root of the universal principle of inconceivability called Prajnaparamita.

Given this irreducible fact of unthinkability—not as a frustrating limit to our understanding, but as a beautiful, blissful openness and freedom from all limits—we know that no authentic expression of Perfect Wisdom will permit us to picture or conceptualize What Is. This revolutionary teaching will always present simply the *pure presence of a transparent, selfless awakeness which is absolutely insubstantial.* The depth of unthinkability—the Mother of the Buddhas—is the rich, radiant presence of What Is. The Sutra's transmission is simplicity itself:

> The transparent presence of the Buddha and the transparent presence of all phenomena are one transparent presence, not multiple or in any way divided or divisible.

The *Prajnaparamita Sutra* makes the same radical point in its startling cosmopoetic mode:

> Tathagatas can lift up any particular billion-world system on their big toe without any process of expansion or contraction, and then replace it again, totally undisturbed. Since they are masters of Perfect Wisdom, it would never occur to these Tathagatas that any independently existing billion-world system is being lifted up by any substantially existing big toe or returned to any describably self-existing location.

At this final horizon of nonduality, language becomes almost non-linguistic. The Sutra can only report: *this unconstructed presence is ever perfect simplicity.* Or as it reveals elsewhere:

> The suchness of pure presence does not emigrate, migrate, transmigrate or emanate. There is no division within pure presence. There is no multiplication of pure presence. Suchness cannot be enumerated, even with the numeral one.

Plunging into this ocean of transcendent insight, we are not entering some trance state, for primordial simplicity is fully evident in

and through the daily world. Suchness, or pure presence, is precisely
the perfectly transparent way that all phenomena actually manifest.
In the benign light of nonduality, we cease to hold even the subtly
adversarial attitude with which religious practitioners regard the world:

> Even those powerful and dangerous structures, such as the selfish pas-
> sions, which religious teaching advises human beings to renounce or
> to destroy, are themselves fluid, open and transparent, inherently empty
> of self-existence.

This adversarial attitude, encoded within various contemplative
methods and religious disciplines, is actually identified by the Sutra
as the last obstacle to awakening:

> The bodhisattva awakens as Prajnaparamita by becoming blissfully
> free from any obsession with battling or obliterating ignorance, habitual
> formulations, personal consciousness, conventional names, finite sense-
> experiences, taking birth or physically degenerating and dying.

In other words, Perfect Wisdom leaves the entire array of mundane
appearances in place—tangibly and coherently functional, yet ontologically transparent.

The radical attitude that later blossomed as the Vajrayana or Tantric tradition of Buddhism is thus contained implicitly in the *Prajnaparamita Sutra*. Both regard the non-self-existing structures of
relativity not as a major obstacle to enlightenment but as a healing
medicine which, when taken under the guidance of a wise physician,
can generate the healthy and relaxed balance which permits the natural
state of universal enlightenment to flower consciously.

> The infinitely diverse structures of relativity, far from being some
> dangerous disease, are actually a healing medicine, for in their intrin-
> sically selfless nature, interdependent structures perfectly express the
> mystery and transmit the spiritual energy of universal friendliness.

Relativity itself, which can be viewed as a limitless expanse of beloved
beings, becomes the eye-medicine to correct the impairment of our

conceptual, emotional and perceptual vision. Now we can spontaneously realize that *all structures, simply as structures, are themselves
essentially Awakened Enlightenment, being perfectly transparent to the
ineffable, all-embracing and all-transcending insight known as Buddhahood.* Thus, without losing the slightest sharpness of compassionate
sensibility, the master of Prajnaparamita *can contemplate the apparently
limited world of forms as being really the limitless expression of
Buddhahood—every facet and every function streaming with the
excellence and goodness of Buddha's positive energy and transcendent
insight.*

The condensed energy of this awakening is startling because it
becomes so concrete, so immediate:

> Material and mental forms are themselves none other than the total
> awakening into Buddhahood. The intrinsic nature of every appear-
> ing form and every mode of consciousness is already and always perfect
> Buddha nature—the simplicity, directness and totality of universal
> enlightenment.

The bodhisattva vow remains in full force, even exponentially increasing in compassionate intensity, yet it is no longer understood as a
vow to change or transform any structure in any way:

> The bodhisattvas vow simply that all beings become conscious of
> universal enlightenment, which is the fact that the intrinsic nature
> of awareness, or life itself, is just Buddha nature—simple, direct, total.

The irreversibly committed bodhisattva who is permeated by the nondualistic attitude of Perfect Wisdom is *intimately near to the awakening experienced by all Buddhas.* About the spiritual capacity of the
bodhisattva, who is actualizing his or her full humanity, the Sutra
confirms:

> It will not be difficult to experience the spontaneous flowering of
> goodness, which displays all the actual and possible structures of
> relativity as a perfectly harmonious and transparent Buddha field, as
> the natural expression of the infinitely beautiful Buddha qualities,

foremost among which is the most tender and loving compassion for all lives.

We need hardly note that compassionate love here retains its position in the forefront of the highest realization, just as the venerable Tsongkhapa rediscovered and demonstrated, logically and empirically, in the vast laboratory of his philosophical, contemplative and religious practices.

The Directionless Direction

The spiritual development of a humble earthly student of Perfect Wisdom is examined in *Sublime Saga of Sadaprarudita*. This noble son of the Buddha family was not a direct disciple of the historical Buddha, but through his enthusiastic love for truth, expressed by ceaseless weeping and longing, he became a direct disciple of Buddha nature. His inspiring quest points out the *directionless direction* in which we all can hope to proceed. As Buddha nature inwardly informed Sadaprarudita:

> You will go beyond the stages of studying and contemplating Prajnaparamita from books or listening to Perfect Wisdom expounded by excellent scholars. You will become able to experience the teaching emanating through diverse human and divine forms directly from the supreme teacher, Prajnaparamita herself, Mother of the Buddhas. With this blessed perception and knowledge, one sees and knows the person who is authentically expounding the Perfection of Wisdom to be none other than the blissful Mother and Wisdom Teacher. What greater spiritual opportunity can there be than this?

We may wonder how we can avail ourselves of this most precious opportunity, which faces us right now as readers of the *Prajnaparamita Sutra*. The Sutra hints at how to open this door of truth:

> One can awaken to the teaching of Prajnaparamita simply by experiencing these resounding declarations themselves, here and now, as the astonishing lion's roar of a fully awakened Buddha.

Should we concentrate on the verbal declarations of the Sutra as they shimmer before us on the printed page, or perhaps close our eyes and visualize them as letters of golden energy streaming through the heart of our awareness? Obviously not. We simply need to look everywhere with the eyes of compassion and transcendent insight, immersing ourselves in the universal music of relativity, in the blissful embrace of the Wisdom Goddess. As the Sutra reveals, *not only these transcendent declarations of Prajnaparamita but every single mundane structure itself is the lion's roar of Perfect Wisdom.*

Even within this explosion of wisdom, the mind streams of the bodhisattvas, those impeccable diamond beings of enlightened compassion, still continue to flow on their precise course. Ever loyal to love, they pursue the interdependent evolutionary careers of conscious beings, remaining inseparable from all that lives. We must not end this discussion with any sense of the primacy of the impersonal, with any sense of mystic merging or nihilistic disappearance. Yet the mode in which bodhisattvas continue to live, laugh, weep, teach and empathize is unthinkable, just as the existential status of all phenomena is unthinkable. As the Sutra suggests:

> The enlightened art of the bodhisattva is to appear to move in the transparent sphere of conventional characteristics and harmoniously functioning causality, while remaining totally awake to the signlessness and causelessness of sheer Reality.

This liberating way of living is not an illusion created by mirrors. The bodhisattvas are emphatically not shadows in a realm of shadows. Honestly and seriously, they manifest on earth and upon other planes of being the irresistible force of awakening, which is the power of Prajnaparamita to clear away every obstacle or obscuration from the lives of conscious beings, who are each supremely precious.

Physical, emotional and spiritual healings are spontaneously generated in the presence of this energy of transcendent insight:

There are no independently self-existing structures which could become infected by disease, nor is disease itself substantially self-existent. This transcendent insight into the total absence of any separate self-existence manifests healing, transforming and illuminating power.

Advanced practitioners of Prajnaparamita heal and protect by the concentrated application of the principle of Perfect Wisdom, a process the Sutra calls *invoking truth energy*. This force is not some provisional countermeasure but is the supremely active principle of nonduality or indivisibility. Yet the Sutra warns about the dangers of self-deception and pride to which thaumaturgic or apparently miraculous actions may expose the immature practitioner.

Engaged in the fullest range of human responsibility, the bodhisattva continuously vows: *I will live and act totally through Perfect Wisdom so that my body, speech and mind, here and now, will be the most radical teaching of the Buddhas that is called Prajnaparamita.* This *diamond vow-I*, completely free from any abstract or habitual notion of substantial or independent *I-ness*, is the irreversibly committed mind stream of the bodhisattva, who lives in constant, heartfelt gratitude to Mother Prajnaparamita and to all her empowered representatives. The bodhisattvas live in tender solicitude for all beloved sentient beings, each of whom expresses the perfect transparency of Prajnaparamita. Bodhisattvas themselves become Goddess Prajnaparamita's fully conscious expression.

> The adamantine awareness who lives and breathes as this transparency is the living, breathing Prajnaparamita—no longer just a narrowly focused conscious being but an omnipresent compassionate awareness, fully awake to universal enlightenment.

By profoundly contemplating the *Prajnaparamita Sutra*, may the ineffable station of bodhisattvahood become manifest! May all conscious beings everywhere evolve swiftly to the point of encountering and appreciating these teachings!

PART II

FORTY SELECTIONS FROM THE
PRAJNAPARAMITA SUTRA IN 8,000 LINES

MAHAYANA IS IMMEASURABILITY

SUBHUTI: O Lord Buddha, what is this Great Vehicle, the Mahayana? What is its point of departure? Its destination? Through what realm does it move? How can one who travels in the Great Vehicle be recognized? Who is the person courageous enough to travel this way?

LORD BUDDHA: Mahayana is synonymous with immeasurability. Immeasurability is synonymous with infinity, and infinity with ineffability. Through selfless cultivation of the six transcendent Perfections—Generosity, Goodness, Patience, Commitment, Meditation and Insight—adamantine awareness travels in the Great Vehicle, the Mahayana. Its point of departure is the triple world, which is comprised of the realm of desire-form, the realm of sublime form and the formless realm and which contains all possible manifestation. Its destination lacks the slightest separate self-existence. Both the point of departure and the destination of the Mahayana are free from the slightest substantial objective or subjective basis or location.

The courageous diamond being, the bodhisattva who travels in this vehicle of immeasurability, is therefore traveling nowhere. Nor is there any separate traveler. Nor does this uncontainable vehicle move through any substantial realm. Simply by its perfect freedom from all notions of location, substance and limitation, the Mahayana already abides as omnipresence and omniscience. No separately self-existing personality is traveling on the Great Vehicle, has ever traveled on the Great Vehicle or will ever travel on the Great Vehicle. Neither the personality structure of the traveler nor the philosophical structure of the Mahayana possess even an atom of substantial or independent self-existence.

Therefore, neither practitioner nor practice can be grasped, crystallized or objectified in any way. What transparent structure can travel in what transparent vehicle? Cultivating this attitude of complete openness and radiant transparency, the bodhisattva is armed with the invincible weapon of Perfect Wisdom and travels in the Great Vehicle, demonstrating the infinitely subtle liberative art that can awaken and mature every unique conscious being.

SUBHUTI: O Lord Buddha, this Great Vehicle appears to travel simply by transcending the triple world, with its countless heavenly, subtle and earthly beings. Mahayana is like boundless space. Therefore, it is called great, immeasurable, ineffable. As within universal space, so within this vehicle of immeasurability, there always remains room for an incalculable number of conscious beings. No one can perceive or conceive the coming or the going of this Great Vehicle, nor does it abide anywhere. Thus no one can discover any beginning or ending to Mahayana, nor even any present state of being called Mahayana. Nonetheless, Mahayana always remains identical everywhere. Because of this wondrous, all-embracing nature, it is called the Great Vehicle.

LORD BUDDHA: Beautifully expounded, Subhuti. This is precisely Mahayana, the wonderful vehicle of bodhisattvas, the diamond beings who, traveling thus, not only will someday reach but have already reached total awakeness or omniscience.

SUBHUTI: The powerful transmission of Buddha nature speaks through me, O Lord, so my words are never inadequate to Perfect Wisdom. Not only is Mahayana immeasurable and ineffable. Bodhisattvas are ineffable as well. These diamond beings cannot be approached from where they begin or from where they end, nor at any point between. Why? Because the personal form, feeling and consciousness of the bodhisattva is equally as boundless, divisionless and ungraspable as the open expanse of the Great Vehicle. Bodhisattvas never entertain the idea: *a bodhisattva is a particular personal form or personal consciousness.* No such conception or experience can exist independently, and therefore the existential status of the bodhisattva cannot be grasped, formulated or entertained in any way.

In every possible mode of clear penetration, I have never apprehended any subjective or objective structures which could constitute a bodhisattva. I do not encounter, O Lord, any separate form of existence to which the terms *bodhisattva* or *mahayana* could point. Neither do I apprehend any separate existence that could be called Prajnaparamita, or Perfect Wisdom, much less do I apprehend some separate state of omniscience, which is the fruit of Perfect Wisdom. Therefore, what unapprehendable structure called a *bodhisattva* should I instruct and encourage in what unapprehendable structure called *prajnaparamita?*

Buddha, bodhisattva, prajnaparamita—these are merely abstract terms, composed of certain sounds and letters, correlated with certain conventional perceptions and concepts. What they point at has never substantially come into being. What they indicate is an uncreated and, hence, ungraspable and unthinkable presence. The same is true of the terms *self* and *universe.* Although we speak conventionally about the personal self, assuming that we are encountering it constantly, no self with separate identity of any kind has ever come substantially into being. That all structures and processes have never been created simply means that they appear vividly and function coherently without possessing any independent essence that can be isolated, grasped or formulated in any way. How can I instruct and encourage a student who has never come into being in a Perfection of Wisdom which never comes into being? How can there be any teacher of Prajnaparamita, since neither Buddhas nor bodhisattvas have ever substantially come into being?

When this most radical truth is unfolded to an aspirant without causing the slightest fear or anxiety, then one can know, with confidence, that the aspirant is a bodhisattva, an adamantine awareness who flows as Perfect Wisdom. With each breath, thought and perception, bodhisattvas investigate and meditate upon Prajnaparamita,

Mother of the Buddhas, spontaneously receiving her healing and illuminating energy and lovingly transmitting this energy of awakening to all conscious beings.

When investigating and meditating upon all structures of relativity
with Perfect Wisdom, there is no direct or indirect approach to or
through any personal form, personal feeling or personal consciousness. There is no going forth of any kind. There is no reviewing of
how forms appear to arise or how they appear to be destroyed.

The absence of the substantial creation of any form is not different
from the radiantly transparent, harmonious and coherent functioning of all forms. Thus absolute openness and relative functioning are
not divided. They are not two alternative dimensions, but utter
simplicity. If one labels and thereby experiences this expansive
simplicity as material form and personal consciousness, one is foolishly
numbering and labeling that which has no multiplicity and no identity. The bodhisattva investigates and meditates upon all structures,
processes and dimensions as simplicity, and therefore does not
approach or even encounter any substantial forms or independent
states of consciousness.

SHARIPUTRA: If I am able to follow this subtle presentation by my
revered brother Subhuti, the bodhisattva, too, is that same indivisible, unthinkable simplicity which has never been created and which
therefore never substantially comes into being in any way. But if this
is true, how can we speak of the bodhisattva going forth on what
is called the most noble and difficult pilgrimage, enduring such suffering and lovingly performing such self-sacrifice for the succor, liberation and enlightenment of all conscious beings?

SUBHUTI: I do not entertain the slightest expectation of discovering even a trace of some person who goes forth on a noble and difficult pilgrimage or who goes forth in any sense at all. The *practitioner* who projects notions of nobility or difficulty is not an awakened
bodhisattva. No one who is limited by any perception of difficulty
can even for an instant work to bring about the well-being and total
illumination of an infinite number of conscious beings, desperately
entrapped by egocentricity and its consequent suffering. Awakened

bodhisattvas operate in precisely the opposite manner. They swim in the sense of limitless ease, freedom and delight generated by Perfect Wisdom. They are imbued with a tender love that regards all conscious beings in the universe without exception as their beloved parents or cherished children. Such is the ecstatic, goalless pilgrimage of the bodhisattvas. They live in communion with and in service of countless living beings who, even closer than parents and children, are essentially their own intimate consciousness.

These diamond beings meditate: *Our longing to be free from suffering is simply the longing of all that lives to be free from suffering.* Bodhisattvas permeate their daily awareness with this commitment: *We can never desert for an instant even one of these beloved beings. We can only live to liberate them all without exception from their terrible burden of delusive suffering. We can never generate the slightest thought of hatred or even irritation toward any of these precious beings, even though they may torture or destroy our bodies during a hundred consecutive lifetimes.* This is the spirit with which bodhisattvas dedicate their mind and heart to conscious beings, recognizing all beings as their very own most intimate consciousness.

One who exists solely as this boundaryless mind and heart of wisdom and love will not perceive difficulties simply because one never perceives separation, substantiality or limit. The ease, freedom and delight of Mother Prajnaparamita flows through the awareness of the bodhisattva, a constant reminder that no personal self exists substantially or independently, just as no apparent structure of the universe exists substantially or independently. This principle of ontological transparency applies to every subjective or objective structure or process that can possibly be experienced by any consciousness. Thus the consecrated heart of love is identical with the clear mind of transcendent insight. There is no substantial coming into being of any difficulty or nobility, just as there is no substantial coming into being of any bodhisattva, pilgrimage or path.

SHARIPUTRA: Is it just the bodhisattva, the awareness dedicated to universal conscious enlightenment, who does not substantially come into being, or also the principles which constitute a bodhisattva?

SUBHUTI: Even the principles which constitute a bodhisattva never independently come into being.

SHARIPUTRA: Does the final, ultimate, transcendent awareness called Buddhahood objectively come into being?

SUBHUTI: Even the total awakeness of omniscience never originates, arises or comes into being, objectively or subjectively.

SHARIPUTRA: What about the millions of ordinary human beings?

SUBHUTI: They, too, have never substantially come into being, nor have the principles which constitute *number*, *humanity* or *ordinariness*.

SHARIPUTRA: If what you say is true and the complete range of manifestation is insubstantial and transparent, then the state of omniscience must be attained instantly, spontaneously and effortlessly.

SUBHUTI: Dear brother, the diamond being has no interest whatsoever in attaining any state, no matter how exalted, for no conscious state ever comes into being. The bodhisattva is not in search of mystic union or reunion with any level of reality, for no such level ever comes into being. A personal structure which has never come into being cannot attain a spiritual goal which never comes into being—whether with effort or without effort, gradually or instantly.

SHARIPUTRA: How, then, is the supremely precious attainment of Buddhahood possible?

SUBHUTI: Dear brother, can what is never created in the first place come into being in the form of some substantial attainment?

SHARIPUTRA: In no way, Subhuti. Yet could one speak, at least metaphorically, of the coming into being of that which never comes into being?

SUBHUTI: Such a statement would contain merely unintelligible words.

SHARIPUTRA: But is it intelligible to speak as you do about uncreated Reality?

SUBHUTI: To reason about uncreated Reality is just to play with words. Yet from this coherent, playful reasoning, lightning bolts flash forth as gnostic intuition—totally insubstantial, not coming into being even for an instant, yet diamond sharp and clear.

SHARIPUTRA: Truly our Dharma brother Subhuti stands foremost among the dialectical masters of Prajnaparamita. Whatever questions are posed, he skillfully turns and opens into sheer illumination. Unswerving from truth, his words and his entire being embody Perfect Wisdom, free from the slightest discrepancy or contradiction.

SUBHUTI: Such clarity is the active compassion of Lord Buddha's transmission expressed through the holders of the lineage, those who neither seek nor perceive the slightest substantial basis or ontological support. Their words never contradict the empty, transparent yet functional nature of relative existence, nor does their awareness ever depart from this true nature. Why? Because they do not rely upon or even perceive any substantial material processes or personal structures, much less any independently existing structures or processes of reasoning. They do not even regard Reality, or Buddha nature, as ever having come independently into being.

SHARIPUTRA: Beautifully spoken, Subhuti. And what is it that permits bodhisattvas never to rely upon or identify with any structure of relativity?

SUBHUTI: The Perfection of Wisdom, the inconceivable power of Prajnaparamita, beneficial to all levels of spiritual practitioners, is what radically opens the bodhisattvas, freeing them from all grasping or identification. If any aspirant remains joyous and relaxed when the inconceivably deep Perfection of Wisdom is being expounded— revealing an infinite expanse of transparently functioning structures, each without any support or identity—then this aspirant can be known to belong to Perfect Wisdom, to have become profoundly attentive and responsive to Prajnaparamita.

SHARIPUTRA: Yet attention and responsiveness are the very nature of consciousness, so all beings must already belong to Perfect Wisdom.

SUBHUTI: Attention and responsiveness are also transparent structures, functioning coherently without any independent essence or identity. Attention does not exist substantially any more than the conscious beings who pay attention exist substantially. Attention is intrinsically free from any abiding basis or foundation, just as the beings who pay attention are intrinsically free from any abiding basis or foundation. Attention is unthinkable and indescribable, just as all conscious beings are unthinkable and indescribable. Attention does not go through either a gradual or an instantaneous process in order to reach enlightenment, just as the beings who pay attention do not go through any such substantial process. This freedom from formulation or crystallization, this depth of unthinkability, is the panoramic attention and tender responsiveness which manifests as the bodhisattva, the diamond being who dwells most powerfully by not dwelling anywhere.

WHERE THE BODHISATTVA STANDS

SUBHUTI: Through the inexhaustible power of Buddha nature, I will now demonstrate to any conscious beings who are prepared to listen how the bodhisattva stands courageously in Perfect Wisdom. Simply by standing in the emptiness or transparency of all conventionally constituted self-existence does the bodhisattva stand in the Perfection of Wisdom. Armed against primordial metaphysical error with the great armor of emptiness, freedom and openness, the bodhisattva is not rooted, focused or established in the perception of material forms or in the experience of personal feelings, perceptions and impulses. The bodhisattva is not rooted, focused or established in any possible state of individual or communal awareness within the cosmic display of earth, water, fire, wind, space and perspectival consciousness. The bodhisattva is not even rooted, focused or established in the practice of mindfulness and other contemplative disciplines, nor in their fruits, the supranormal powers. The bodhisattva is not identified with exalted levels of the spiritual path, including gnostic sainthood or solitary sagehood, nor even with the supreme goal of Buddhahood.

The diamond being who stands courageously in Perfect Wisdom experiences no identification with the noble Stream Enterer, who begins to flow as the stream of realization, nor with the noble Once Returner, who has only one more incarnation before achieving com-

51

plete personal liberation, nor with the noble Never Returner, who will achieve complete personal liberation at the moment of death. Nor does the bodhisattva identify with or idolize even the sublime Arhat, or gnostic saint, who has already achieved complete personal liberation while living out this present lifetime.

The diamond being who stands courageously in Perfect Wisdom does not identify with any idea, statement or doctrine from common experience or from any philosophical or religious framework, beginning with the conventional assumption, *the world consists of material forms*, all the way to the exalted teaching, *the world consists of Buddha nature*.

The bodhisattva is not rooted, focused or established in any philosophical analysis, either Buddhist or non-Buddhist, which concludes that the principle of form is impermanent or that it is permanent. The bodhisattva does not identify truth with the assertion that the processes of form constitute suffering or that they constitute happiness, that the processes of form are not the self or are the self, that the processes of form are repulsive or attractive, or that form is inherently empty of substantiality or inherently substantial. The bodhisattva is not identified with any philosophical or religious notion that the fruits of the holy life of Buddhist or non-Buddhist practice derive their value and dignity from a separate, unconditioned Reality. The bodhisattva does not seek to become established in the sublime station of a self-realized sage nor even in the supremely wondrous state of a fully awakened Buddha, when such is conceived as a separate individual state above or apart from all conscious beings.

The diamond being who courageously stands in Perfect Wisdom does not adopt or lean for support upon the notion that any advanced level of Buddhist or non-Buddhist attainment is worthy of earthly or heavenly praise, honor or reward. The bodhisattva does not even lean for support upon the inspiring idea of the supreme praiseworthiness of a Buddha who has attained Final Nirvana — that state of absolute fulfillment that leaves behind no impurity or suffering whatsoever. The bodhisattva does not objectify even this heroic Buddha, who has succeeded in bringing about the physical and spiritual well-

being of countless living beings and has led to Nirvana, or total liberation, thousands of millions of billions of beings, maturing them
gradually through the stages of common experience, then through
discipleship, sainthood, sagehood and Buddhahood. The bodhisattva
who stands courageously in Perfect Wisdom is not fixated even upon
the imageless image of total liberation.

While listening to this radical discourse by his Dharma brother
Subhuti, incomparable master of Prajnaparamita and noble companion
of Shakyamuni Buddha, the holy elder Shariputra experiences a flash
of thought: *If the bodhisattva cannot be rooted, focused or established
in the ideal of liberation, how is it possible to train and to stand authentically in Perfect Wisdom?* Through the power of Buddha nature,
Subhuti discerns the thought of his spiritual brother and addresses
him tenderly.

SUBHUTI: O inseparable friend, consider our gentle Master who has
disappeared so beautifully into pure presence, the transcendent
Tathagata who has gone completely beyond any conventional view.
Where does he stand? How does he stand?
SHARIPUTRA: Nowhere does the wondrous Tathagata stand.
Nowhere does he root, focus, establish or identify himself. Nowhere
does Awakened Enlightenment seek base or support. He is never to
be found, neither within the play of conditions nor within some
separate realm of unconditioned reality.
SUBHUTI: Precisely so, beloved brother. And this traceless way of
the transcendent Tathagatas is the very way the bodhisattva trains
and stands in Perfect Wisdom. With ultimate courage and adamantine conviction, the bodhisattva goes completely beyond convention,
vowing: *Just as Awakened Enlightenment does not focus itself as any
description or as any thought pattern — neither standing anywhere nor
not standing anywhere, neither standing apart from everywhere nor
not standing apart from everywhere — precisely with this modeless insight
and this enlightened energy will I train and stand in Perfect Wisdom.
Exactly as the Tathagata is stationed in the stationless transparency of*

all phenomena, so will I be stationed without further delay – perfectly
stationed, because free from the experience of any independent substance
or separate individuality upon which to be established, perfectly stationed
because without the slightest physical or metaphysical ground upon which
to stand.

When diamond beings generate the infinite courage to live existentially in this spirit, their entire awareness becomes aligned with Prajnaparamita, absorbed in Perfect Wisdom. Inseparable from every
breath of every conscious being, their heartfelt meditation on Perfect
Wisdom never ceases, even for a moment.

UNTHINKABLE AND UNFINDABLE

*T*HE fully realized master of Perfect Wisdom, the venerable Subhuti, queries his supreme guide and illuminator, the radiant Buddha.

SUBHUTI: O Lord Buddha, when the conventional mind speaks about the bodhisattva, the one committed to universal conscious enlightenment, to what substantial, independent being does this term refer? After profound investigation, I still cannot discover any such bodhisattva. Neither can I find any subjective or objective structure corresponding to the term *prajnaparamita,* or Perfect Wisdom. Therefore, what bodhisattva should be instructed in what Prajnaparamita?

By means of the power streaming through Subhuti directly from Buddha nature, the answer is revealed through his own voice and words.

SUBHUTI: When the truth of unthinkability and undefinability is revealed, the heart of the diamond being is not shocked nor even slightly disturbed, nor is the adamantine commitment to all-embracing compassion dissolved or even dimmed. The bodhisattva's mind is not frightened or even faintly dismayed by the absence of any recognizable, definable or findable being called a *bodhisattva.*

Precisely this diamond being who does not tremble or waver when hearing the truth is the one who should be instructed and who will make great advances in Perfect Wisdom. This marvelous courage of the bodhisattva in the face of the infinite expansiveness and indefinability of Reality is the direct gift of Prajnaparamita, Mother of the Buddhas.

As the aspirant intensively cultivates this Perfection of Wisdom— indescribable, indefinable, unfindable—no personal pride can arise from some thought of the noble role of the bodhisattva, for all thoughts, as well as their subjects and objects, are recognized as luminous transparency, without the slightest substantial self-existence or independent self-awareness. Who is there to think what proud thoughts?

SHARIPUTRA: Revered brother disciple of the Lord, though luminous and transparent, are not the thinking subject, the thought and its object still some reality which actually exists?

SUBHUTI: Can assertions such as *it exists* or *it does not exist* apply to pure presence, which is entirely without modification and hence remains untouched by any possible discrimination or definition?

SHARIPUTRA: Well spoken, noble Subhuti, whom Lord Buddha rightfully calls the foremost among those who dwell in the inconceivable peace of Perfect Wisdom. Precisely through such clear recognition of the ontological transparency of subjects and objects does the bodhisattva become unwaveringly focused upon universal enlightenment. There is no possibility of losing this focus, because the diamond being is ceaselessly engaging in Perfect Wisdom with the entire process of thought and perception. There is nothing other than Prajnaparamita.

To validate and intensify whatever contemplative training one undertakes, on whatever level of universality, one should pursue the Perfection of Wisdom. One should embrace Perfect Wisdom with one's whole being, constantly bearing its principles in heart and mind, venerating its scriptural form devotedly, chanting it melodiously, studying it critically and awakening others to it with stainless reasoning and dynamic enthusiasm. The only proper motive for engaging with

Prajnaparamita is to unfold the subtle characteristics of all-embracing compassion and all-transcending insight which constitute the bodhisattva, one who is lovingly dedicated to the enlightenment of all conscious beings and who displays an astonishing array of liberative skills to awaken these beings. The dedication of a bodhisattva gradually matures into the universal conscious enlightenment of a Buddha.

SUBHUTI: Brother Shariputra, although you state the case eloquently, I still cannot discover any independently self-existing structures to correspond with these wonderful words *bodhisattva* and *prajnaparamita*. My question remains, what bodhisattva should be instructed in what Perfection of Wisdom? What good is it to play with words if one cannot discover some reality to which they actually refer?

Once again, the power streaming through Subhuti directly from Buddha nature responds perfectly to this question through the elder's own speech.

SUBHUTI: The Reality which these and all other terms refer is ungraspable and inconceivable, possessing no physical or metaphysical self-existence. The spiritual aspirant who does not become even subtly anxious when this unthinkable depth of Perfect Wisdom is invoked should be recognized as already a bodhisattva immersed in Prajnaparamita, authentically established in truth by being free from any personal claim to truth.

The adamantine awareness who flows as Perfect Wisdom does not define, formulate and thereby experience Reality in terms of personal forms, personal feelings or personal consciousness. This would be the way of personality, not the way of Prajnaparamita. Whoever remains crystalized as personality cannot melt and flow as the Perfection of Wisdom. Spontaneous and selfless flow alone is the authentic practice of Prajnaparamita. While remaining a separate personality, constantly attempting to grasp and to define the ungraspable and the indefinable, one can never blossom into the omniscience which is total awakeness. Prajnaparamita never attempts to grasp or define

What Is. Prajnaparamita can never be grasped or defined. With selfless freedom and openness alone can the bodhisattva truly flow as Perfect Wisdom.

The transcendent insight of the diamond being is called *the vision which simultaneously sees and sees through all subjective and objective structures without remaining to grasp or even encounter them.* This gnostic vision is limitless, unwavering, sublime. It is not attained by any aspirant whose practice is even partially sustained by motives of self-service or self-liberation.

Obviously, omniscience cannot be grasped. By its very allness, it is precluded from possessing any particular mark, sign or limit which the mind might actually cognize or even attempt to cognize. If total awakeness manifested a sign by which it could be defined, discriminated and separately encountered, it would not be total. One should generate adamantine faith and confidence in omniscience which participates in omniscience directly, never regarding it through any limited focus whatsoever. One should not attempt to locate omniscience anywhere within the processes of personal form, personal feeling and personal consciousness, nor outside or beyond these processes, as some separate reality other than form, feeling and consciousness. The omniscience or total awakeness of Buddhahood can simply not be located or formulated.

Taking as sole guideline the true nature of all structures, which is the absence in them of any substantial self-existence, one should generate powerful conviction concerning the essential selflessness and signlessness of What Is, so as no longer to assume, even unconsciously or instinctively, the independent self-existence of any structure which one might then attempt to grasp, isolate, cognize and encounter separately. One should not attempt to encounter separately some state of final release, or Nirvana, because desiring or even acknowledging final release implies that there exists some independent structure of consciousness which is released at a certain moment. There is only Prajnaparamita.

Thus the Perfect Wisdom of the bodhisattva does not grasp, isolate and encounter either form or formlessness. Adamantine awareness never seeks Nirvana but flowers transparently as the illuminating presence of a Tathagata—one who has disappeared into complete wakefulness, radiating miraculously liberating wisdom energy through all conscious beings.

The courageous practitioner who engages in this Perfection of Wisdom meditates ceaselessly on its transparency and always recalls the ontological transparency of the one who engages in it—a transparency which possesses absolutely no self-existence, no solidity, no limits and which therefore cannot be grasped or even subtly apprehended in any way. When these most radical teachings do not evoke anxiety or even slightly disconcert the mind, then the aspirant can be known as already authentically immersed in Prajnaparamita.

SHARIPUTRA: But how can a bodhisattva be recognized as immersed in Perfect Wisdom when the personal form of the bodhisattva does not possess any independent or substantial self-existence, when even the wisdom of the bodhisattva does not possess independent or substantial self-existence, when omniscience or total awakeness does not possess even a trace of independent or substantial self-existence?

SUBHUTI: Well spoken, Shariputra. It is precisely as you say. All the intricate forms which are encountered as the universe do not actually, under close investigation, possess any characteristic marks of form. The Perfection of Wisdom, even though it can be spoken about clearly and pointed out authentically, does not, under close investigation, actually possess any characteristic marks of Perfect Wisdom. Even characteristic marks which may appear unequivocal do not themselves actually possess the slightest characteristic. Even essence does not possess the slightest self-existing essentiality.

SHARIPUTRA: And still there is a bodhisattva who, cultivating this Perfect Wisdom, will attain omniscience?

SUBHUTI: My noble brother, of course there is! Simply by this clear recognition that no processes, structures or characteristics of any kind are substantially generated, the bodhisattva blossoms as total awakeness. The thought flow and even the physical body of an awakened bodhisattva become perfectly pure, because they manifest solely for the sake of guiding and maturing all conscious beings. With body and thought flow completely purified from subtle egocentricity, the bodhisattva, who actually embodies the omniscience of Prajnaparamita, will meet spontaneously with living Buddhas upon all planes of being and awareness.

Immature practitioners retain the instinctive notion that their own personal form, personal feeling and personal consciousness possess some sort of recognizable and invariable set of characteristic marks. These persons are engaged in the false assumption that form, feeling and consciousness have been substantially produced and, therefore, they remain anxious to control or transcend these processes.

Immature practitioners can even become entrapped by self-consciously proclaiming the doctrine, *form is empty,* or by the self-involved notion, *I am practicing Prajnaparamita,* thereby giving play to false suppositions concerning separate self-existence. When such persons speculate, even for an instant, that *the one who practices and contemplates in this way certainly will develop Perfect Wisdom,* they become tangled in mere signs, words and limited assertions which they falsely suppose to exist in some subtle yet substantial manner.

SHARIPUTRA: Given the intense rigor of your analysis, revered brother, how can a bodhisattva be consciously committed to the practice and contemplation of Prajnaparamita?

SUBHUTI: The awakened bodhisattva does not indulge in analyzing and constantly reviewing the *skandhas,* or structural processes of personality, nor even in contemplating the advanced notion that the *skandhas* themselves are mere signs. Much less does the bodhisattva observe any apparent arising, diminishing or destruction of the *skandhas.* The awakened bodhisattva does not even indulge in contemplating the assertion from the wisdom tradition that the *skandhas* are empty of self-existence, much less does the personal affirmation arise, *I am practicing* or *I am a bodhisattva.* It never occurs to the diamond being, even for an instant, that *the one who practices and contemplates in this way certainly will develop Perfect Wisdom.*

The bodhisattva trains rigorously but never becomes even slightly distracted by the self-congratulation, *I am truly training in Prajnaparamita,* nor by the self-doubt, *I may not be truly training in Pra-*

jnaparamita. The mature practitioner does not even approach or thematically represent any separate things, any structure of relativity. Why? Because all beings and events, by their very nature are inconceivable and therefore unapproachable, ungraspable, unfindable, unrepresentable. Thus the awakened bodhisattva manifests spontaneously the transcendent insight known as *not grasping any separate thing*—the omniscient insight which is limitless, unwavering, sublime. This panoramic awakeness transcends even the widest vision of any contemplative practitioner who remains subtly self-conscious and self-involved.

When they flow indivisibly as Perfect Wisdom, bodhisattvas inherit the full enlightenment which Buddhas of past aeons have predicted for them. But even while remaining immersed in Prajnaparamita, the adamantine awareness never forms or entertains any self-conscious notion such as *I am now deep in sublime concentration* or *I have now entered the meditation beyond all meditation.* For the awakened bodhisattva, the entire spectrum of spiritual levels and degrees of realization possesses absolutely no substantial self-existence.

SHARIPUTRA: Can this selfless contemplation called Prajnaparamita be demonstrated or recognized in any way?

SUBHUTI: In no way, Shariputra. The son or daughter of the Buddha family who awakens as Prajnaparamita does not thematize, objectify or perceive any method or goal of contemplation called Perfect Wisdom.

LORD BUDDHA: Precisely so, Subhuti. By not objectifying, isolating, formulating or even encountering Prajnaparamita in any way is Prajnaparamita truly practiced, demonstrated and transmitted.

SUBHUTI: One wonders, O Lord, when the bodhisattva practices the Perfection of Wisdom in this radical way, what exactly is being practiced or engaged in? Responding through the power of Buddha nature, one can answer that no process whatsoever is being practiced or engaged in by the bodhisattva. Why? Because no processes—either subjective, objective or transcendent—ever exist with the physical or metaphysical solidity and separateness assumed by naive perceivers and immature contemplatives.

SHARIPUTRA: Supremely revered Lord Buddha, in what surprising mode or manner, then, do all the structures and processes which are conventionally encountered actually exist?

LORD BUDDHA: They exist free from self-consciousness and self-objectification. The appearance of separately self-aware and substantially self-existing beings and events is the result of the primordial ignorance which unconsciously and instinctively projects the notions of individuality, substance and separation. Persons who naively take their perceptual and conceptual experience, or even their contemplative experience, as literal or complete are attempting to root themselves existentially on the level of mere abstract conventional constructs. They indulge, obviously or subtly, in the false reasoning that presumes a structure must exhibit substantiality or encounterability in order to exist at all. This largely unconscious reasoning blinds naive realists and even naive contemplatives to the transparent, insubstantial and yet totally functional existence of all structures and processes, forcing such persons to live instead within complex sets of worldly or religious abstractions and conventions which they presume to be solid, findable and therefore real. They project this abstract solidity and encounterability onto their notions of the past, the future and the present moment. They attempt to crystalize Reality temporarily or permanently into names and forms.

Although these constructions or structurings of personal and communal consciousness do not possess the slightest degree of self-existence, they nonetheless veil the path of insight, the spiritual path which reveals the ontological openness, freedom and radiant transparency of What Is. Whether worldly or religious, naive perceivers cannot awaken from this veiled awareness, which is the triple world of mundane form, sublime form and formlessness. They remain asleep to the pure presence, or total awakeness, which constitutes all worlds and dimensions. The fundamental ignorance which they take to be their own direct, reliable experience is simply the naivete of the conventional, habitual mind. These persons need to develop faith and confidence in the radical teachings of Prajnaparamita. The bodhisattva is one who no longer naively or literally accepts any of the innumerable constructs of consciousness to be self-existent.

SHARIPUTRA: O Lord Buddha, when bodhisattvas cultivate this radical insight of Perfect Wisdom, are they cultivating omniscience?

LORD BUDDHA: The diamond being never covets or cultivates the omniscience of Buddhahood. The very attitude of noncultivation reveals all possible structures, from sense objects to Buddhas, to be ontologically transparent. This radiant transparency, in turn, is simply the total awakeness of all Buddhas. The awakened bodhisattva thus becomes immersed in omniscience and spontaneously blossoms as omniscience.

SUBHUTI: O Lord, how can a dream person, an imaginary person or a fictional person become immersed in omniscience and blossom as omniscience?

LORD BUDDHA: Consider carefully, most brilliant Subhuti. Is the dimension of objective form separate from the dimensions of dream or imagination?

SUBHUTI: No, Lord. Because all dimensions of experience are completely interrelated and interdependent.

LORD BUDDHA: Consider also, Subhuti. Is the being who is committed to universal enlightenment, the bodhisattva, some supersubstantial existence outside the insubstantial structures of consciousness?

SUBHUTI: No, Lord. Because there is, in reality, no substantial self-existence of any description whatsoever—whether bodhisattva or naive person, dreamed person or fictional person—although the strange sense of being a dream character often arises spontaneously in the bodhisattva's awareness. None of the constructs of consciousness possess the slightest degree of independent self-existence, whether they be sense organs, sense objects, complete personalities or entire universes.

SHARIPUTRA: O sublime Lord, will not those who have only recently committed themselves to the Bodhisattva Way become unsettled or even despondent when they hear your teaching about the unthinkable and unfindable existential status of the bodhisattva?

LORD BUDDHA: Beginners will become unsettled or despondent only if they hear these teachings of radical insight from immature or nihilistic teachers, who have the same distracting and disintegrating effect on the mind as bad worldly companions. But there will be no despondency, distortion or even the slightest distraction if aspirants receive these revolutionary teachings from mature teachers, who are called supremely good friends. These cherished guides of humanity and benefactors of all sentient beings inspire an intimate love and trust more intense than that experienced between best friends. They wisely and skillfully encourage the aspirant to develop the selfless Perfections of Generosity, Goodness, Patience, Commitment and Meditation, as well as the peerless Perfection of Insight that constitutes the central core of the Bodhisattva way.

These supremely good friends also tirelessly and unerringly point out the tendencies toward negativity and self-deception which spring from the active principle of egocentricity, Mara the Tempter, until the aspirant learns clearly to recognize and carefully to avoid every such tendency. These supremely good friends are indispensable to the diamond being, the bodhisattva, who learns to wield the most subtle weapon of peace, Perfect Wisdom, traveling with inconceivable swiftness on the Great Vehicle, the Mahayana, along the way of universal conscious enlightenment.

ABSOLUTELY NOTHING
TO UNDERSTAND

*A*s they listen to Subhuti discourse on Prajnaparamita, an astonishing thought arises in the pure minds of the highest heavenly beings: *The arcane secrets which beings on the subtle planes whisper among themselves, we can understand instantly with our heavenly modes of perception and our divine intellection. Yet what the noble Subhuti discourses upon openly and clearly, we cannot begin to understand.*

Subhuti, through the power of Buddha nature, hears these celestial minds thinking in concert and replies: *Dear friends, you cannot understand because there is absolutely nothing finite to understand. You are not lacking in refinement of intellect. There is simply nothing separate or substantial in Prajnaparamita to which the intellect can be applied, because Perfect Wisdom does not present any graspable or thinkable doctrine and offers no describable method of contemplation.*

Thereupon, the exalted beings of the Heavenly Realm aspire collectively, with great intensity: *May this holy disciple of Awakened Enlightenment expand upon his paradoxical assertion that there is nothing to understand. The subtle teaching which the marvelous Subhuti is now unfolding through his illumined intellect and demonstrating with his entire being is more arcane than the arcane, more secret than the secret, more profound than the profound.*

Subhuti again reads their divine thoughts and replies: *No one can truly taste any level of realization – from the beginning point of entering wholeheartedly into the stream of contemplative cultivation to the final goal of full enlightenment – without patiently accepting the ultimate elusiveness of truth. The nature of What Is can be demonstrated clearly and pointed out authentically by Prajnaparamita, but always remains beyond finite or conventional teaching, beyond explanation, description or designation.*

With sincere longing to penetrate this mysterious teaching beyond all teaching, the denizens of the Thirty-Three Heaven ponder silently: *With what attitude should we regard ourselves in order to be receptive to the profound and elusive truth indicated and demonstrated by Subhuti?*

Subhuti discerns even this silent pondering and replies: *Those conscious beings who are mature enough to receive the radical teaching of Perfect Wisdom regard themselves simply as a display of magical power without any substantial self-existence. There should be no residual tendency to hear and grasp as some independent reality the words of the teaching, nor to isolate and reify their meaning, nor to experience as a separate reality whatever they are indicating.*

DIVINE REALM: But if conscious beings seriously consider themselves to be magical display, is this not tantamount to regarding their own existence as illusory?

SUBHUTI: The phrases *magical display, dream display, own existence* and *all conscious beings* are simply synonymous. Every objective or subjective structure that is directly experienced as factual or palpable should be regarded as magical display, as dream display. Even the various kinds of saintly or realized beings—from those at the beginning point of entering wholeheartedly into the stream of contemplative cultivation to those who have reached the final goal of full enlightenment—are magical display, dream display.

DIVINE REALM: Can you be suggesting, venerable Subhuti, that even a fully awakened Buddha is a magical display? Or even that the ultimate principle of Buddha nature, from which all Buddhas emerge, is a dream?

SUBHUTI: Absolutely. Even Final Nirvana, the cessation of all phenomenal manifestation, is purely magical display, purely dream display.

DIVINE REALM: How is it possible, Subhuti, that Nirvana, the supreme release from all projection and structuring, can be regarded as some form of magic or dream?

SUBHUTI: Dear divine friends, even if there could be any reality more perfect, more transcendent or more liberated than Final Nirvana, that, too, would be magical or dreamlike. The terms *magical display, dream display, Buddha* and *Nirvana* are synonymous.

At this electrifying moment in Subhuti's discourse, the venerable Shariputra, tenderhearted master of Perfect Wisdom, the venerable Purna, exalted cousin of Shakyamuni Buddha, the venerable Mahakatyayana and the venerable Mahakashyapa, adepts of the wondrous power of truth, as well as other realized companions of Lord Buddha, along with many thousand awakened bodhisattvas committed to universal conscious enlightenment, open their minds and hearts in a single ecstatic exclamation: *O noble Subhuti, who can possibly understand Prajnaparamita as you so radically elucidate it?*

SUBHUTI: Absolutely no one can grasp the Perfection of Wisdom here elucidated. For no independently existing objective or subjective teaching whatsoever is being presented by any isolated teacher, nor are there any separate, substantially existing students or listeners with whom to communicate. There is only Prajnaparamita.

TRUE INFINITUDE

SHAKRA: O holy Subhuti, an inconceivably great perfection shines forth as this Perfection of Wisdom. The radiance of its perfectness is limitless, immeasurable, infinite.

SUBHUTI: Your view of Perfect Wisdom is dawning, noble king of the heavenly realm. But one must remember that Prajnaparamita is inconceivably great, limitless, immeasurable and infinite simply because whatever the conventional mind separates and discriminates as material forms and conscious states are known by Prajnaparamita to be its own inconceivability, immeasurability and infinity. There is no reason to become fixated upon or to extol the Perfection of Wisdom as some isolated form of greatness or perfectness, because Prajnaparamita recognizes every single being, event and perception as precisely the same limitless, immeasurable, infinite perfection. This recognition is what constitutes the greatness of Perfect Wisdom.

The perfection of Prajnaparamita is infinite because it demonstrates that no one can isolate or analyze the genesis, evolution or goal of any subjective or objective process. The perfection of Prajnaparamita is infinite because it recognizes that all processes are inherently infinite and, therefore, ungraspable and unthinkable. This freedom from being perceptually and conceptually confined by the habitual mind, this opening to the limitlessness, immeasurability and infinity of all realms and dimensions is why Prajnaparamita is an inconceivably great perfection.

SHAKRA: O holy elder, how is the infinitude of worlds and beings related to the infinitude of Perfect Wisdom?

SUBHUTI: Prajnaparamita is not infinite in the same sense as either the exceedingly large number of conscious beings or the unimaginably vast expanse of living worlds.

SHAKRA: Why, then, do you teach that recognizing the limitlessness, immeasurability and infinity of beings, realms and dimensions makes Prajnaparamita an inconceivably great perfection?

SUBHUTI: Consider carefully, O celestial intelligence. What precisely is an individual being in the first place?

SHAKRA: According to your own clear teaching, the term *individual being* does not indicate any independently existing structure. This term is just an arbitrary sound, an abstraction floating in the realm of linguistic and perceptual abstractions which are conventionally experienced as the world.

SUBHUTI: Well stated, noble king. So when someone uses the terms *individual being, substantial being* or *independent being*, is any structure actually indicated thereby?

SHAKRA: In no way, venerable Subhuti.

SUBHUTI: If not even a single separate being can be authentically indicated, how can there be an exceedingly large number of them? Suppose that a fully awakened Buddha—with the miraculous voice that reaches all beings, realms and dimensions simultaneously—were to call out with great power, during aeons as numberless as the grains of sand in the River Ganges, the term *individual being*, would this authenticate even one substantially self-existing being? Would this miraculous Buddha voice, with all its liberating power, be able to produce any such solid self-existence?

SHAKRA: In no way, venerable Subhuti. Because Prajnaparamita teaches that every structure which appears as an individual being or a substantial world is unthinkably pure, open and transparent from beginningless time.

SUBHUTI: Truly spoken. This ungraspable purity, openness and transparency is precisely what is meant by the limitlessness, immeasurability and infinity of all beings, realms and dimensions. Recognizing this purity, openness and transparency everywhere is what constitutes the inconceivable greatness of Prajnaparamita. Rather than infinity of number or infinity of extension in space and time, this transparent depth of unthinkability is the true infinitude. This alone makes Perfect Wisdom supremely perfect.

At this moment of heavenly time, the divine beings who inhabit the sublime realm under the kingship of Shakra, as well as the constellation of souls who have ascended into this celestial realm of consciousness through appropriate forms of worship, all cry out with great ecstasy, expressing themselves through the power of Buddha nature.

DIVINE REALM: Victory to truth! Supreme is the teaching of Prajnaparamita! Beautifully and wondrously has the illumined master Subhuti demonstrated Perfect Wisdom. Mother Prajnaparamita is the mysterious womb of infinitude which gives birthless birth to Awakened Enlightenment, transparently appearing everywhere as Buddhas, the humble Lords of Enlightenment who emanate rays of bodhisattvas, their spiritual daughters and sons. The bodhisattva who has awakened to the true infinitude of Prajnaparamita and who lives, moves and breathes as this plenitude of Perfect Wisdom, certainly is an embryonic Tathagata, worthy of the awe and love that all beings spontaneously experience for a fully awakened Buddha.

LORD BUDDHA: O divine beings and souls elevated by heavenly knowledge, you have discerned correctly. Your further evolution is assured. You now clearly understand the bodhisattva as the plenitude of Prajnaparamita.

During an ancient aeon, I lived the Bodhisattva Way, moving and breathing as the plenitude of Prajnaparamita. One blessed day, I encountered the Tathagata Dipankara in the dusty bazaar of a royal city. The Tathagata glanced at me and perceived an embryonic

Tathagata. He immediately predicted my full spiritual evolution, indicating that my mind stream would flow for aeons in compassionate service to conscious beings, while clearly recognizing them as the true infinitude of Perfect Wisdom. Tathagata Dipankara also predicted precisely when my mind stream would plunge into the ocean of pure presence as the Buddha Shakyamuni—becoming an overflowing fountain of goodness and liberating knowledge for future ages, one who is awakened beyond waking and dream, a complete manifestation of omniscience, an incomparable tamer of wild consciousness, a consummate teacher of both divine and human beings.

DIVINE REALM: It is wonderful, O Lord of Enlightenment, inconceivably wonderful, how Mother Prajnaparamita unveils conscious beings as omniscience through the oceanic presence of the Buddhas and their embryos, the bodhisattvas.

OVERWHELMING, O LORD

SHAKRA: O glorious Lord Buddha, please clarify the relative power of transferable meritorious energy generated by the following two practitioners. The first one, a loyal son or daughter of the Buddha family, writes by hand, with clear concentration and deep reverence, a copy of the *Prajnaparamita Sutra*. This precious copy, beautifully bound, perhaps illuminated with gold, is placed upon a holy shrine, kept perfectly clean and venerated as a living symbol of Buddha nature by the prayerful offering of blossoms, incense, rare perfumes, garlands, sandalwood powder, scarves of fine white cloth, silk banners of the primary colors, strings of delicate silver bells, rows of butter lamps and various other sublime offerings.

The second practitioner, perhaps an emperor, constructs many imposing stupas, each one enshrining a relic from the Buddha's miraculous physical body—a sanctifying relic, streaming with healing and illuminating power. These graceful stupas are reverently circumambulated thousands of times hourly and are venerated daily with precisely the same traditional forms of worship as the first practitioner uses to venerate the *Prajnaparamita Sutra*.

Which of these two equally sincere persons, O Lord, will generate the greater spiritual energy for the awakening of all conscious beings?

LORD BUDDHA: O Shakra, Buddha nature will question you on this point, so you can awaken to its intuitive power that streams through you. Consider carefully and respond. When the Tathagatas disappear into the shoreless ocean of pure presence, going completely beyond any conventional perspective, in what spiritual refreshment and teaching do they engage with their entire body, speech and mind, even though abiding as omniscience?

SHAKRA: The Tathagatas awaken as omniscience solely through the practice of Prajnaparamita and continue to function as Tathagatas, radiating light for all living beings, solely by the refreshing power of Mother Prajnaparamita flowing and teaching through them.

LORD BUDDHA: Excellent, O aspiring heavenly king. The Buddha, or Awakened One, does not receive this most exalted spiritual rank because he has generated a miraculous body but because he has awakened as omniscience, coming forth from the timeless womb of Prajnaparamita, Mother of the Buddhas.

Various miraculously generated bodies of holy energy, called by the name Shakyamuni and by other names, appear as living Buddhas before astonished eyes of disciples and share the human condition of mental effort and physical suffering. Yet these earthly bodies are simply a result of the compassionate, liberative art flowing from Perfect Wisdom. She alone is the teacher.

The physical emanation-bodies of the Buddhas are no doubt unimaginably precious. The voice and energy of Prajnaparamita clearly manifest through these human forms for the evolution and eventual enlightenment of all conscious beings, generating the redeeming organism of the spiritual community and the spiritual teachings. The graceful, serene, fragrant, golden-colored body of a living Buddha is the supreme instrument for playing the exquisite music of Perfect Wisdom, which delights all beings in all realms of being, attracting them inexorably toward the total awakeness of omniscience. Therefore the Buddha emanation-bodies, including the relics from these physical forms, become sacred shrines, worthy of being venerated, saluted and honored by means of all perennial modes of worship, including prostration and circumambulation. The religious practice of revering Buddha relics generates powerful streams of reverence and adoration. After I have disappeared completely from conventional view into Final Nirvana, O Shakra, the relics of my physical form will certainly be enshrined and worshipped in this way, generating healing and illumination for devoted worshippers and for the whole world.

However, the practitioner who studies, venerates, copies by hand, recites to others or in any other way reproduces and prayerfully disseminates the *Prajnaparamita Sutra,* generates vastly greater reservoirs of transferable meritorious energy. Why? Because this person is directly venerating, absorbing and radiating Perfect Wisdom, which is the very power of sanctification, while the other person is venerating relics which have become infused with the power of Prajnaparamita and thereby sanctified. Engagement with the Sutra is direct, circumambulation of the stupa indirect.

SHAKRA: You have made crystal clear, omniscient Lord, the inestimable value of communing directly with the *Prajnaparamita Sutra.* How is it possible, then, that sensitive human beings upon the earth, who have direct access to this sanctifying scripture of Perfect Wisdom, do not study, venerate, copy, recite or in other ways reproduce and disseminate Prajnaparamita? How is it possible that they have not heard from the beautiful Buddha emanation-bodies this unequivocal teaching that the prayerful study of Prajnaparamita is incomparably more powerful and beneficial to all beings than even the veneration of Buddha relics? Either people have never heard this teaching or they are lacking the clarity and confidence of perfect faith in Mother Prajnaparamita.

LORD BUDDHA: Consider carefully, Shakra. How many of the human level beings on all the inhabited planets where this present Buddha form simultaneously manifests have developed unshakable faith in the mystical body of the Buddha community and the Buddha teachings?

SHAKRA: Relatively few, O Lord.

LORD BUDDHA: Precisely so. Only a tiny percentage of the intensely self-aware streams of consciousness that are called human have developed this liberating faith. And how few even among this small number have actually entered into the path of rapid and radical spiritual evolution? Fewer still have attained the various levels of gnostic sainthood. Even fewer are those whose sainthood has reached its culmination while they are still living on earth. Fewer still are those who have transcended sainthood and awakened as solitary sages. More rare even than these self-perfected, self-realized ones are the bodhisattvas, diamond beings who have intensified their aspiration to the supreme degree, longing only for the conscious enlightenment of all mind streams without exception. Rare even among such rare practitioners are those who ceaselessly increase the fire of this longing, until it consumes the entire self-involved world, including self-centered forms of religious practice. Among these vast compassionate hearts, these radical lovers of all living beings, only a few engage in total concentration on Prajnaparamita. Among these supremely courageous ones, few indeed flow consciously as Mother Prajnaparamita. Among such superb masters alone are found the irreversible bodhisattvas, and only a few of these awaken to full enlightenment during any given aeon.

The irreversible bodhisattvas who have known full enlightenment are therefore the most rare and excellent guardians and transmitters of Prajnaparamita. To hear the teaching of transcendent insight and liberative art directly from them inspires every member of the Buddha family to the most earnest intentions and the most vigorous efforts. Then alone will aspirants train with every heartbeat in this sublime Perfection of Wisdom. Then they will study it prayerfully and ardently venerate its visible symbol, the scriptural text, through traditional modes of worship, absorbing its subtle energy fully and directly, as nourishment is absorbed into the bloodstream. But the opportunity to meet a true guardian and transmitter of Prajnaparamita is exceedingly rare.

One cannot approach the living presence of Mother Prajnaparamita with a mind stream that is not completely dynamic and utterly tireless. One cannot approach her with a mind stream tainted by fundamentally selfish motivation or even by passing thoughts of self-service or self-aggrandizement. Persons who come into the direct presence of Perfect Wisdom will begin to hear and contemplate her teaching, awake or asleep, through all processes of perception, thought and even physical actions such as breathing and walking. These persons will gradually realize and be humbled by the realization that in some previous incarnation they were trained directly by a living Buddha. They have inherited and, with unbroken moral and spiritual continuity, incarnated the precious mind stream of a bodhisattva. This realization will deepen even further until the illuminating recognition dawns that Prajnaparamita, Mother of the Buddhas, is the sole teacher and the sole Reality. The emanation-bodies of Buddhas and awakened bodhisattvas appear and disappear, whereas the Wisdom Light of Mother Prajnaparamita is always shining.

LORD BUDDHA: Consider carefully, King Shakra. Could a sincere practitioner generate a vast treasure of transferable merit for aspiring beings by constructing, over many lifetimes, billions of large stupas, enshrining the sanctified and sanctifying relics of Tathagatas—imposing monuments, composed of the seven gemlike substances, whose great beauty would attract many heavenly and earthly beings to perform prostrations and circumambulations?

SHAKRA: A shared treasure vast beyond imagination, O Lord.

LORD BUDDHA: Astonishing as it may seem, even greater treasures of fruitful energy with which to accelerate the spiritual quest of conscious beings can be generated by persons who totally accept Prajnaparamita: serenely and trustingly submitting their entire life energy to her; indefatigably presenting profound questions and receiving illuminating responses directly from Mother Prajnaparamita; intent on Perfect Wisdom even during the blinking of the eyes; every thought dedicated only to the conscious enlightenment of all beings; hearing Prajnaparamita chanted internally at all times, waking or sleeping; reciting Prajnaparamita melodiously to other aspirants; elucidating Prajnaparamita verbally and demonstrating it subtly with every movement of the body; uncovering and investigating its hidden levels and dimensions; debating, clarifying and commenting upon its finest details.

Inconceivably vast resources of transferable meritorious energy can be generated by even a single practitioner, who uses innate insight to absorb and transmit the transcendent insight of Prajnaparamita, who copies the text by hand and carefully preserves the copy so that this supremely excellent teaching will not disappear from the arena of human civilization and so that the mind streams of bodhisattvas can continue to receive assistance and guidance from the written form of Prajnaparamita. This practitioner not only studies and recites but also venerates the scriptural symbol of Perfect Wisdom with ceremonial offerings of exquisite beauty. Why? In order to assimilate and radiate to all beings more fully the sanctifying and liberating energy which emanates from Mother Prajnaparamita.

Vaster is the power for universal conscious enlightenment flowing from this single lover of Perfect Wisdom than from all the devout emperors in the universe who erect billions of precious stupas that enshrine the holy relics of Tathagatas and that are ceaselessly circumambulated. The inexhaustible spiritual power flowing from this single lover of Perfect Wisdom surpasses even the unimaginable blessings which would result if every human being in an entire billion-world system were to construct and devoutly worship sacred reliquary stupas bearing the sanctified and sanctifying relics of Tathagatas. A more impossible case can provide an even more accurate illustration: the power of transformation generated by a totally consecrated practitioner of Prajnaparamita exceeds even the blessing waves which would result if all the miniscule living beings in an entire billion-world system miraculously became devout religious persons, built holy stupas and venerated them intensively for an entire aeon.

SHAKRA: Overwhelming, O Lord. The practitioner who honors Prajnaparamita is invoking and transmitting the indivisible presence and total power of the Awakened Ones who have appeared in all world systems from beginningless time and who will continue to appear into the incalculable expanse of the future. The full implications and fruitfulness of this cumulative wisdom energy can be comprehended only by the infinitely expanded intellect of a Tathagata. The consecrated person who honors the glorious Prajnaparamita, source, protectress and guide of all Buddhas, will generate more power for universal awakening than if the living beings in billion-world systems as numerous as the grains of sand in the Ganges River were to build sacred reliquary stupas and honor them with perfect purity of intention for an entire thousand-Buddha aeon.

LORD BUDDHA: O noble Shakra, listen to Buddha nature clearly speaking through you.

PROTECTIVE POWER OF MANTRA

*S*HAKRA: A vast trove of esoteric lore is contained in the inconceivable recesses of Prajnaparamita—a measureless store of unsurpassable knowledge, an incomparable secret treasury which is actually none other than the incomparability of Reality.

LORD BUDDHA: Precisely so, Shakra. Thanks to just this all-embracing and all-transcending knowledge, this Perfection of Wisdom, the Awakened Ones of past and future have known and will know full enlightenment, radiating and transmitting Prajnaparamita spontaneously and lovingly to all conscious beings. Simply because of the powerful presence of this Perfection of Wisdom, the ten wholesome modes of purifying and healing activity gradually become manifest in the conscious streams called living beings. Simply because of her subliminal influence, the four levels of boundless concentration develop. From them, in turn, spring the subtle refinements called the thirty-seven mystic limbs of enlightenment, which open access to the four spheres of formlessness, as well as their corollary, the six miraculous modes of super-knowledge.

O king, this measureless body of wisdom, Mother Prajnaparamita, is the living ground for all eighty-four thousand teachings which culminate in Buddha knowledge—the knowledge of Reality, the inconceivable knowing that is without subject, object, structure or process.

Whenever there are no Buddhas outwardly manifest in a particular system of inhabited planets and heavenly realms, the teaching responsibility there devolves upon the bodhisattvas, compassionate diamond minds wholly committed to the enlightenment of every conscious being. These bodhisattvas are endowed with astonishing skills in expression, communication and direct transmission, as a result of hearing the rich outpourings of Perfect Wisdom from living Buddhas during past aeons.

When Buddhas are invisible, bodhisattvas must unfold the potent knowledge of Prajnaparamita into the ten modes of purifying and healing activity, the four levels of boundless concentration, the thirty-seven limbs of enlightenment, the four spheres of formlessness and the six modes of super-knowledge.

As the full moon illuminates both tiny herbs and the night sky full of constellations, just so, after the blazing sun of the Buddha has disappeared from ordinary vision by manifesting the teaching of physical death, do moonlike bodhisattvas illuminate for living beings whatever righteous, dignified, excellent and wholesome ways of life can be envisioned and practically manifested in the world. These inspiring and refined values and virtues are elicited from conscious beings of varying degrees of maturity by the skillfulness of the bodhisattvas, whose abilities in expression, communication and transmission shine forth solely from the luminous source called Prajnaparamita.

Aspirants who are devoted to the Perfection of Wisdom clearly know that not only exalted supramundane attainments with which to guide and mature conscious beings but also countless mundane blessings of success, refreshment and protection stream forth from Mother Prajnaparamita.

SHAKRA: O omniscient Lord, what are some of these mundane blessings?

LORD BUDDHA: Those who are thoroughly devoted to Prajnaparamita will not die suddenly or unexpectedly, neither from poison nor any kind of weapon, nor from fire, water or other natural elements, nor from violence of any kind from any quarter, unless they choose to manifest such suffering as a skillful teaching or as some other form of compassionate action.

Adepts and lovers of Prajnaparamita bring to mind and heart the protectress and matrix of all Buddhas and bodhisattvas by repeating her mantra. These seed sounds contain the entirety of Perfect Wisdom: *om gaté gaté paragaté parasamgaté bodhi swaha* – gone, gone, gone beyond, gone beyond even the beyond into full enlightenment, so be it.

If any arrogantly self-appointed powers, human or demonic, try to harm a person who constantly brings to mind and heart this Perfection of Wisdom—whether by reading the holy scripture silently, chanting its text melodiously or repeating it in condensed mantra form— these negative forces will certainly not succeed. Why? Because Prajnaparamita unveils all phenomena, all structures of relativity, as the boundless expanse of openness and luminous transparency.

When tyrants and other powerful and dangerous human or subtle beings approach the adepts of Perfect Wisdom with violent or other harmful intentions, they will instead spontaneously decide to greet the lovers of Prajnaparamita in a polite or even friendly and sympathetic manner. This occurs because the Perfection of Wisdom radiates intense friendliness and joyful sympathy toward all conscious beings, automatically generating a similar response.

If persons deeply devoted to and therefore instinctively aligned with Prajnaparamita are lost in a wilderness infested by poisonous serpents, the physical environment will become friendly toward them and no harm will befall them. Neither human beings nor wandering spirits can injure them in any way, unless the devotees of Mother Prajnaparamita decide to accept such injury voluntarily to demonstrate the Perfection of Patience or as an expiation for various negative thoughts and actions of living beings.

During Lord Buddha's inspiring exposition, vicious thoughts occur to Mara, the principle of negative and rebellious egocentricity: *The fourfold assembly of the Tathagata—the one who has disappeared into pure presence—is now seated face to face with their teacher, fervently attending to his discourse on the Perfection of Wisdom. This assembly includes monks and nuns, laymen and laywomen. In the companionship of Awakened Enlightenment also gather various divine beings from the heavenly realm who are certain to be predicted as future bodhisattvas during this assembly. I must approach now to blind them with arrogance before it is too late.*

Shakra, profoundly sensitized by having received the transmission of the Prajnaparamita mantra directly from Lord Buddha, notices immediately the stealthy approach of Mara's delusive forces. These forces are not some human or physical army and therefore cannot be defeated through any ordinary means. Such forces of negativity are perpetually intent on finding a way to invade novices as well as advanced practitioners, bent on wounding them spiritually and even destroying them. The noble Shakra decides to bring to mind and heart the Mother of the Buddhas, holding her clearly before his eye of intuition and radiating her incomparable power through his entire being by repeating the seed sounds *om gaté gaté paragaté parasamgaté bodhi swaha.* The all-pervading wisdom energy of this mantra of all mantras instantly spreads Prajnaparamita, infusing all minds and hearts. Mara the Adversary immediately turns away from the luminous Buddha assembly and retreats into peripheral darkness.

Amazed by this powerful demonstration of the Prajnaparamita mantra, the beings from the Thirty-Three Heaven who received the protection of this most esoteric knowledge scatter miraculously generated flowers of great beauty and fragrance over the majestic golden figure of the living Buddha, exulting in triumphal and harmonious tones.

DIVINE REALM: Wonderful! Wonderful! How wonderful that the Perfection of Wisdom is perennially revealed to human beings on the planetary plane and to subtle and heavenly beings as well. Mara's demonic forces will find no way to invade any consciousness that recalls, reveres, contemplates, chants, communicates, embodies and radiates Prajnaparamita. Those who possess a general comprehension of Perfect Wisdom, or even those who study only a few verses of the scriptural text, are endowed with wholesome roots of goodness which will inevitably sprout, blossom and flourish. Even those who simply hear about the *Prajnaparamita Sutra,* respecting it without studying it, must have served fully awakened spiritual conquerors in past aeons to have received this blessing. How much more intensely connected with Buddhas of past, present and future are those who carefully investigate and reverently chant the holy text, who become thoroughly trained and attuned to Reality, who become immersed in Reality, making heroic spiritual endeavors to plunge into the pure presence which is Reality. These are surely aspirants who during past, present and future have, are and will be honoring and serving the Tathagatas, the Awakened Ones who have disappeared completely into Reality.

As miraculous wish-fulfilling jewels are known to be generated in the depths of the great ocean, and should be searched for there, just so the supreme Buddha jewel of omniscience, or total awakeness, should be searched for in the unthinkable depths of the boundless ocean of Prajnaparamita.

SIX TRANSCENDENT PERFECTIONS

*A*NANDA: The omniscient Lord Buddha, embodiment of universal enlightenment, does not single out for praise the Perfection of Generosity, the Perfection of Goodness, the Perfection of Patience, the Perfection of Commitment or the Perfection of Meditation. Only the peerless Perfection of Wisdom, transcendent insight into the insubstantiality and transparent functioning of all possible phenomena, does Lord Buddha continuously mention, ecstatically praise, intensively teach and radiantly transmit.

LORD BUDDHA: You have observed accurately, beloved Ananda. The Perfection of Wisdom alone generates and sustains the other five transcendent Perfections that constitute the way of the bodhisattva, the translation into selflessness of the conventional, egocentric universe.

Consider, Ananda, some particular act of giving which is not released and illuminated by the principle of Prajnaparamita—the bright emptiness, insubstantiality and transparent functioning of all apparent self-existence. This act is not radically transformed by being dedicated to the awakening of all conscious beings. Can any such conventionally generous action ever qualify as Danaparamita, the Perfection of Generosity, in which no independent giver or receiver, no gift and no substantial process of giving are recognized or crystallized?

ANANDA: In no way, precious Lord.

LORD BUDDHA: Precisely the same evaluation holds good for the other four Perfections—selfless goodness, selfless patience, selfless commitment and selfless meditation. Each paramita can be sustained only by the conscious presence of Prajnaparamita. Beyond any possible measure or conception is the value of Perfect Wisdom, which empowers the entire contemplative practice, thought and conduct of the bodhisattvas, transforming into liberating energy for all living beings their ceaseless acts of giving, their spontaneous disciplines of goodness, their patient sacrifices, their active commitment to the spiritual path and their profoundly concentrated meditation.

Perfect Wisdom continuously generates, offers, dedicates and contributes the immeasurable meritorious energy of selfless thought and action. Why? To bring about the awakening of all lives into the bliss of Buddhahood.

ANANDA: O precious Lord, the value of Perfect Wisdom for the whole universe is absolutely immeasurable and inconceivable.

LORD BUDDHA: The glorious name Prajnaparamita derives from the Sanskrit words *prajna,* insight, and *parama,* the supreme excellence which transcends all that is excellent. From the supremely excellent insight of Prajnaparamita alone do the other boundless spiritual qualities and radiant universal efforts of the bodhisattva receive the sublime designation *paramita* and attain the stature of transcendent excellence.

The Perfection of Wisdom subsumes these five areas of illuminating thought and healing action, transforming them into selflessness and consecrating them solely for the awakening of all conscious beings. This is why it is taught that Perfect Wisdom alone animates, subtly unfolds and crowns the other five transcendent Perfections, the Paramitas of Goodness, Patience, Commitment and Meditation, clearly establishing the primacy of the Perfection of Wisdom. The other Perfections shine forth through the indivisibility and unthinkability of Prajnaparamita, whose blissful transparency is the fulfillment of all the highest ideals and aspirations of human life. Therefore, beloved Ananda, when the Buddha declares the truth and transmits the healing energy of Perfect Wisdom, the other five transcendent Perfections are simultaneously being declared and transmitted.

As precious gemstones evolve deep in the earth wherever conditions are correct, the earth itself with its rich potentialities being their sole source, just so do all precious moral and spiritual qualities grow within the mysterious profundity of Prajnaparamita, evolving spontaneously from the Perfection of Wisdom which is the omniscience, the panoramic subjectless and objectless knowing, enjoyed by all the Awakened Ones.

Only when absorbed and radically transmuted by the power of Perfect Wisdom, as unrefined matter is transformed into diamond, do positive thoughts and actions attain the peerless stature of transcendent Perfection. Prajnaparamita alone animates, subtly unfolds and gloriously crowns all supreme excellence.

MIRACULOUS GEMS

SHAKRA: Prajnaparamita is the ultimate among wish-fulfilling gems —those miraculous jewels, spontaneously generated within heavenly realms or subtle spheres, which manifest the power to prevent wandering spirits with malevolent intentions from entering their radiant and sacred ambiance. If someone is possessed or oppressed by any wandering spirit or demonic being, one of these supernal jewels can instantly effect the person's liberation. If someone is afflicted by an imbalance in physical or psychic energy, by applying one of these empowered crystals to the body, the particular energies in question will be tempered and harmonized. Such mystic gems can illuminate their surroundings, even in the dense darkness of a moonless night. They can cool habitations in the desert and warm retreat caves high among snow mountains. Their powerful healing radiation can clear an area of poisonous serpents, stinging insects and other dangerous creatures. Even the sight of such a gem can act as antidote for fatal venom.

If these subtle crystals manifest various astonishing characteristics, how much more so does the supremely precious diamond of Perfect Wisdom. These miraculous gems can be understood as metaphors for the functioning of Prajnaparamita.

If the eyes of a person are afflicted, or eyesight is impaired in any way, merely placing one of these heavenly crystals upon the eyes will heal them and vastly clarify their vision. When bound in a white cloth and placed in water, the wish-fulfilling gem will cause that water to dye clothing white. When bound in cloth of another color—such as dark blue, yellow or crimson—the water into which the mysterious gem is placed will dye clothing that color. These unearthly crystals, colorless in themselves just as the diamond of Prajnaparamita is perfectly transparent, can clear away any impurity that may exist in water, as Perfect Wisdom clears away any limit or obscuration that may exist in awareness.

ANANDA: O noble king of celestial beings, do these wish-fulfilling gems belong solely to the exalted realms of your jurisdiction or to the planetary plane of existence as well?

SHAKRA: Such miraculous gems are generated solely in heavenly or subtle planes of being and awareness. The precious stones that originate in the earthly sphere are small and unrefined, possessing few if any of the powerful characteristics of their heavenly or subtle counterparts. If one of these supernal gems were to manifest on earth and touch a common straw basket, through the radiant power transmitted by this touch, the basket would become a healing object worthy to be longed for by one's whole heart and mind. It is the same with the transcendent diamond of Prajnaparamita, which transmits omniscience by its very touch, so that the physical body of the practitioner, like the straw basket, becomes intensely precious. This is why the holy relics of the Tathagatas, after they have entered the Final Nirvana of pure presence, are worthy of being cherished, adored and worshipped. They have been touched by the adamantine jewel of Prajnaparamita and have thus become reservoirs for the inconceivable energy of omniscience.

The incarnation and demonstration of truth by living Buddhas in all world systems occurs through precisely the same miraculous touch of the supreme diamond of Perfect Wisdom. This powerful touch pervades as well every authentic teacher and transmitter of Prajnaparamita. As a king should be revered because his royal authority and charisma give strength, succor and inspiration to a vast number of people, so should the teachers of Perfect Wisdom be revered, because, through the power transmitted by Mother Prajnaparamita, they offer strength, succor and inspiration, as well as liberation and enlightenment, to a limitless number of sentient beings. For the same reason that the relics of the Buddhas are cherished, adored and worshipped, so should one bow down in reverence before the pure demonstration of truth that flows through authentic teachers of Perfect Wisdom, for such teaching is the healing and illuminating touch of the diamond of infinite facets, the incandescent Prajnaparamita.

INCOMPARABLE AND MEASURELESS JOY

*L*ORD BUDDHA: Fervently dedicated to the enlightenment of every conscious being, the bodhisattva contemplates the expanse of manifestation, extending beginninglessly and infinitely in every direction and through every dimension.

Ceaselessly, the diamond being contemplates world systems beyond this planetary system—an expanse of inhabited worlds immeasurable in extent, beyond reckoning in number, inconceivable in their essential nature, infinite in the complexity of their life forms and limitless in the subtlety of their civilizations.

The bodhisattva observes the range of past aeons in each of these world systems, envisioning the Buddhas, or fully Awakened Ones, who have appeared there wisely to guide and tenderly to mature conscious beings—Buddhas immeasurable in spiritual stature, beyond reckoning in number, inconceivable in essential nature, infinitely powerful in liberative art and boundless in transcendent insight.

Adamantine awareness flawlessly visualizes these ancient Buddhas at the moment when they blissfully enter Final Nirvana, the state of absolute fulfillment which leaves behind no trace of the suffering of any being—perceiving how their tracks suddenly cease, how their path instantly disappears, how their obstacles and the obstacles of all beings in their Buddha fields utterly dissolve.

The bodhisattva now contemplates with jubilation the marvelous process by which these ancient Buddhas were guided to the final goal of evolution, where tears for themselves and for others disappeared forever, where inner blockages and outer obstacles were broken through forever, where personal burdens and those of others were laid down forever, where even their highly developed sense of perpetual change and the suffering of sentient beings involved in change was extinguished and their altruistic thoughts were released entirely, their minds having become the highest perfection of harmony, diamond persistence and pure presence.

The meditator now carefully appreciates the long careers of these Buddhas, beginning from the moment when they first generated the clear conviction that enlightenment for the sake of all beings is possible, committing themselves to this possibility and continuing to struggle for the sake of others through innumerable lifetimes until they attained enlightenment and blissfully entered Final Nirvana.

The bodhisattva includes in this joyous contemplation the entire time span of the rich teachings and holy lineages which each of these innumerable Buddhas left behind and which radiated truth throughout thousands of years until the good Dharma that each one had embodied and transmitted gradually waned and at last disappeared.

The diamond being now weighs and considers with great delight the inconceivably vast accumulation of crystal clear concentration and enlightening meditation, the inconceivably vast accumulation of merit from the compassionate service and liberation of living beings and the inconceivably vast accumulation of supreme insight into the innate freedom of conscious beings developed over uncountable aeons by all these majestic Buddhas.

The bodhisattva surveys and considers with ecstatic awe the deep reservoir of transferable meritorious energy accumulated along their way by these fully Awakened Ones through their practice of the six transcendent Perfections—total Generosity, ceaseless Goodness, selfless Patience, utter Commitment, all-embracing Meditation and all-penetrating Insight. The bodhisattva considers as well the astonishing energy generated by their limitlessly powerful Buddha qualities after they reached the goal, including their adamantine courage and confidence, their sublime and miraculous ways of knowing, their intimate comprehension and tender sympathy for the minds and hearts of all beings and their vow to sacrifice themselves for the smallest act of service as well as for the liberation and enlightenment of every conscious being. The meditator visualizes the shining treasury of transferable merit generated by these Buddhas in all world systems through their awakening into omniscience — joined with tender solicitude toward all beings and the other immeasurable and incalculable characteristics of Buddhahood.

With increasing rapture, adamantine awareness now contemplates the indescribable bliss experienced by these Buddhas beyond number when attaining full enlightenment. The bodhisattva meditates upon their sublime awareness of being sovereign over all the structures of relativity and upon their great joy in wielding selflessly the supreme miraculous powers which overcome every obstacle and nonviolently conquer every adversary. Above all, the bodhisattva contemplates the Buddha power beyond miracles — the indivisible, panoramic, subjectless, objectless knowing of What Is. Without any veils, attachments or obstructions this power of omniscience is actually the measurelessness of Reality. The diamond being contemplates the inconceivable scope and intensity of this Buddha knowledge, which utterly transcends all clairvoyant powers and which is pervaded by the kindness of Buddha skill and the relaxed ease which results from Buddha confidence.

Gazing intently in visionary contemplation upon these Awakened Ones of past and present aeons, the meditator considers their realizing and giving of the most radical teaching — that Buddha nature is fully evident and openly expressed through all the structures of relativity without exception. Before the intuitive vision of the bodhisattva now appear all the turnings of the wheel of this revolutionary teaching of Dharma, all the victorious efforts to carry the brilliant torch of Dharma, to beat the thunderous drum of Dharma, to fill with timeless nectar the auspicious white conch shell of Dharma, to wield the nonviolent sword of Dharma. The illumined meditator clearly witnesses the careers of all Buddhas as the spontaneous pouring down of the rain of Dharma and the refreshment of all living beings with the subtly appropriate nourishment of Dharma, presented directly to them as the purest gift—their own true nature.

The bodhisattva now extends this rapturous meditation to include the reservoir of healing and transforming energy accumulated by all conscious beings who were and are to any degree educated, inspired or spiritually awakened by these innumerable demonstrations of Dharma—not just by radiant world teachers but also by solitary sages and ascetic practitioners.

The diamond being greatly expands this meditation by envisioning as well the inconceivable waves of future energy which the countless aspirants who have witnessed, accepted and assimilated these demonstrations of Dharma generate as they, in turn, inevitably reach full enlightenment and become victorious spiritual conquerors.

The contemplative now focuses with inexpressible joy on the treasury of transferable merit already being selflessly generated through Generosity, Goodness, Patience, Commitment, Meditation and Insight by awakened bodhisattvas in all world systems, diamond beings whose full enlightenment has already been predicted and assured by Buddhas of past aeons.

The meditative scope is once again expanded, this time to include the merit dedicated to universal conscious enlightenment which was and is being generated by the excellent practitioners in the fourfold assembly surrounding every ancient and contemporary Buddha— the radiant and joyful assembly that consists of monks, nuns, laymen and laywomen, surrounded by various heavenly and subtle beings.

Finally, the bodhisattva contemplates with the greatest intensity of sympathetic joy and gratitude every single seed of goodness planted during beginningless aeons in all world systems—on every planet where Buddhas or emanations of Buddhas have demonstrated truth and entered into Final Nirvana. This contemplation extends to the goodness and the potential for future goodness generated not only by human beings but also by exalted heavenly beings, as well as by subtle beings on every plane of being, all the way down the scale of consciousness to elemental spirits, including even confused spirits wandering in the planetary sphere who may have engaged in a single good action or intention. The bodhisattva contemplates as well the countless seeds of goodness planted in their conscious streams by animals on every rung of the evolutionary scale when they help one another or serve more highly developed conscious beings.

At the culmination of this ecstatic meditation, with vastly expanded and reconsecrated mind and heart, the bodhisattva gives thanks for the supreme teaching of Reality, gives thanks to the fourfold communities that gather around every Buddha to assure the dissemination of this most precious teaching, gives thanks to all conscious beings who are even to the slightest degree cultivating goodness by training their minds to be selflessly compassionate.

At this summit, filled with the most sublime sense of jubilation and limitless gratitude, the bodhisattva gathers and fuses into a single diamond all the goodness, meritorious energy and bliss which has been visualized, contemplated and directly experienced—not leaving out even the smallest good intention from past, present or future. Delicately, the bodhisattva holds this inconceivable diamond in the center of awareness, rejoicing over it in the purest ecstasy of joy—a joy unapproached by any other joy, a rejoicing which is actually the incomparability of Reality.

Having celebrated thus in unthinkable delight, the bodhisattva prays: *I now offer and dedicate to the eventual enlightenment of every conscious being the boundless meritorious energy of this incomparable and measureless joy.*

MYSTIC HYMN TO THE WISDOM MOTHER

SHARIPUTRA: This Perfection of Wisdom, O radiant Lord, is none other than the total awakeness which is omniscience.

LORD BUDDHA: So it is, noble Shariputra, precisely as you say.

SHARIPUTRA: The Perfection of Wisdom shines forth as a sublime light, O Buddha nature. I sing this spontaneous hymn of light to praise Mother Prajnaparamita. She is worthy of infinite praise. She is utterly unstained, because nothing in this insubstantial world can possibly stain her. She is an ever-flowing fountain of incomparable light, and from every conscious being on every plane, she removes the faintest trace of illusory darkness. She leads living beings into her clear light from the blindness and obscurity caused by moral and spiritual impurity as well as by partial or distorted views of Reality. In her alone can we find true refuge. Sublime and excellent are her revelations through all persons of wisdom. She inspires and guides us to seek the safety and certainty of the bright wings of enlightenment. She pours forth her nectar of healing light to those who have made themselves appear blind. She provides the illumination through which all fear and despair can be utterly renounced.

She manifests the five mystic eyes of wisdom, the vision and penetration of each one more exalted than the last. She clearly and constantly points out the path of wisdom to every conscious being with the direct pointing that is her transmission and empowerment. She is an infinite eye of wisdom. She dissipates entirely the mental gloom of delusion. She does not manipulate any structures of relativity. Simply by shining spontaneously, she guides to the spiritual path whatever beings have wandered into dangerous, negative, self-centered ways.

Mother Prajnaparamita is total awakeness. She never substantially creates any limited structure because she experiences none of the tendencies of living beings to grasp, project or conceptualize. Neither does she substantially dismantle or destroy any limited structure, for she encounters no solid limits. She is the Perfect Wisdom which never comes into being and therefore never goes out of being. She is known as the Great Mother by those spiritually mature beings who dedicate their mind streams to the liberation and full enlightenment of all that lives.

She is not marked by fundamental characteristics. This absence of characteristics is her transcendent, mystic motherhood, the radiant blackness of her womb. She is the universal benefactress who presents, as a sublime offering to truth, the limitless jewel of all Buddha qualities, the miraculous gem which generates the ten inconceivable powers of a Buddha to elevate living beings into consciousness of their innate Buddha nature. She can never be defeated in any way, on any level. She lovingly protects vulnerable conscious beings who cannot protect themselves, gradually generating in them unshakable fearlessness and diamond confidence. She is the perfect antidote to the poisonous view which affirms the cycle of birth and death to be a substantial reality. She is the clear knowledge of the open and transparent mode of being shared by all relative structures and events. Her transcendent knowing never wavers. She is the Perfect Wisdom who gives birthless birth to all Buddhas. And through these sublimely Awakened Ones, it is Mother Prajnaparamita alone who turns the wheel of true teaching.

LORD BUDDHA: Precisely so, beloved Shariputra.

FROM WHERE DO THEY INCARNATE?

S HARIPUTRA: O omniscient Lord, from where do they incarnate, these bodhisattvas totally dedicated to universal conscious enlightenment, these diamond beings who accept the unthinkable Perfection of Wisdom without the slightest hesitation, doubt or sense of shock? For how many incarnations have they heard and practiced the true teachings that they so readily follow this great Perfection, easily absorbing its radical meaning, eloquently instructing and authentically initiating and directing others into its astonishing subtlety?

LORD BUDDHA: Such bodhisattvas manifest rebirth in this world system after manifesting in many world systems, where they have devotedly served and directly questioned many fully Awakened Ones. This explains the spontaneous recognition and acceptance which such aspirants experience, even when they first encounter this amazing depth of unthinkability. They immediately recognize Perfect Wisdom as the sole teacher, the very principle of Buddhahood, the tender Mother of the Buddhas. They clearly sense upon hearing this sublime teaching that they are once again seated face to face with one of the humble Lords of Enlightenment, bowing in utmost reverence and listening with the crystal clear attention that never grows weary of the wisdom teaching. Such diamond beings have practiced Dharma for aeons and have been initiated into Prajnaparamita by many victorious Buddhas.

SUBHUTI: O Lord Buddha, is it really possible to discern the Perfection of Wisdom, to discriminate and analyze it, to make valid, rational statements concerning it, presenting it in the light of discrete intellectual categories? Can one explain Prajnaparamita in terms of levels or degrees? Can one isolate certain attributes or marks that will always identify Perfect Wisdom and always disqualify whatever is not Perfect Wisdom?

LORD BUDDHA: In no way, Subhuti. The Perfection of Wisdom cannot be discursively expounded or learned, nor isolated or described, nor stated in words, nor reflected upon by means of or in terms of any limited patterns of awareness. This unformulatability and unapproachability is a consequence of the fact that all structures of relativity, on all levels of experience, are inherently unformulatable and unapproachable. Even the most fundamental principles are totally empty of independent self-existence—unthinkably pure, calm and blissful. The very same inconceivable peacefulness and innate bliss is manifest through every detail of existence. Prajnaparamita is not aloof or separate from the countless structures of relativity. No division exists between the absolute and the relative. Nothing can actually be grasped, apprehended or reified. Precisely this unthinkability of What Is is conventionally designated by the term *Perfect Wisdom*, though this phrase is merely a word, merely a sound.

DANGERS OF NEGATIVITY

*L*ORD BUDDHA: Astonishing as it may sound, Prajnaparamita is so exalted and so radical that some mind streams may not be able to develop total faith and confidence in Perfect Wisdom, even though they have practiced contemplative life under the direct guidance of hundreds of Buddhas during past aeons—or even in the inspiring presence of thousands of past Buddhas, or hundreds of thousands of past Buddhas.

The reason for this is simple. Even though the reverence and commitment of these aspirants was strong, when the Buddhas of past aeons began to expound Prajnaparamita, the most radical teaching of truth, these practitioners did not cherish profound respect for Perfect Wisdom, much less did they fully understand it. Because intense respect and veneration was lacking, they did not have the necessary burning desire to learn more about Perfect Wisdom, nor did they generate the longing necessary to assimilate and realize it. Since they did not honor it far above all other teachings of the Buddhas, they did not develop the adamantine intention to pose penetrating questions about Perfect Wisdom.

Some of those who lacked faith in Prajnaparamita even walked out of the radiant Buddha assemblies where this unthinkably precious teaching was being expounded. Because from the distant past such practitioners have gradually accumulated this habitual energy ruinous to faith in Prajnaparamita, they also walk out of assemblies in the present whenever the depth of unthinkability is being presented. Without instinctive respect, heartfelt faith and total intellectual confidence in Prajnaparamita, the body and mind of the practitioner subtly fall out of harmony. This creates a circular self-imprisonment, for without sensitivity and harmony of awareness, it is difficult even to hear the Perfection of Wisdom, much less to understand it intimately, transmit it and thereby deepen one's spiritual connection with it.

From a lack of reverence for Prajnaparamita, follows a loss of the ability to hear the wisdom teaching clearly. After this, one's overall vision of Dharma begins to dim, and one ceases to be able to recognize the radical teachings of truth, even when they are clearly unfolded. Through this process, one gradually and almost imperceptibly accumulates habitual energy which runs counter to contemplation and penetration. Lacking the intensity of selfless contemplative practice, the previous experience of transcendent insight is seriously weakened. This weakening inevitably causes careless practitioners at first to resist and then to reject or even revile Prajnaparamita, the essence of the spiritual path. They may even walk out of an assembly where Perfect Wisdom is being expounded and demonstrated. By negating the Perfection of Wisdom, such disintegrating practitioners become involved in the total absurdity of negating the clear and limitless knowledge unveiled by all past, present and future Buddhas. Such negation can threaten the continuity and integrity of contemplative practice on less advanced levels of teaching as well.

This rebellion against the subtle kindness of Mother Prajnaparamita can be further compounded by the mad attempt to poison the minds of vulnerable persons, turning them away from transcendent insight. These persons may possess less native intelligence; their experience of insight may not yet be strong; they may be lacking somewhat in the meritorious energy brought about by good actions and intentions; or their faith may be somewhat tenuous. Such vulnerable persons are not yet completely permeated with reverence for truth, serenity of mind and the active commitment to study and contemplate the Perfection of Wisdom. By attacking beginners who are just developing the extensive qualifications necessary to approach Prajnaparamita, those who negate Perfect Wisdom with the blasphemous assertion that it is not the highest teaching of all Buddhas dissipate their own precious mind streams. To attack Prajnaparamita is to attack omniscience. It is an attempt to discredit the Awakened Ones of past, present and future. By adopting this extreme course of thought and action, negative mind streams remove themselves from the living presence of the Buddha, deprive themselves of the healing and illumination of the Dharma, and excommunicate themselves from the spiritual friendship and support of the Sangha, the community of sublime lovers of Perfect Wisdom.

These rebellious ones gradually become disassociated in every dimension of their being from the Triple Gem of Buddha, Dharma and Sangha, which consists of Awakened Enlightenment, its teachings and its practitioners. Because the thoughts and actions of these increasingly negative persons both subtly and openly diminish the goodness of other beings, they gradually accumulate habitual energy which creates the conscious environment called hell. A hellish consciousness feeds on itself and inevitably generates even more extreme conditions of rebellion—a process which may extend within a particular mind stream for hundreds of years. Then, reaching an even more critical level of negativity, this hell consciousness can become demonic, persisting through thousands of aeons—a bitter karma extending not only across generations but also throughout the creation and final dissolution in fire of entire world systems. Its subtle tendencies may even persist into fresh universes, as a poisonous stream of unimaginable anger, hatred and pain. There are future Maras as well as future Buddhas.

UNTHINKABLE DEPTH OF PURITY

SUBHUTI: It is extremely difficult to develop confidence in Prajnaparamita if one is not a consistent practitioner of truth, if one lacks the wholesome roots of ceaseless commitment to goodness or if one falls under the influence of an immature spiritual guide.

LORD BUDDHA: Indeed, Subhuti. It is also extremely difficult to develop confidence in Prajnaparamita if one is inexperienced in deep meditation, has put forth only shallow roots of extensive compassionate action, is lacking discipline and precision of mind and carefulness of life, is lacking in the eagerness and capability to learn, adopts any doctrinal form of divisive or partial understanding, relies on low-level spiritual teachers, is inhibited in asking penetrating questions or is lacking the gratitude and delight generated by truly good teachings.

SUBHUTI: O victorious Buddha, it is difficult to gain unshakable confidence in Prajnaparamita primarily because Perfect Wisdom is so intensive, so elusive, so deep.

LORD BUDDHA: Indeed, Subhuti. Prajnaparamita is unthinkably difficult because unthinkably deep. Perfect Wisdom reveals that none of the material or mental forms that we encounter are actually involved in impeding or imprisoning mind streams, nor are such forms involved in liberating mind streams. Nor is the principle of form either imprisoned or freed, because no form and no principle possess even the slightest inherent self-existence.

The apparent starting point of any process is neither circumscribed within boundaries nor liberated from boundaries, because it lacks the slightest independent or substantial self-existence. Just so, the apparent final stage of any process is neither circumscribed within boundaries nor liberated from boundaries, because it is equally empty of self-existence. Even in the midst of any apparent process of development, whatever material or mental structures may appear possess no solid self-existence and are therefore neither circumscribed nor liberated. Even the conventional sense of present time, or the present moment, does not possess an atom of self-existence.

Precisely this same clear insight holds true for every pattern of experience, including perceptions, conceptions, impulses and other limited modes of awareness. No structure is ever imprisoned or released. No structure is ever circumscribed by boundaries and therefore no structure is ever liberated from boundaries.

SUBHUTI: It is difficult to gain adamantine confidence in Prajnaparamita if one lacks constant practice in this way of clear insight, if one fails to plant seeds of kind and helpful actions, if one is guided by someone of superficial understanding, if one falls under the subtle influence of the sense of negativity, if one is lacking in spiritual intensity, reverence and passionate commitment or if clarity of awareness and sharpness of discernment are dulled.

LORD BUDDHA: Indeed, Subhuti. Prajnaparamita is unthinkably deep because the intrinsic purity, freedom, emptiness, openness and transparency of all material and mental structures is identical with the radiant transparency of the highest spiritual realization. The sublime purity of transcendent insight is identical with the natural, spontaneous purity of the countless configurations that present themselves as the universe in all its multidimensionality. The intrinsic purity and peacefulness of all structures of relativity and the blissful purity of total awakeness are not two separate realities. They cannot be divided into different levels or dimensions, nor broken down into different categories, nor cut apart in any way by discursive analysis. The intrinsic purity, or unthinkable depth, of all appearing forms is the direct expression of the unthinkable depth of the highest fruition of transcendent insight. The pure, selfless transparency of every single form is identical with the pure, selfless transparency of omniscience or total awakeness. That which is true of form is true as well of perception, conception and any other possible mode of experience or object of experience. There is only the unthinkable depth of Prajnaparamita.

SHARIPUTRA: Most elusive of the elusive and deepest of the deep, O victorious One, is the unthinkable depth of Prajnaparamita.

LORD BUDDHA: Because of its intrinsic purity.

SHARIPUTRA: A constant source of all-pervading illumination is Prajnaparamita.

LORD BUDDHA: Because of its selfless and transparent purity.

SHARIPUTRA: Nothing but sheer illumination is Mother Prajnaparamita.

LORD BUDDHA: Because of her radiant purity.

SHARIPUTRA: Free from notions of dying or being reborn is Perfect Wisdom.

LORD BUDDHA: Because of its infinite depth of purity.

SHARIPUTRA: Impossible to stain or profane in any way is Perfect Wisdom.

LORD BUDDHA: Because of its diamond purity.

SHARIPUTRA: Free from any concept of spiritual attainment or mystical union is Perfect Wisdom.

LORD BUDDHA: Because of its radical purity.

SHARIPUTRA: Prajnaparamita does not give birth to any reality separate from herself. She does not even reproduce herself.

LORD BUDDHA: Because of her virginal purity.

SHARIPUTRA: Prajnaparamita is not divided in any way among the realms of material existence, mental existence or transcendent being.

LORD BUDDHA: Because of its most simple purity.

SHARIPUTRA: Perfect Wisdom neither knows nor perceives any separate or substantial process or structure, whether material or mental.

LORD BUDDHA: Because of its non-self-existing purity.

SHARIPUTRA: Prajnaparamita neither brings about nor cancels any mode of awareness, including omniscient awareness.

LORD BUDDHA: Because of its uncreated purity.

SHARIPUTRA: Prajnaparamita neither accepts nor rejects any teaching, neither embraces nor renounces any world or dimension of existence.

LORD BUDDHA: Because of its enlightened purity.

SUBHUTI: O radiant Buddha nature, the purity of the supreme spiritual fruition of omniscience is essentially the pure selflessness of whatever appears as the self.

LORD BUDDHA: This is the unalloyed purity of Perfect Wisdom.

SUBHUTI: O radiant Buddha nature, the lack of intrinsic boundaries circumscribing any material or mental structure is essentially the lack of intrinsic boundaries circumscribing whatever appears as the self.

LORD BUDDHA: This is the unmitigated and unimaginable purity of Perfect Wisdom.

SUBHUTI: The courageous bodhisattva, committed to the full enlightenment of all conscious beings, by understanding every appearing structure, including the self, in this undivided and comprehensive way, perfectly demonstrates Prajnaparamita.

LORD BUDDHA: Through its indivisible purity.

SUBHUTI: Prajnaparamita cannot be described as standing on this shore or on the farther shore or as standing simultaneously within immanence and transcendence.

LORD BUDDHA: Because of its unthinkable depth of undifferentiated purity.

SUBHUTI: The diamond being, who lives only for universal conscious enlightenment, does not treat any of these radical insights as separate objects of consciousness, for that would be to part from Prajnaparamita by opening up an illusory distance or distinction between the knower and what is known.

LORD BUDDHA: This is the nondual purity of Perfect Wisdom.

BEHOLD THE PERFECTION
OF WISDOM

SHARIPUTRA: The Perfection of Wisdom is the perfection of what is not, as empty space is the presence of what is not. Perfect Wisdom is unequaled, because it does not apprehend any substantial structures that equal it or fail to equal it. This wisdom is both all-embracing and all-transcending, because it is void of any conceptual notion or instinctive sense of separate self-existence.

The Perfection of Wisdom can never be obstructed or suppressed, because no substantial or independent force to accomplish any such action can be apprehended. Such wisdom is beginningless, pathless and goalless because of the absence of any separate or substantial body or mind. Perfect Wisdom manifests no independent existence of its own, because it neither comes nor goes, arises nor dissipates, expands nor diminishes, is spoken nor heard. Prajnaparamita is not expressible, or even identifiable, because it does not discursively apprehend or grasp any other structures, much less some supposed structure of its own.

The Perfection of Wisdom is nameless, because none of the structures which assign or receive names are apprehended as substantial. This wisdom cannot be destroyed, because nothing is ever substantially created or destroyed. No one can personally appropriate or claim Prajnaparamita, because there is nothing that can be isolated, grasped or owned. Perfect Wisdom is inexhaustible, because truth is inexhaustible.

The Perfection of Wisdom has no beginning, because nothing exhibits a separate point of departure. This wisdom does not engage in action, nor is it passive, because no separate agent is ever apprehended. Perfect Wisdom possesses neither practicing subject nor cognitive object, because none of the subjects or objects that appear in conventional experience actually possess the slightest independent self-existence. Prajnaparamita never ceases to be total awakeness, because no awareness ever substantially sleeps or wakes, dies or is reborn.

The Perfection of Wisdom cannot be identified with or approached by any mode of contemplative discipline, because it does not discriminate any temporality—neither past, future nor even present—within which to engage in any discipline. Perfect Wisdom resembles dreams, echoes and reflections, for none of these events, although remaining coherently functional, can be found to possess the slightest independent or substantial self-existence.

The Perfection of Wisdom is spontaneously free from moral impurity, because it clearly perceives that greed, hatred and delusion possess no inherent self-existence. Therefore, Prajnaparamita does not apprehend or recommend any substantial process of purification, nor does it posit any independently self-existing receptacle to be purified. This wisdom is stainless, as empty space is stainless. This Wisdom encounters no inherently existent obstacles or adversaries, because it does not adopt negative mental attitudes toward any appearing process or structure.

Since the Perfection of Wisdom is free from any conceptual or instinctive discrimination that assumes separate self-existence, it remains steady and imperturbable. Because of the perfect poise and balance of this all-liberating wisdom, it remains unwavering and unfading. Prajnaparamita is untouched by even the most subtle forms of acquisitiveness, because it perceives absolutely no lack anywhere.

The Perfection of Wisdom does not suddenly arise as an experience in a person, because it does not discursively apprehend any persons, much less does it apprehend itself as an isolated subjective or objective experience. Perfect Wisdom is wonderfully quiet, calm, peaceful and blissful, because it does not consist of the apprehension or suppression of any particular sign or situation.

The Perfection of Wisdom is flawless and faultless, because it is the spontaneous fulfillment of all moral and spiritual values and aspirations. Perfect Wisdom is undistracted and undissipated by any imaginings, rudimentary or sophisticated, because it perceives that the imagination possesses no inherent self-existence. No separate living being is isolated and then encountered by Prajnaparamita, for it does not limit or divide Reality. This wisdom knows no limits, because no limits manifest as independent or substantial.

The Perfection of Wisdom does not engage or indulge in the duality of opposites, because it does not confine itself within any particular pattern of experience. This wisdom cannot be subdivided or differentiated, any more than any appearing structures can be fundamentally divided or differentiated. Perfect Wisdom is untarnished by various modes of personal ambition. No stages or dimensions of Prajnaparamita can be discerned, because no separately self-existing practitioners can be apprehended and no inherently existing levels or degrees of realization can be discriminated.

The Perfection of Wisdom is infinite, because truth is infinite. Perfect Wisdom is not attached, joined or correlated to any subject or object. This wisdom is unconditional, just as all apparently conditioned structures are fundamentally unconditioned. Prajnaparamita is not relational, because the nature of truth is like open space, possessing no separate parts or interrelated components.

Void of the slightest separate self-existence is this wisdom, just as all appearing structures and events are essentially void of separate self-existence. Perfectly selfless is this wisdom, which therefore comes to rest nowhere. Without any characteristic marks is this wisdom, just as no structure or process essentially possesses primary or secondary characteristics, permanent or impermanent. Prajnaparamita is the panoramic vision of the emptiness of self-existence, because it is without any partition, boundary or fixed perspective.

The Perfection of Wisdom is the complete fulfillment of all contemplative practices, because it does not discriminate contemplative practices as separate realities. This wisdom is the radical opening of all avenues to enlightenment, because it never apprehends any separately self-existing avenues. This wisdom is the natural, effortless realization of every level of spiritual experience, because it never apprehends any separately self-existing levels.

The Perfection of Wisdom is the comprehensive application of the basic principles of spiritual discipline, because these basic principles are not apprehended as separate or substantial. Prajnaparamita is the perfection of perfections, the perfection of powers, the perfection of courage and confidence. This wisdom is the completion of all forms of analytic and intuitive knowledge, because it is not concerned with attaining any knowledge—not even subjectless, objectless omniscience—and hence its pure flow remains unobstructed, undistracted and unobscured.

The Perfection of Wisdom is the plenitude of all the enlightened qualities of a Buddha, or fully Awakened One, which are uncountable because never perceived by Prajnaparamita to be separate or substantial qualities. This wisdom is the spiritual plenitude of a Buddha, who has awakened as pure presence, as sheer Reality. Why? Because Prajnaparamita perceives neither absence nor unreality anywhere.

The Perfection of Wisdom is the perfect simplicity of What Is, because there are no separate, substantially existing beings or events apart from What Is. This wisdom expresses omniscience, because it fully comprehends and clearly illuminates for all living beings the selflessness and modelessness of all possible phenomena on every plane of being and awareness.

LORD BUDDHA: Felicitations, noble Shariputra. Behold the Perfection of Wisdom!

INTREPID PRACTITIONERS OF PRAJNAPARAMITA

SHARIPUTRA: O Awakened Enlightenment, will there exist future bodhisattvas in northern and other distant lands who will immerse themselves in the study and practice of this exceedingly profound Perfection of Wisdom?

LORD BUDDHA: There will be a generous number of aspirants everywhere, sincerely training to develop compassion for all conscious beings. However, surprisingly few among them will have the requisite stamina, intensity of character and radical intelligence to immerse themselves in Prajnaparamita to the point of fully embodying Perfect Wisdom. Even among those aspirants who encounter the authentic exposition of Prajnaparamita, few will be able to absorb the impact of its unthinkable profundity. Few will not be disconcerted, depressed or shocked by this unequivocal teaching about the absence of any substantially underlying ground or basis, either physical or meta-physical.

Those few who can fully and joyously immerse themselves in the Perfection of Wisdom should be recognized as precious mind streams that have flowed for aeons through the immeasurability of Mahayana. They have sought out the fully Awakened Ones and fearlessly questioned them, devoutly contemplating and devotedly venerating the exalted Buddha body, Buddha speech and Buddha mind. These blessed streams of consciousness have become perfect in moral action, which is to say that even their slightest movements and intentions care for, guide and elevate countless beings by orienting them toward the omniscience, or total awakeness, which simply is all Buddhas of past, present and future.

Precisely for the sake of these intrepid practitioners of Prajnaparamita have the spiritual conquerors offered their most radical teaching, the omniscience that knows all possible phenomena to be empty of substantial self-existence. These intrepid practitioners retain consciously from rebirth to rebirth the intense wisdom energy generated by ceaseless engagement with Prajnaparamita. Wherever these mind streams may flow and manifest, they rejoice solely in this most compassionate teaching that reveals all beings and events to be already and forever free from the illusory limits of self-existence, this most radical teaching that leads to and itself constitutes universal conscious enlightenment.

Lifetime after lifetime, these pure streams of consciousness always belong to Mother Prajnaparamita, always remain entirely immersed in her, essentially undifferentiable from her. The powerful, subtle and dangerous principle of egocentricity and negativity, Mara the Adversary, will never be able to divert these awakened bodhisattvas from the Perfection of Wisdom. However, even if Mara approaches them—manifesting through advanced adepts by diverting the refined power of their wills or by channeling negative energy through delusive trances—these bodhisattvas will not for a moment be deceived or distracted.

These invincible diamond beings, through great love for Mother Prajnaparamita, have developed irreversible commitment to universal conscious enlightenment. They are both adamantine and tender. By constantly drinking in and assimilating the beautiful teachings of Perfect Wisdom, these practitioners are filled with spiritual delight, boundless energy and confident serenity. Many persons will be attracted by these bodhisattvas to plant the selfless seeds of kindness and clarity which eventually blossom into full enlightenment.

Face to face with living Buddhas, who are simply Awakened Enlightenment, such diamond beings have proclaimed the supreme vow: *By practicing the sublime Bodhisattva Way of the six transcendent Perfections, its central core the Perfection of Wisdom, we will attract and confirm thousands of conscious beings on their way to enlightenment in our present lifetime, as well as billions of conscious beings in our future lifetimes. We shall ceaselessly articulate and demonstrate Prajnaparamita—awakening, inciting and encouraging conscious beings to imbue themselves with this teaching, to train selflessly according to this teaching, to be born anew out of this mysterious matrix and to be established irreversibly in the process of universal conscious enlightenment.*

Upon hearing this magnificent vow, the humble Lord of Enlightenment greets and rejoices, mind to mind, with these noble sons and daughters of the Buddha family. As a result of this direct transmission from Buddha mind, they become even more powerfully confirmed in their gnostic faith. With this new intensity and empowerment, they become irreversible bodhisattvas, able to direct their mind streams voluntarily to be reborn in various Buddha fields. During each incarnation, they will have the precious opportunity to sit face to face with living Buddhas, receiving the clear demonstration and ineffable transmission of the purest Dharma, the perfectly articulated Prajnaparamita. In widely scattered Buddha fields, such bodhisattvas will attract and confirm countless living beings along the way of conscious evolution into omniscience—tenderly helping, sustaining and guiding them in every possible manner.

SHARIPUTRA: How amazing that there is not even a single being or event, during past, future or present, that those who have disappeared into pure presence, the Tathagatas, have not directly perceived and recognized as empty of inherent self-existence. There is no thought or action of any conscious being which extends beyond or occurs outside this all-encompassing Buddha awareness. The infinitely compassionate Tathagatas clearly perceive each future effort of the bodhisattvas who are inflamed with intense commitment to unveil universal enlightenment. Most lovingly do these spiritual conquerors protect and encourage those who have consecrated their mind streams entirely to the arduous process of universal awakening, guiding all streams of consciousness without exception into the open ocean of truth.

O Awakened Enlightenment, please reveal the reason why some of these sons and daughters of the Buddha family, after great efforts, attain the supreme benediction of Prajnaparamita, while others, whose efforts are intense and sincere, do not. Why are still others granted the consummate encounter with Perfect Wisdom after no appreciable struggle at all?

LORD BUDDHA: Noble Shariputra, you have observed accurately the boundless nature of Buddha awareness. There is absolutely no being or event, whether past, future or present, which the Tathagatas do not experience intimately by recognizing it to be empty of independent or substantial self-existence. You have understood correctly, as well, that during degenerating ages and civilizations, some bodhisattvas who search intensely and sincerely for Prajnaparamita are not able to encounter an authentic expression of the supreme teaching, much less to attain the full realization of Perfect Wisdom. Other bodhisattvas, in more blessed eras, will experience the inestimable good fortune of encountering Prajnaparamita without much search or personal sacrifice. But this rare opportunity is always generated by habitual energies and thought tendencies acquired during previous ages and civilizations, when heroic personal efforts were made to encounter, study, assimilate and perpetuate the Perfection of Wisdom. Practitioners whose mind streams are inextricably connected with Prajnaparamita will spontaneously attract to themselves various auspicious expressions of the supreme teaching, which may take the form of scriptures revealed in various languages and mature spiritual guides, kind and generous.

Know with certainty, O Shariputra, that if any bodhisattva, acting solely from compassion for all living beings, longs and diligently searches for this most radical teaching, the intensity of this quest establishes the good fortune, after one or two incarnations, that enables this stream of consciousness to attract various auspicious manifestations of the principle of Prajnaparamita, which remains always essentially the same. This process of search, however, must never be rooted in any form of self-concern but in heroic efforts of personal sacrifice to awaken, encourage and confirm countless conscious beings on the way to full enlightenment. Then alone will these revolutionary teachings and skilled teachers appear to the aspirant—teachings which reveal the total absence of any underlying ground or basis, either physical or metaphysical, teachers who brilliantly unveil the emptiness of self-existence. Here and now, these teachers generate the energetic fullness and effectiveness of Prajnaparamita as the Perfections of Giving, Goodness, Patience, Commitment, Meditation and Insight.

MOTHER OF THE BUDDHAS

*L*ORD BUDDHA: Consider a mother who has many children—not just five or ten self-centered ones, but a thousand enlightened children, totally devoted to her. If she were to become infirm, they would commit themselves to caring for her with great love and intensity, aware that they owe their very existence to her. With selfless sacrifice and intense labor she brought them into the world. During their childhood, she carefully and wisely instructed them about the nature of human existence—its joys and dangers, its goal and the path to that goal. How sensitively they would care for her, providing every condition that might make her happy, protecting her and lavishing tenderness upon her, imbued with the longing that she should be free from any pain or discomfort coming from her own body or caused by stinging insects, human intruders, demonic spirits or physical mishaps. Thus would enlightened children naturally honor and serve their beloved mother.

In a similar way do the Tathagatas—the ones who have disappeared into Reality, the thousand Buddhas of this aeon—reverently regard their Mother Prajnaparamita, keeping her constantly in heart and mind, longing only to serve her and facilitate her wishes. This devoted connection with the Wisdom Mother generates the waves of blessing that enable those on the path of universal conscious enlighten-

115

ment to venerate, memorize, study, chant, copy and transmit the *Prajnaparamita Sutra*. Not only Tathagatas from this billion-world system, but fully Awakened Ones who dwell in other universes as well, constantly express the Perfection of Wisdom through body, speech and mind, thereby generating happiness and fulfillment for countless living beings. They remain aflame with intense compassion for the illusory suffering of all limited forms of consciousness—heavenly, subtle and earthly beings on all levels of awareness. Buddhas without number exercise superhuman efforts so that the Perfection of Wisdom can remain culturally available and spiritually accessible, never becoming obscured or forgotten. These conquerors exercise all Buddha skills so that Mara and the forces of egocentric negativity will not impede Perfect Wisdom from being widely disseminated, authentically transmitted and carefully practiced.

Unthinkably deep is the loving commitment of Buddhas and bodhisattvas to Mother Prajnaparamita—cherishing her, protecting her and receiving her protection. She is their true nature, matrix, guide, power and bliss. She alone has revealed unobstructed and spontaneous omniscience to them as total awakeness. She has patiently instructed them to deal skillfully with the empty, transparent nature of existence, tenderly awakening all living beings from the dream of individuality, substantiality and separation. From her compassion and wisdom alone have the Tathagatas miraculously come forth. She alone shows them the world as it really is. The pure presence of the Awakened Ones comes from her and is simply her plenitude. All Buddhas from the beginningless past, from the infinite dimensions of the present and from the inconceivable expanse of the future reach full enlightenment thanks to their one universal Wisdom Mother.

WHAT BUDDHA MIND KNOWS

*L*ORD BUDDHA: O brilliant friend, Subhuti. Consider how Tatha-gatas, who have disappeared into pure presence, sensitively know the immeasurable array and incalculable number of conscious beings precisely as they are. This is accomplished through the principle of Prajnaparamita alone. Tathagatas compassionately know the intentions and actions of all living beings, simply by knowing that neither actions nor intentions possess any substantial or independent self-existence.

Tathagatas, who have gone completely beyond conventional views, know clearly the complex collective thoughts of conscious beings precisely as they are. How? By knowing without doubt that as individual thoughts possess no independent self-existence, neither are collective thoughts independent or substantial, and further, by knowing that the very principles of insubstantiality and interdependence also possess no separate substance.

Similarly, omniscient spiritual conquerors know the desperately distracted thoughts of conscious beings precisely as they are. How? By knowing with certainty that distractedness and desperation possess no self-existence, nor are distracted thoughts characterized by any specific marks, never coming into being and therefore never needing to be extinguished. Desperately distracted thoughts are inherently neither distracted nor desperate.

Awakened Ones know the minds of living beings as intrinsically infinite and inexhaustible. Through all-embracing compassion, living Buddhas manifest an all-embracing mind which blissfully recognizes that just as empty space cannot disintegrate or be destroyed, neither can the infinitely open space of all minds ever be narrowed or extinguished. The inconceivably marvelous Buddha mind which knows this openness—which simply is this openness—can itself never be extinguished. Why? Because it never comes into being in the first place, and therefore possesses no duration through time that can be interrupted.

Buddha mind is the one mind of all beings—fully awakened, fully matured, fully sensitized, fully liberated. Buddha mind does not support or ground any phenomena, and since it is infinite, no possible standard or rule exists by which it could be measured. Nor can its creative power of transparent manifestation be exhausted, any more than truth could ever be used up.

Tathagatas compassionately know the polluted thoughts of conscious beings precisely as they are. How? By realizing directly that the minds of those living beings who do not practice any spiritual disciplines are not actually stained by the pollution of false viewpoints. Wrong ideas possess absolutely no substantial self-existence, nor do the conventional minds in which they are claimed to lodge possess any such self-existence. Similarly, Tathagatas know pristine, unpolluted thoughts precisely as they are. How? By realizing directly that minds, transparently luminous in their intrinsic nature, cannot provide substantial residence for even true viewpoints, because correct ideas as well possess no independent self-existence. Buddha mind equally recognizes as inherently empty any illumined thoughts attained by contemplative practitioners who have become free from the drain of outflowing attachments or obsessions.

According to the cardinal principle of Prajnaparamita, Awakened Enlightenment knows lazy thoughts precisely as they are, with nothing to rest upon and thus no way to be lazy. Awakened Enlightenment equally knows positively active thoughts precisely as they are, for even if such thoughts appear active in the effort to win libera-

tion, there is no independent self-existence about which or with which
to be active. Buddha mind knows outflowing or obsessive thoughts
of ordinary persons to be without any substantial self-existence which
could flow in any direction and thus as empty representations or projections of an outflow.

Tathagatas know directly all greedy thoughts by intuitively realizing that the open space of mind can never be greedy. Tathagatas equally
know that thoughts liberated from greed are not actually liberated,
because they never were intrinsically greedy in the first place. The
same intuition applies to thoughts that are hateful and those that are
loving, as well as to deluded thoughts and illumined ones. Mistaken
thoughts are known just as they are—not connected with the coherently relational world of transparent functioning. Appropriate
thoughts are also known precisely as they are—as transparently functional manifestations of Reality, neither inherently increasing,
diminishing nor disappearing.

Ordinary daily thoughts do not come from anywhere, nor go
anywhere, nor can they be encountered independently during present time, for even the present moment possesses absolutely no substantial self-existence. Powerful contemplative thoughts are simply the
spontaneous comprehension of the absence of self-existence, including
the absence of their own independent self-existence. Unlimited
thoughts are not definable or describable as self-existent, because they
do not relate to any conceptual limit. Thoughts apparently bound
by perceptual or conceptual limits are known clearly by Buddha mind
to be transparent manifestations of precisely the same non-self-
existence as unlimited thoughts are. Transcendent insights—free from
any perceptual or conceptual attributes, untouched by any distinguishing mark or by any object or subject of thought and unen-
cumbered by physical or intellectual vision—are known by the Buddha mind as transparent to pure presence.

Tathagatas kindly know that reactive thoughts react simply to their
own false representations of Reality—representations which, whether
subjective or objective, are empty of substantial self-existence. Tathagatas equally know nonreactive, harmonious, peaceful thoughts to

be the total simplicity of Reality, never independently existing in themselves.

Unrefined thoughts are known to be inherently free from their own common characteristic, which is self-involved imagining. Refined thoughts are known as unimpeded, because consciously transparent to the absence of any substantial self-existence and therefore free from self-involved imagining.

Unconcentrated thoughts appear to wander about in perceptual and conceptual realms of conflict and difference, yet the principle of Prajnaparamita reveals that no conflicts or differences are in any way substantial. Concentrated thoughts are known as spontaneous expressions of Prajnaparamita and therefore are as insubstantial as open space. Unemancipated thoughts are known to be intrinsically liberated from any trace of independent self-existence. Emancipated thoughts are known not to exist inherently as past, future or even present self-awareness.

All possible thoughts are known by Buddha mind to be unencounterable, because they never exist independently and therefore never constitute an entity which could be perceived by any level of perception, however refined. Nor can thoughts be discerned as self-existing entities by any level of cognition or contemplative vision, however refined—not by the supreme eye of transcendent insight, nor by the heavenly eye of sublime vision, much less by the ordinary mental eye.

Awakened Enlightenment sympathetically knows, precisely as they are, the ingrained tendencies of countless conscious beings to engage in literal affirmations and negations concerning the transparent structures of relativity. Such beings—themselves constructs—take their own linguistic constructions at face value to be solidly self-existing entities. Awakened Enlightenment clearly knows that these kaleidoscopic affirmations and negations arise like a play of reflected light beams from the constituent processes of personal awareness called form, feeling, impulse, perception and consciousness. How? Because Buddha mind realizes that all possible statements have reference not to Reality but only to the transparent processes and structures called personal awareness. Included in this mere kaleidoscopic play are various metaphysical statements about the Tathagata—that the Tathagata does or does not continue to exist after physical death; that the Tathagata in some sense does and in some sense does not exist after death; or that the Tathagata cannot be said either to exist or not to exist after death. None of these statements, however refined, refer directly to Awakened Enlightenment—birthless as well as deathless.

Buddha mind, unveiling the inherent emptiness of self-existence, dissolves metaphysical assumptions, such as the doctrine that the self and its consciousness are eternal and that all other phenomena are mere delusion. Equally inadmissible as truth are statements that the self and its consciousness are eternal, temporal, both eternal and temporal or neither eternal nor temporal. It is inadmissible as well to maintain that the self and its consciousness are finite, infinite, both or neither. Referring also to false abstractions and projections and not to Reality are doctrines which claim that the soul is confined to or identical with the body or that the soul is independent from the body and from other structures of relativity.

Through the unwavering principle of Prajnaparamita, Tathagatas know all possible positive or negative assertions precisely as they are, for Buddha mind realizes the transparent processes and structures of personal and communal awareness to be simply suchness, or pure presence. Through awakening fully as pure presence, the Tathagatas know the suchness of all beings and events and of all statements about them. The whole image of phenomenal manifestation is the play of universal enlightenment through the constituents of individual and communal awareness. All is simply suchness.

Therefore, noble Subhuti, the pure presence of the constituents of personal and communal awareness is the pure presence of what we call the world, the pure presence of all phenomena without exception, including the contemplative life in all its subtle degrees, from novitiate to sagehood to complete Buddhahood. All material and mental structures manifest as one continuous presence, one absolute depth of unthinkable purity, without any trace of positive or negative assertion. This pure presence is inextinguishable, indistinguishable simplicity. Precisely this pure presence is what Tathagatas have fully known through the blessings of Prajnaparamita. This is how Mother Prajnaparamita carefully and lovingly instructs all the Awakened Ones. And this is exactly how the Awakened Ones patiently reveal to the superficial, intoxicated and inharmonious awareness of living beings what the apparent world really is.

After receiving the inestimable blessing of this instruction, aspirants experience insight into the true nature of What Is. Thus does Perfect Wisdom function as Great Mother—generating countless Tathagatas, awakening them and revealing herself through them to all conscious beings. Tathagatas, whose enlightenment is composed of suchness alone, blissfully recognize the whole world as precisely this same suchness, never as false or as changing. This is why the mysterious title *Tathagata* is conferred upon the Buddhas, for *Tathagata* means the one who has disappeared entirely and beautifully into suchness.

SUBHUTI: O Lord Buddha, surely the uttermost unthinkable depth of the teaching is suchness, or pure presence. The very enlightenment of all Buddhas shines forth as pure presence alone. No one can have total confidence in this teaching of suchness except a bodhisattva who is irreversibly on the path of universal conscious enlightenment or a liberated sage or a practitioner who has at least attained a clear, penetrating understanding of Prajnaparamita. The uttermost depth of unthinkability is therefore presented by Tathagatas as simple suchness only to these three—irreversible bodhisattva, realized sage and profound student of Prajnaparamita.

LORD BUDDHA: Precisely, Subhuti. And pure presence, which Buddha mind fully knows and spontaneously reveals, is inexhaustible Reality. Awakened Ones, after full enlightenment, always joyously teach and indicate with every word and wordless gesture the absolute inexhaustibility of pure presence.

PURE GRATITUDE, INFINITE THANKFULNESS

SUBHUTI: Perfection of Wisdom is a boundless field of subjectless and objectless awareness where, without trace, the Tathagatas freely and joyfully roam.

LORD BUDDHA: So it is, beloved Subhuti. In this free and joyful atmosphere, the Wisdom Mother—through the sublime body, speech and mind of the Buddhas—tenderly instructs bodhisattvas about the true nature of manifestation. Tathagatas live and move in the most intimate relationship with truth, and thereby understand thoroughly the transparent structures of relativity, which manifest spontaneously and without beginning. Buddhas are able to be all-knowing by not assuming finite or fixed positions within any cultural, philosophical or religious system of knowledge. They abide only in, through and as Perfect Wisdom. They devotedly contemplate the spontaneously revealing Goddess Prajnaparamita with deep consecration and respect —revering, worshiping and ecstatically adoring her, for they know that truth, the openness and harmony of all structures of relativity, is none other than the Wisdom Mother.

The omniscience which knows without finite cognition and which alone constitutes Buddhahood springs from Mother Prajnaparamita, and therefore all Buddhas and bodhisattvas are intensely grateful and thankful to her and only to her. They are, in fact, nothing but pure gratitude, infinite thankfulness. This gratitude takes the form of their constantly cherishing and embodying the Mahayana—the immeasurable vehicle upon which universal loving awareness is borne, the contemplative practice by which heart and mind become fully illumined. The pure thankfulness of adamantine awareness takes the form of recognizing the transparent structures of relativity as never brought together and therefore never taken apart, as never created and therefore never destroyed. Through their selfless gratitude and thankfulness, the Wisdom Mother continues to instruct her enlightened children about the true nature of What Is.

SUBHUTI: Lord, how can Prajnaparamita actually instruct anyone about What Is, since the true nature of manifestation is unknowable and inconceivable?

LORD BUDDHA: It is excellent, Subhuti, that you choose to pose this question directly to the Buddha. All possible structures of relativity are unthinkable and ungraspable. Why? They are perfectly empty of self-existence, because no structure springs from any underlying root, ground or source. Thanks to the Perfection of Wisdom—through its very unidentifiability and unthinkability—all structures are penetrated and fully known. Thanks to the intimate instructions of the Wisdom Mother, Buddhas and bodhisattvas know the transparent nature of the world by not viewing themselves and by not viewing the world.

SUBHUTI: Lord, how is such viewless knowing possible?

LORD BUDDHA: When the universal panorama is clearly seen to manifest without any objective or subjective supports, viewless knowing awakens spontaneously. Simply by not reviewing any appearing structures, one establishes the true view of What Is. This viewless or nonperspectival view is what constitutes Buddha nature and acts dynamically as the Wisdom Mother, revealing whatever is simply as what it is—empty of substantial self-existence, unchartable and uncharacterizable, calmly quiet and already blissfully awakened. Mother Prajnaparamita compassionately reveals the world as purified from any false concepts or misguided instincts of worldhood or worldliness. She alone makes the inexpressible truth known by pointing it out directly and by embodying it miraculously.

UNIVERSAL PRINCIPLE
OF INCONCEIVABILITY

*S*UBHUTI: Deep and elusive beyond all doctrine and all recognition, O Lord, is this Perfection of Wisdom. The supreme enterprise beyond all others is this Perfection of Wisdom—an unthinkable enterprise, an unimaginable enterprise, an unapproachable enterprise, an incalibratable enterprise, a totally unique enterprise which reaches the unreachable and attains the unattainable.

LORD BUDDHA: Precisely so, most brilliant Subhuti. And why is Perfect Wisdom unthinkable? Because unthinkably profound are all its points of reference: *Tathagata*, the disappearance into pure presence; *Buddha nature*, the Reality which is simply awakeness; *spontaneous selflessness*, the essenceless essence of all phenomena; and *luminous omniscience*, which knows without knower, knowing or known. Upon none of these points can thought be focused, because they are not objects or subjects. They cannot be imagined or willed, perceived or felt. They cannot be touched or approached in any way by any finite mode or procedure of consciousness.

Why is Perfect Wisdom incalibratable? Because there is no way to focus upon, much less to compare with other known phenomena or to measure against any known standard, either *Tathagata, Buddha nature, selflessness* or *omniscience*. Why is the enterprise of Perfect Wisdom unique? Because nothing can in any way approach, much less equal, *Tathagata, Buddha nature, selflessness* and *omniscience*.

SUBHUTI: Lord, do the attributes of infinity—including unthink-ability, incalibratability and uniqueness—apply only to *Tathagata, Buddha nature, selflessness* and *omniscience,* or do they apply as well to every structure of relativity, to every appearance without exception?

LORD BUDDHA: These attributes of infinity, or absolute incon-ceivability, apply equally to every possible point of reference, to every possible mode of manifestation, to every existential detail. The con-stituents of limited personal awareness are just as unthinkable as is limitless Buddha nature. The basic structures of every finite manifesta-tion are as unimaginable, unapproachable, incalibratable, indecipher-able and indescribable as is infinite Buddha nature.

Suppose one attempts to approach the essential nature of form, or patterning. No thought or imagination applies, no intentionality is appropriate, no feelings or perceptions of any kind are relevant, no process of comparison or reasoning is possible. The intrinsic nature of form remains elusive, impenetrable, unformulatable. This same principle of inconceivability applies to all general structures or par-ticular phenomena whatsoever, which are beyond measuring, coun-ting or discriminating because they are not separately self-existing but are like the essential indivisibility of space.

Consider carefully, Subhuti. Can you count, compare, measure, conceive, imagine, perceive, touch or divide the principle of space? Can you approach, reach or attain space? Can space even be described as infinite?

SUBHUTI: In no way, Lord Buddha.

LORD BUDDHA: In precisely the same manner as the principle of space are all appearances whatsoever unthinkable, unimaginable, incalibratable, unapproachable, unattainable, incomparable. For all phenomena are Buddha phenomena, arising as the open space of total awakeness, in which dividing, discriminating and discursive thought is absent, in which no comparison is feasible. Every possible subject or object of consciousness is in exactly this manner inconceivable, indescribable and unattainable. Because of the fundamental impossi-bility of measuring, calculating or comparing, all structures and phenomena are Buddha structures and Buddha phenomena, essentially like open space. No beings or events substantially exist side by side, any more than space can exist side by side with itself or with some other expanse or nonexpanse. This impossibility of any comparison is the core of the universal principle of inconceivability called Prajnaparamita.

MIRROR IMAGE OF PURE PRESENCE

SUBHUTI: This radical teaching of truth is openly presented as a nonteaching. Therefore, nothing can obstruct this teaching, which is as all-embracing and ungraspable as space, no trace of which can ever be found, crystallized, isolated, divided, tested or analyzed. This teaching of truth is not related to any other teachings, because it does not preserve the concept of otherness, nor does it encounter any adversarial positions, because it does not proclaim any principle of opposition. It is a traceless teaching because it is utterly spontaneous—not brought into being by various causes or influences. This teaching has never been taught or displayed in any way, because it does not accept as substantial any coming into being or going out of being. It is a nonteaching without any path to its realization, because no separate mode of access is recognized to exist inherently.

SHAKRA: A precise mirror reflection of the Awakened One is this perfect disciple, the holy sage Subhuti, for whenever he demonstrates truth, he begins, moves and concludes in the absolute transparency called non-self-existence.

SUBHUTI: Only because the one now speaking has never been born, does he manifest as an utterly insubstantial mirror image of the Tathagata, the Awakened Enlightenment that just is. The one now speaking is simply an image of the pure presence into which the

Tathagata has disappeared. Neither arriving from anywhere, abiding anywhere nor going anywhere, neither evolving, continuing, devolving or dissolving is the pure presence which is the essenceless essence of the Tathagata—and of Subhuti as well.

There has never been a time in which the loyal disciple Subhuti has not been an image of the pure presence, or suchness, of the Tathagata. Why? Because the suchness of the Tathagata, the one who has disappeared by awakening as Reality, is the very same as the suchness of all possible structures of relativity. So the pure presence of Subhuti the Elder is universal pure presence. Born without birth as the mirror image of pure presence is Subhuti; born only as the mirror image of ever-perfect Buddhahood is the one now speaking.

Suchness is not substantial in any sense. Only as a mirror image of ontologically transparent or insubstantial suchness has Subhuti spontaneously arisen without beginning. This is the only sense in which the one now speaking can be said to manifest as a living image of Lord Buddha, who is the pure presence of a transparent, selfless awakeness which is absolutely insubstantial yet functions coherently as a relative body, speech and mind. This suchness called Subhuti is not some self-existence which changes or transforms in any way, nor can it be discriminated or differentiated as any separate mind stream which changes or remains the same. Precisely the same is true of the Tathagata. Thus it can be said that the unidentifiable Subhuti now speaking is simply indivisible, undifferentiated suchness and is therefore a living image of universal Buddha nature.

Just as the pure presence of the Tathagata, which never transforms or divides, does not encounter any obstruction, barrier or frontier, so it is with the pure presence of all phenomena, which never transforms by dividing or multiplying in any way and which never experiences any contact or encounter. The transparent suchness of Buddha and the transparent suchness of all phenomena are simply suchness—not divided or divisible, not multiple, not even single.

This pure presence, without any second reality or subreality, is not located anywhere, nor does it come from anywhere, nor does it belong anywhere, much less is it going anywhere or evolving in any way. It is precisely because this pure presence does not belong anywhere that it is total and simple.

Just by being awake as unconstructed presence is the speaker of these words a living image of universal Buddha nature. An unconstructed presence, never put together or taken apart, is at no time not present. It is ever-perfect, ever-present simplicity. This is why the present speaker is a living image of the universal Buddhahood of all conscious beings.

At all times, and timelessly, suchness remains without substantial structure and therefore without essential description, although it appears effortlessly as Subhuti, as Shakyamuni Buddha and as all phenomena. Although there may seem to be two beings—that is, Subhuti the disciple as a separate image of Buddha, his master—nothing has been broken away from the original Buddha presence which can now be called the image of Subhuti, because pure presence remains unbroken and unbreakable. There is no substantial agent apart from suchness which could break or divide it into two or which could reflect suchness by functioning as a separate mirror or perceiver. In this divisionless sense alone can Subhuti be said to be a living image of universal Buddha nature.

The pure presence of the Tathagata does not exist somewhere else, outside or beyond the pure presence of all phenomena. The same can be said about the pure presence of the one who is now speaking. Since the suchness of Buddhahood is not outside or beyond any phenomenon, there is no phenomenon that is not Buddhahood. The simple suchness of Subhuti is therefore precisely the same as the suchness of all the structures of relativity and all the Awakened Ones.

The present speaker knows directly the pure presence of all structures and processes by reflecting it spontaneously in the unchanging and insubstantial mirror of his own pure presence. But no reflection takes place in a mode of separation. It is therefore only in a processless, imageless, inseparable sense that Subhuti is a mirror reflection of the Tathagata. Why? Because the pure presence of the Tathagata is neither past nor future, nor is it to be found in the false abstraction called present time. Exactly thus is the suchness of all phenomena. So Subhuti could just as easily be called the timeless mirror image of all phenomena, not just the reflection of his master.

However, only through the pure presence of Shakyamuni Buddha does Subhuti actually awaken to his own pure presence as being simply that of all phenomena. Only through the total simplicity, or suchness, of his great master does Subhuti awaken to the total simplicity of all manifestation in the past, future and present. But Subhuti now recognizes no essential distinction whatsoever between the pure presence of the master and the pure presence of the disciple.

Within the all-embracing simplicity of Reality, there is no distinction or division between the pure presence of Subhuti, the pure presence of Shakyamuni Buddha and the pure presence of all phenomena. The suchness of Shakyamuni while he is strenuously sacrificing his energy for others during five hundred preparatory lifetimes as a bodhisattva is precisely the suchness of Shakyamuni when he attains full enlightenment, sitting perfectly at ease beneath the bodhi tree, now manifest as Lord Buddha. This inexhaustible suchness alone constitutes the Buddha nature of all conscious beings.

As this incomparable demonstration of pure presence shines forth in the miraculously unified awareness of Subhuti, King Shakra and the assembled denizens of the Thirty-Three Heaven, the universe quakes in all six dimensions of its being—trembling and rumbling melodiously with ecstasy, precisely as it did when Shakyamuni Buddha attained complete enlightenment.

SUBHUTI: It is only in this way, O heavenly beings who seek truth, that the one now speaking can be said to be a living mirror image of the Tathagata. But the present speaker is not the reflection of any holy form nor of any stage of contemplative attainment, ranging from wholeheartedly entering the path to tasting the fullest fruition of the path. For no holy forms or attainments, external or internal, actually

possess the slightest substantial self-existence, nor can they be grasped
or objectified in any way. Only in this uncrystallizable sense can
Subhuti be called a mirror image of universal Buddha nature.

SHARIPUTRA: O Lord Buddha, according to this brilliant exposition by the Elder Subhuti, pure presence constitutes the unspeakable,
unthinkable depth of the teaching.

LORD BUDDHA: Indeed it does, Shariputra.

As this totally effective demonstration of suchness shines forth with
great initiatory power in the Buddha's radiant assembly, the well-
prepared minds of three hundred holy monks are liberated from all
notions of gain or loss and from every conceivable form of grasping
or clinging. Five hundred well-prepared holy nuns blissfully open
the pure, dispassionate and perfectly unstained eye that perceives truth
alone. Five thousand exalted heavenly beings, who have trained in
Prajnaparamita during previous precious human lifetimes, now
awaken to the transcendent Patience which lovingly accepts and
embraces all structures of relativity, knowing that no structures have
ever substantially come into being. And the profoundly compassionate
minds of six thousand male and six thousand female bodhisattvas are
suddenly released into the astonishing delight and freedom of Perfect
Wisdom.

WHO ATTAINS ENLIGHTENMENT?

*S*UBHUTI: How can the venerable Lord Buddha assert that complete enlightenment is difficult to realize, even supremely difficult to realize? Prajnaparamita so clearly teaches, according to the principle by which all phenomena without exception are recognized as empty of substantial self-existence, that no structure exists independently which could be said to perform any such difficult or supremely difficult realization. All structures are fluid, open and transparent, free from any obstructing or confining substantiality. Even powerful and dangerous structures, such as the selfish passions, which religious teaching advises human beings to renounce or even to destroy, are themselves fluid, open and transparent, inherently empty of independent self-existence.

Any particular being who would become illumined by reaching enlightenment—that is, the individual mind stream of any practitioner who would recognize the state of full enlightenment upon arriving there—simply does not exist independently or substantially. In this light, O Lord of Enlightenment, one might just as accurately assert that enlightenment is easy to realize, even supremely easy to realize. There is only universal enlightenment.

LORD BUDDHA: Most brilliant Subhuti, only in the radical sense that it could never be attained by any separate individual is enlightenment said to be supremely difficult to attain. Neither practitioner nor path nor enlightenment is a self-existing entity which can be isolated, perceived or conceived. The conventional appearance of individual beings—as coherently functioning relations and perspectives, as meaningful perceptual and mental constructions—possesses not an atom of substantial self-existence.

SHARIPUTRA: Noble brother Subhuti, enlightenment is difficult to attain only because no thought or act of attaining enlightenment can be said to occur in reality, any more than open space decides to attain its own openness or reach its own spaciousness. Enlightenment is nothing other than the spontaneous experience of all possible structures as equivalent to open space.

However, if enlightenment could be described as easy to attain, as you suggest, why would so many practitioners, even very advanced ones, lose nerve and allow their intention to attain enlightenment to degenerate? Precisely because so many practitioners do turn away from the radical commitment to universal conscious enlightenment can it be called difficult to realize, even supremely difficult to realize.

SUBHUTI: Shariputra, can one say that form, perception or any other constituent process of personal awareness loses nerve and turns its back on the commitment to enlightenment?

SHARIPUTRA: Obviously one cannot.

SUBHUTI: Or, Shariputra, could one assert that the practitioner who loses nerve and turns away is some substantial entity apart from the fluid, transparent, insubstantial processes which constitute personal awareness?

SHARIPUTRA: Obviously one could not.

SUBHUTI: Then is it the suchness, or pure presence, of these constituents which loses nerve and turns away?

SHARIPUTRA: Clearly not, Subhuti.

SUBHUTI: Is that which loses nerve and turns away from its commitment some reality independent from the suchness of the constituent structures of awareness?

SHARIPUTRA: Clearly not, Subhuti.

SUBHUTI: For that matter, Shariputra, could one assert that form or perception or any other constituent of personal awareness experiences full enlightenment?

SHARIPUTRA: Certainly not, Subhuti.

SUBHUTI: And yet is that which experiences enlightenment some reality independent from personal awareness?

SHARIPUTRA: Certainly not, Subhuti.

SUBHUTI: Could one even say, Shariputra, that the pure presence of awareness reaches enlightenment?

SHARIPUTRA: Not accurately, Subhuti.

SUBHUTI: For that matter, Shariputra, what precisely is experienced by total awakeness? Is it material forms and mental states or is it some reality independent from material forms and mental states?

SHARIPUTRA: One cannot truly say that total awakeness, which is like open space, self-consciously experiences any limited situation whatsoever.

SUBHUTI: So one cannot even describe what enlightenment experiences, much less what it is that allegedly loses nerve and turns away from the commitment to attain enlightenment. Shariputra, can Reality lose nerve and turn away from full enlightenment?

SHARIPUTRA: Certainly not, Subhuti.

SUBHUTI: Is there any second reality independent from Reality which might lose nerve and turn away?

SHARIPUTRA: Certainly not, Subhuti.

SUBHUTI: What, then, is this structure called a practitioner who has lost nerve and allowed commitment to degenerate? We can only consider this question adequately by recognizing the fluidity, transparency, openness and insubstantiality of all possible structures, reifying none of them. Is it this fluidity, transparency, openness and insubstantiality which loses nerve and turns away from attaining enlightenment?

SHARIPUTRA: Absolutely not, Subhuti.

SUBHUTI: So finally, in the clear light of truth, how can one assert that there are any practitioners who attain enlightenment or any who lose nerve and turn away from enlightenment?

SHARIPUTRA: When one approaches this question as the insightful Subhuti has done, with the uncompromising application of the principle of Prajnaparamita, viewing all possible phenomena in their essential nature alone, there is certainly no practitioner who loses nerve and veers away from the supreme goal of the universal conscious enlightenment of all beings. But how, then, can one validate the method taught by the Tathagata for distinguishing those who have set out wholeheartedly in the direction of enlightenment into three groups or vehicles? According to the radical approach of the venerable Subhuti, there appears to be only one authentic way to enlightenment—the all-inclusive, indivisible, timeless Buddha Way, the principle of Prajnaparamita that discerns Reality alone.

PURNA: Before you pose this question, Shariputra, you should inquire of Subhuti, the unsurpassable master of dialectic and radical insight, whether he admits the independent existence of any practitioners, using any of the traditional three vehicles, or methods—whether personal liberation, solitary self-realization or universal conscious enlightenment.

SHARIPUTRA: O Subhuti, do you admit the objective existence of a group of practitioners who vow in a heartfelt manner to attain enlightenment and who use either of the two individual vehicles of liberation or isolation, or the universal vehicle of compassionate commitment?

SUBHUTI: Brother Shariputra, does transcendent insight perceive or cognize in the total simplicity of pure presence even one single independent being who is committed to some independent state called enlightenment and who is using some independently existing vehicle, or method, to attain this goal?

SHARIPUTRA: Certainly not, Subhuti. The total simplicity of suchness is not divisible into vehicles or practitioners who use them, nor is it oriented toward any goal whatsoever. So is there only one way?

SUBHUTI: Can pure presence, or suchness, even be characterized as being *one* or as being *a way?*

SHARIPUTRA: No, indeed, Subhuti.

SUBHUTI: Reality, which is the transparent manner in which phenomena actually manifest, never projects any substantial or independently self-existing structure called a spiritual practitioner. So how can the notion arise that certain practitioners belong to a personal liberation vehicle, others to a solitary self-realization vehicle and still others to a universal enlightenment vehicle? How can the further notion arise of only one vehicle?

If aspirants who are unreservedly committed to the enlightenment of all conscious beings hear this teaching and realize that there can be no crystallization of practitioners and no differentiation between methods, since they are all merely expressions of the same pure presence, and if these aspirants are not shocked, depressed or dissuaded by this radical teaching from their authentic commitment to the enlightenment of all, then one can be assured that such diamond beings will soon awaken as irreversible bodhisattvas.

LORD BUDDHA: Well-argued and incisively expressed, O Subhuti. Only through the truth power of the Buddha, who is simply awakeness, have you declared these unfindable, inexpressible and ungraspable teachings.

SUBHUTI: O Lord Buddha, to what inconceivable enlightenment does the bodhisattva awaken who no longer discriminates and differentiates any separate practitioner or any separate vehicle whatsoever?

LORD BUDDHA: To the full, perfect, spontaneous, supreme and universal enlightenment of all living beings.

HOW TO RECOGNIZE
THE BODHISATTVA

*L*ORD BUDDHA: The bodhisattva who is irreversibly established in the principle of Mahayana—utter consecration to universal conscious enlightenment—no longer pays the slightest attention to the narrowly focused path of individual liberation or to the isolated realization of the solitary sage but proceeds, continuously and without distraction, toward the omniscience of Buddhahood that shines through all phenomena equally. The spiritual evolution of this diamond being remains always clearly directed and profoundly sensitized by the most tender compassion. Whatever high realm of meditative attainment may be mastered, this compassionate mind stream does not focus or abide there, during the present life or in future lifetimes, but remains so concentrated on the suffering beings in the sensory plane of desire form that its voluntary rebirth will not occur in any of the refined realms of sublime form or blissful formlessness. This unwavering focus on the realm of intensely suffering beings is the characteristic sign of the irreversibly established bodhisattva.

This mind stream of complete commitment, though fundamentally elusive in nature, may be recognized through certain indications. Bodhisattvas attach no importance whatsoever to personal names, to impressive secular or religious titles or to widespread recognition and acceptance—whether it concerns their own station or the station of others. Furthermore, bodhisattvas are never distracted or depressed, because they abide solely as panoramic concern for the present well-being and future spiritual evolution of all conscious forms of life. Wherever these diamond beings move, through blissful spiritual realms or comfortable physical environments, their heart awareness does not wander even for an instant from the suffering of all living beings. This totally consecrated Mahayana heart is never shattered or even agitated by negative conditions, however frightful these may become, remaining ever mindful, peaceful and blissful because immersed perpetually in Prajnaparamita. When bodhisattvas appear as married persons with extensive family and social responsibilities, they remain free from any obsessive longing for the pleasant experiences of life, accepting wealth and delight or poverty and pain with the same quiet dignity.

Consider this parable. If one were lost with family and friends in a wilderness inhabited by dangerous animals and by bands of ruthless highwaymen, one could certainly not enjoy life complacently but would remain active and alert, ceaselessly contemplating possible ways of protection and escape. So it is with irreversible bodhisattvas, whether lay or monastic, who live the true life of responsibility. They never remain focused on whatever personal pleasure or difficulty may arise: Rather, they accept their lives gracefully and deal with their surroundings effectively, without once ceasing to contemplate possible ways of protection and escape for all conscious beings. The awakened bodhisattva engages fully in the five dimensions of sensual pleasure and commits intensively to some righteous form of livelihood or concrete service to humanity, while remaining untouched by any impurity, never dying in an unconscious or unmindful manner and never willfully inflicting obvious or subtle suffering upon any living being. Such bodhisattvas exist only to inspire conscious beings to embrace the way of universal joy and fulfillment, the Mahayana, the ineffable fusion of wisdom and compassion.

Bodhisattvas, whether recognized as such or not, are the human beings who have become worthy of their own humanity, who manifest the true magnificence of humanity. They alone can be called the ultimate evolutionary step of humanity and of the whole universe.

They are persons of true excellence, beings of true splendor. They
are the noble elephants of humankind. They are the valiant spiritual
warriors and the heroic leaders of humankind. They are beautiful,
fragrant lotuses of humankind, thoroughbreds of humankind, wise
dragons and royal lions of humankind. They are the sensitive educators
of humanity and of all conscious beings.

Bodhisattvas can live this exalted life of consecration within the
sphere of every imaginable responsibility because they have been
infused by Perfect Wisdom and have merged with the living power
of Prajnaparamita. The irreversible commitment of these diamond
beings is simply Prajnaparamita. Transcendent streams of consciousness, such as the magnificent protector Vajrapani, constantly
abide with, sustain and accelerate the irreversible bodhisattva. Surrounded invisibly by such adamantine protecting and illuminating
presences, these awakened bodhisattvas cannot even be touched, much
less defeated or destroyed, either by human adversaries or by cun-
ning negative forces from other planes of being, unless they accept
such suffering as a form of skillful teaching. Fanatic or demonic forces
find it difficult even to encounter much less to attack an irreversible
bodhisattva, whose calm mind, without the slightest anxiety, merely
notes their existence as empty or transparent.

The physical, intellectual, moral and spiritual faculties of such
bodhisattvas are complete, and their mind streams, dedicated to universal conscious enlightenment, suffer no substantial deficiency on any
level. The vital organs of bodhisattvas are not those of weak or impo-
tent persons. These diamond beings do not rely for protection or
healing upon superstitious or superficial forms of magical ceremony,
upon fanciful medicines or hypnotic suggestion. Such misplaced
respect and reliance is the hallmark of persons who have allowed
themselves to become mentally and therefore physically debilitated
and distracted.

Bodhisattvas earn an honest living or receive the gift of sustenance
in some way that serves and elevates beings, rather than in any way
which would exploit or corrupt them. These diamond beings inter-
relate with people in ways which are harmonious rather than argumen-

tative, serving rather than demanding. Dedicated to and acting upon principles of the highest intellectual, moral and spiritual refinement, bodhisattvas never praise or even subtly overestimate themselves and never denigrate or even subtly underestimate others.

There are innumerable noble qualities which characterize the bodhisattvas who are irreversibly committed to the spiritual awakening of all conscious streams. These diamond beings do not engage in superficial feats of psychic prediction, such as whether a son or a daughter will be born into a certain wealthy family, regarding such dramatic predictions or other flamboyant manifestations of mental power as mere forms of ingratiation and self-elevation.

Listen with boundless joy, O Subhuti, to the truly marvelous attributes of those who are irreversibly established in the universal love called Mahayana. These practitioners never become preoccupied and thereby diverted by contemplating as substantial the constituents of personal and communal awareness which project the sense of separate individuality. Nor do they review, reify or crystallize the various fields of sense experience, including mental experience. Nor do they concretize the existence of the physical elements, nor objectify the structures of causality which coherently unite all these dimensions of experience.

Much less are bodhisattvas preoccupied and thereby diverted by the conventional conversation which is prevalent in any society—habitual talk about kings or government officials, about criminals, about armies and battles, about the problems of villages, cities, nations and their capitals. Bodhisattvas are freed from obsessively speaking about themselves and are not obsessed either with discussing prime ministers or other men and women of worldly power or religious authority. Bodhisattvas do not have any overwhelming impulse to talk about possible journeys, beautiful parks, remote monasteries or sumptuous palaces with reflecting pools, lotus ponds, gardens and game preserves. Nor do the diamond beings talk obsessively about the supernatural landscape, which is populated by fascinating forces, including endless varieties of ghosts and demons.

They do not purposelessly discuss the preparation of food and drink, the design of clothing and jewelry or the preparation of flower garlands, perfumes and soothing ointments. They do not experience any compulsion to talk about highways, crossroads, streets, shops or vehicles, nor about popular songs and unusual performers, dances and dancers, theaters and actors. Nor do these beings of consistent purpose and compassion ever become obsessively engaged in whatever random form of discussion may arise, such as the scope of oceans, the course of rivers or the number of islands, continents or worlds.

Awakened bodhisattvas do not allow any possible subject of thought or conversation to obstruct or obscure their continuous contemplation of truth. They always bear the Perfection of Wisdom carefully in mind, discussing it at every opportunity with great sensitivity and enthusiasm. They are beings whose entire mental and perceptual activity is oriented solely toward omniscience. They experience no prurient delight in discussing degeneration or violence, nor in gratuitously analyzing various personal, political or legal disputes. Nevertheless, they are totally committed to what is righteous and just in any particular situation, never even considering the slightest concession to what is criminal, base or in any way destructive or heedless. They evaluate situations calmly, free from judgmental or divisive attitudes and unconscious presuppositions. Their approach always heals differences rather than causing further dissension. They stand for universal friendship, not for pervasive mistrust and its consequent personal and social disintegration and degradation. They teach universal truth, not the proliferation of limited viewpoints or sectarian doctrines.

These irreversible bodhisattvas live their humble, invisible lives of wisdom and compassion consecrated to the purpose of meeting with fully Awakened Ones, within whatever world system or on whatever plane of being they may be abiding. Why? To become capable of generating even greater energy for universal awakening. Such diamond beings seek to be reborn in radiant Buddha assemblies, wherever they may manifest, in order to receive the precious teachings of Prajnaparamita directly from Awakened Enlightenment, thus becoming able to transmit these teachings more powerfully to all beings.

Irreversible bodhisattvas are never deprived of either the inward communion or the external encounter with great spiritual conquerors. These diamond beings are never, even for an instant, denied the supreme opportunity of honoring and serving the humble Lords of Enlightenment.

Furthermore, awakened bodhisattvas have finished with the seductive experience of being reborn into realms of heavenly delight – whether limited sensuous heavens, sublimely formed contemplative heavens or even exalted heavens of formless bliss. Instead, they consciously direct their reincarnational streams into the suffering planetary plane, incarnating wherever living Buddhas or their active lineages of radical teaching can be found. Diamond beings usually avoid being born on planets or in geographical locations where there exist only very few persons of high spiritual refinement – those with knowledge of iconography, mystic poetry, mantra meditation, secrets of Perfect Wisdom, interpretation of omens and complete understanding of the levels of experience along the path to full enlightenment. Being continuously reborn into refined spiritual cultures, as a base for the efforts of universal education, is often a characteristic of irreversibility.

It never occurs to irreversible bodhisattvas to wonder whether they are irreversible or not, for absolutely no doubt arises in their hearts and minds concerning their own total and final commitment to protecting, educating and awakening all beings. They never for a single moment depart from this ideal. Just as persons who authentically enter the spiritual path do not doubt that they have gained access to the true way, precisely so the selfless mind streams which achieve irreversible commitment to the liberation and enlightenment of all beings never doubt the adamantine nature of this commitment which they have blessedly attained and which they will never abandon.

Awakened bodhisattvas instantly see through any negative or demonic deception that may arise, and thus never come under the subtle influence of Mara, the non-self-existing adversary of Truth. Persons who submit to negative or demonic influences and, as a result, commit capital crimes against humanity, cannot forget their terrible actions, the impact of which persists even after physical death. The

mind streams of awakened bodhisattvas, by contrast, are completely
suffused with blissful commitment, throughout this and future
lifetimes. This commitment to kindness and insight cannot be reversed,
even if the whole universe—including divine beings, subtle beings and
human beings—would try by psychic power, argument, ruse or
violence to divert the consecrated mind from its sacred vow.

Irreversible bodhisattvas are free from personal, cultural or demonic
illusion. They are not attracted by the limited notions of separate
individual liberation or the self-realization of the solitary sage. Even
after innumerable lifetimes of selfless, relentless and even thankless
struggle to awaken and mature living beings and to kindle within
them the pure longing for universal conscious enlightenment, irreversible bodhisattvas never cry out: *Alas, we shall never be able to awaken
all sentient beings and establish them on the path to enlightenment.*
Instead, the compassionate mind streams committed to enlightenment
for all fearlessly proclaim: *We will certainly be able to generate universal
awakening, because our commitment is absolutely irreversible and we
know that it is.* Such fully consecrated practitioners can no longer
be seduced into uncertainty or vacillation.

Because these bodhisattvas have merited and attained irreversibility,
their joyful spirit of commitment can never be obliterated, dissipated
or even slightly dimmed. These magnificent practitioners are so
intensely dedicated to universal love that their minds become impeccable and impervious, their transcendent insight unsurpassable and
imperishable. Suppose the impostor Mara were to simulate the golden
form of a Buddha, which would then deceptively proclaim: *Strive
to attain individual liberation. Universal love is an illusion. You are
not destined to reach full enlightenment, as is clear from your obvious
lack of sublime attributes and the absence of any miraculous signs.*

If a newly avowed bodhisattva listens seriously to this simulated
Buddha and experiences a loss of nerve, then such a bodhisattva has
not yet matured into the stature of irreversibility. An irreversible
bodhisattva, upon hearing such delusive words, immediately thinks:
*This golden form is none other than the impostor Mara, who has
magically projected it, for the Buddha speaks only in terms of attaining*

enlightenment and elevating all conscious beings to enlightenment.
Thereupon, Mara's magically fabricated double of the Buddha dissolves
instantaneously, dissipated by the truth force of irreversibility. Victory in such confrontations with negativity and delusion is the only
sublime attribute and miraculous sign necessary to confirm, beyond
the slightest doubt, that the bodhisattva has been predicted to full
enlightenment by Buddhas of past aeons and has become irreversible
in the Mahayana, the all-embracing vehicle, the union of Perfect
Wisdom and liberative art.

Awakened bodhisattvas always strive to hear and practice the purest
teachings of truth, whether such heroic efforts cost them their entire
wealth or even their lives. All that functions in these fully consecrated
mind streams is the most intense love and profound respect for the
humble Lords of Enlightenment and the inextinguishable longing
to emulate these radiant Buddhas of past, present and future. Because
of their intense love and profound respect for truth alone, such lovers
of truth inevitably encounter and assimilate the most excellent
teachings. Through their longing to embody truth, these selfless mind
streams fuse with the wisdom transmission not only of all past
Awakened Ones but of all present and future Awakened Ones as well.
The irreversible bodhisattvas have joined the noble company of those
beautiful beings who are the Buddhas of the future, who have been
specifically predicted by Awakened Enlightenment to attain Buddhahood and thus to become miraculous embodiments of truth.

Clearly aware of this unimaginable and unthinkable blessing and
responsibility, irreversible bodhisattvas are filled with equally unimaginable and unthinkable gratitude, inspiration and energy, geometrically increasing their efforts to merge their mind streams and
those of all conscious beings into the ocean of truth. Spontaneously,
they renounce every obvious and subtle strand of egocentric possession, satisfaction or ambition, never losing nerve or becoming
spiritually idle even for an instant, never hesitating to accept and
assimilate even the most unexpected demonstration of Prajnaparamita
that emanates from the Tathagatas.

Diamond beings who have acquired infinite patience with the beginningless arising of all structures of relativity, knowing them to be empty of independent or substantial self-existence, never hesitate to embrace and transmit the most revolutionary teachings about the limitless and identityless nature of Reality. These active contemplatives rejoice ceaselessly in Perfect Wisdom, which can never be obstructed or obscured by any phenomenon but which is, instead, expressed openly by the transparent mode of being shared by all possible phenomena.

Such joyful acceptance and skillful transmission of Prajnaparamita is the most sublime attribute and miraculous sign of bodhisattvas who are irreversibly established in the principle of Mahayana—dedication to the conscious enlightenment of all living beings without exception.

THOUGHT FLASHES

*S*UBHUTI: Fathomless beyond all measure of thought, O Lord of Enlightenment, is your teaching about the ontological transparency and harmonious functioning of the entire range of interdependent manifestation—this beginningless, boundless and divisionless expanse of living worlds.

LORD BUDDHA: Consider, Subhuti, what you have just thought and expressed. Will any such momentary flash of thought be reproduced again exactly at any future time?

SUBHUTI: No, Lord, it will not.

LORD BUDDHA: Is not every flash of thought which may appear compelled by its own ephemeral nature to disappear again?

SUBHUTI: Yes, Lord, it is.

LORD BUDDHA: Although compelled by its ephemeral nature to disappear, is there any flash of thought which thereby substantially ceases or is destroyed?

SUBHUTI: No, Lord, because no flash of thought is ever substantially produced in the first place.

LORD BUDDHA: Shift focus to the future, Subhuti. Can thought flashes which have not yet appeared cease or be destroyed?

SUBHUTI: No, Lord, for precisely the same reason. Without substantial production, there can be no substantial destruction.

LORD BUDDHA: Precisely so. The essence of all thought flashes is that they are never substantially produced and therefore never substantially destroyed. Is this essence of thought some independent reality which arises and ceases or which remains constant?

SUBHUTI: Neither, Lord. The ephemeral and non-self-existent nature of thought flashes does not constitute an independent reality of any kind.

LORD BUDDHA: By extension, can the nature of any appearing structure of relativity cease or be destroyed?

SUBHUTI: No, Lord, because no structure or process of relativity is ever substantially produced.

LORD BUDDHA: Is not the bodhisattva consciously and unwaveringly established as the simple, transparent modelessness by which all phenomena manifest coherently, without ever substantially arising or ceasing?

SUBHUTI: Yes, O Lord of Enlightenment.

LORD BUDDHA: That pure presence, that harmoniously functioning ontological transparency, that sheer Reality which neither arises nor ceases—is it in danger of becoming destabilized or crystallized in any way?

SUBHUTI: In no way, Lord.

LORD BUDDHA: Profound beyond any conception, any penetration and any doctrine is this suchness of Reality.

SUBHUTI: It is the depth of unthinkability, O Lord.

LORD BUDDHA: Do thought flashes either reflect or reflect upon this suchness, this pure presence?

SUBHUTI: No, Lord, for pure presence has no surface and no content.

LORD BUDDHA: Can any thought process whatsoever be identified or correlated with pure presence?

SUBHUTI: No, Lord, because the total simplicity of suchness is identityless, processless and uncorrelatable.

LORD BUDDHA: Does the process of thinking constitute a provisionally separate reality apart from pure presence?

SUBHUTI: No, Lord, because all-embracing simplicity contains no borders, parts or dimensions, either final or provisional.

LORD BUDDHA: Can suchness be conceived or perceived in any way?

SUBHUTI: In no way, Lord.

LORD BUDDHA: Where is the bodhisattva actually going while flowing as the unthinkable current of pure presence?

SUBHUTI: The awakened bodhisattva is going nowhere at all and holds no habitual or self-conscious notions whatsoever about personal performance, personal location or personal destination.

LORD BUDDHA: When manifesting entirely as the unthinkable depth of Perfect Wisdom, exactly who or what is the bodhisattva?

SUBHUTI: Such a bodhisattva is sheer Reality.

LORD BUDDHA: Is there any sign which indicates this Reality?

SUBHUTI: Pure presence possesses absolutely no characteristic mark.

LORD BUDDHA: Are there any characteristic marks, obvious or subtle, in the conscious stream of such a bodhisattva—substantial marks which have not yet been unveiled as transparency by advancement in the contemplation of Perfect Wisdom?

SUBHUTI: No, Lord.

LORD BUDDHA: Can such a bodhisattva, therefore, be characterized as having erased or destroyed all personal marks by advanced meditation on Prajnaparamita?

SUBHUTI: No, Lord. Such bodhisattvas are not in the least engaged in personal efforts to erase or destroy personal characteristics, nor do they monitor or even acknowledge personal spiritual advancement. This would constitute entrapment in reified notions of self-centered contemplative practice. The enlightened and enlightening art of the bodhisattva is to move in the transparent sphere of conventional characteristics and harmoniously functioning causality, while remaining totally merged in the signlessness and causelessness of sheer Reality.

LORD BUDDHA: O noble Subhuti, it is precisely as you say.

VICTORY OVER FEAR

*L*ORD BUDDHA: The bodhisattva whose mind stream flows as Perfect Wisdom is never terrified or even subtly anxious. Why? Because totally imbued with the living power of Mother Prajnaparamita, the practitioner has the physical, moral, intellectual and spiritual strength to remain unwavering and undivided in transcendent contemplation, while ceaselessly and skillfully engaging in compassionate action. This diamond awareness consists of a single concentrated current of prayer: *May living beings never be diverted from the path of universal conscious enlightenment, which is their own true nature, empty of any separate or self-existence.* The selfless and luminous mind stream that flows onward in this unthinkable manner is flowing as Prajnaparamita.

The bodhisattva is not in the least fearful when surrounded by a trackless forest in which carnivorous animals roam—an accurate symbol of the egocentric world. The Mahayana heart of universal empathy spontaneously renounces every possession, including even physical life, for the benefit of other living beings, calmly expressing this attitude: *If the hungry predators in this forest should attack me, I will lovingly offer this body as nourishment for them. Such sacrifice will provide a precious opportunity for the transcendent Perfection of Generosity to develop in this mind stream. The universal enlightenment of conscious beings will be unveiled, displaying ontological trans-*

150

parency and harmonious functioning as a miraculously pure field of Buddha manifestation, where beings do not live by the motivation to kill, where compassion is the only true nourishment.

The bodhisattva is not in the least fearful when surrounded by an uninhabitable wasteland in which merciless bandits roam—an accurate symbol of the egocentric world. The being of universal empathy takes genuine delight in the spiritual practice of renouncing all sense of selfish power and satisfaction. The bodhisattva is ready at every moment to cast away this physical form or to forego comforts or even the basic needs of life, not as a self-involved act of austerity but as an act of sheer altruism, vowing: *If someone steals my surplus wealth or even the bare necessities of life, I will transform this into a loving gift. If someone threatens or takes my physical life, I will respond without anger or even the slightest negativity. I will initiate no violent action—either through body, speech or mind. Such sacrifice will provide a precious opportunity for the transcendent Perfections of Generosity, Patience and Meditation to develop in this mind stream. The universal enlightenment of conscious beings will be unveiled, displaying ontological transparency and harmonious functioning as a miraculously pure field of Buddha manifestation, where beings do not live by the motivation to compete, where obvious or subtle violence is inconceivable, where compassion is the only true wealth.*

The bodhisattva is not in the least fearful when surrounded by a treeless desert without life-sustaining water—an accurate symbol of the egocentric world. Through constant training in selfless compassion, the Mahayana mind of universal empathy is oriented only toward removing the physical needs and the burning spiritual thirst of all beings. Concerned so intimately with the panorama of suffering, bodhisattvas do not isolate their own hunger or thirst, nor feel apprehension at the prospect of dying from deprivation and the difficult after-death experiences such a death might generate. Diamond beings simply remain immersed in the infinitely wise and tender compassion of Mahayana that embraces all lives equally, contemplating: *What intense negativity conscious beings must engage in to manifest such terrible suffering! I will ceaselessly reintensify my commitment to sacrifice limited happiness and personal liberation in order to relieve suffering on all levels. Such sacrifice will provide a precious opportunity for the transcendent Perfection of Commitment to develop in this mind stream. The universal enlightenment of conscious beings will be unveiled, displaying ontological transparency and harmonious functioning as a miraculously pure field of Buddha manifestation, where beings are free from the terrible thirst of selfish grasping. Their way of life will be constituted by the very principle of authentic happiness, bliss and freedom which is Prajnaparamita. I will continue to act solely from the motivation to elevate the intentions and ideals of all. Just as heavenly beings in the thirty-three progressively more subtle realms can generate whatever they desire simply by contemplating it, so will I develop the most intense and consistent clarity of awareness, in order that all living beings realize freedom from selfish desire. They will be able to generate sustenance and benign environments solely through selfless contemplative power. In order that the natural needs and positive intentions of all should be fulfilled, I will train tirelessly to establish the transcendent Perfections of Meditation and Insight in this mind stream.*

The bodhisattva is not in the least fearful when visiting an area infested by contagious, painful or fatal diseases—an accurate symbol for the egocentric world. Through constant contemplation of Prajnaparamita, the adept of Perfect Wisdom exclaims spontaneously: *There are no independently self-existing structures which could become infected by disease, nor is disease itself substantially self-existent.* This transcendent insight into the total absence of any separate self-existence manifests healing, transforming and illuminating power. The fearless diamond being acts valiantly in the most dangerous regions of manifestation filled with deadly plagues. Wearing the shining armor of Perfect Wisdom, the bodhisattva generates the adamantine vow: *I will constantly reintensify my commitment until universal enlightenment consciously dawns, revealing ontological transparency and harmonious functioning as a miraculously pure field of Buddha manifestation, where beings do not attribute substantial self-existence to disease or to any other obstacle. I will live and act totally in and through Perfect*

Wisdom so that my body, speech and mind, here and now, will fully express the most radical teaching of the Buddhas.

The bodhisattva never indulges in imagining that enlightenment can occur only in some distant future, for every single thought flash reveals the absence of limits, separation and distance. The awakened bodhisattva, therefore, never concentrates on supposed limits, difficulties or obstacles but lives as the limitlessness and unobstructedness of Prajnaparamita. Free from the slightest self-orientation, the diamond being never considers how long it will take to attain full enlightenment and thereby to unveil ontological transparency and harmonious functioning as a miraculously pure field of Buddha manifestation. When no hesitation or anxiety of any kind arises to cause the bodhisattva to waver, it is clear that this son or daughter of the Buddha family is capable of awakening, here and now, into the perfect wakefulness enjoyed by all the Buddhas.

GODDESS OF THE GANGES

A divine feminine being now enters the radiant assembly of the Buddha and quietly joins its blissful atmosphere. Suddenly, she arises from her meditation seat, wraps her robe so as humbly to bare the right shoulder, makes triple obeisance to the embodiment of enlightenment, joins her palms and fearlessly proclaims: *O Lord Buddha, whenever I finally reach deep realization and receive extensive spiritual responsibility, without being the least self-conscious or anxious, I will demonstrate truth to all living beings.*

Immediately the Awakened One, his body like burnished gold, forms a delicate smile. The radiance of this smile illuminates the vistas of all world systems, rising as a luminous wave even to the highest heavenly realm. Returning instantly across the hierarchy of manifestation, and swirling thrice around the Lord, the golden wave merges again into the golden Buddha.

When the wisdom being perceives this rare smile, she miraculously brings forth golden flowers, joyously and reverently scattering them over the embodiment of enlightenment. These magnificent full blossoms—neither substantially self-existent, nor merely nonexistent—do not fall to the floor of the assembly but remain suspended in a golden cloud about the serene figure of the Awakened One.

The most devoted, intimate and loving disciple, the blessed Ananda, now intercedes with the Lord, in order that all future practitioners of Dharma might know the precise reason for this rare and sublime Buddha smile.

LORD BUDDHA: Beloved Ananda, this wisdom being is now manifest as the Goddess of the Ganges. In a cosmic future, called the Great Starlike Aeon, she will attain full enlightenment. She will become a Tathagata named Golden Flower — a victorious one, insurpassable in transcendent insight and liberative art, one who has disappeared into pure presence and who knows the nature of all phenomena to be pure presence, a compassionate tamer of wild consciousness, a skillful educator of divine and human beings, a Buddha, a humble Lord of Enlightenment.

In preparation for this attainment, when she transmigrates from her present divine lifetime, vast in duration, she will be reborn in the magnificent pure Buddha field of the Tathagata Akshobya, in whose august presence she will lead an intensive life of contemplation. Transmigrating from that blessed lifetime, vast in duration, she will pass from Buddha field to Buddha field, never deprived of the beautiful vision and the precious teaching of a fully Awakened One, always choosing to incarnate in the direct presence of a living Buddha.

Just as a universal emperor on the earthly plane passes from palace to palace, the soles of his feet never once in his entire lifetime touching rough or thorny ground, so will this Goddess who aspires to Buddhahood pass from pure Buddha field to pure Buddha field, never residing anywhere except within the jewel palaces of Buddhas, until she attains enlightenment. Diamond beings who are reborn into transmundane contemplative environments, such as the Buddha field of the Tathagata Akshobya, are known as fortunate ones who have fully emerged from the veils of mundane realms, fortunate ones who are irreversibly and rapidly approaching the total awakeness of Buddhahood.

The disciples of this future Tathagata Golden Flower will not be limited in number. Spreading throughout the entire Buddha field of the Tathagata Golden Flower will be an astonishingly vast spiritual family called the immeasurable, inconceivable community of Perfect Wisdom. This future Buddha field will be transmundane — manifesting no jungles inhabited by carnivores, no lonely highways attacked by brigands, no deserts without springs, no districts decimated by disease or famine. In this pure Buddha field, inauspicious or terrible circumstances will not be present or even conceivable.

ANANDA: O omniscient Lord, who was the ancient Tathagata in whose holy presence this feminine being planted the supreme seed of goodness, the commitment to attain enlightenment and to dedicate the energy of that attainment toward the enlightenment of all conscious beings?

LORD BUDDHA: She made her original vow in the sublime presence of the Tathagata Dipankara. In that remote aeon, she scattered earthly flowers over the Tathagata as she vowed with total intensity to become enlightened for the sake of all living beings. She longed then with her entire heart and mind that a Tathagata would someday, with great initiatory power, predict her full enlightenment. Now this prediction is being proclaimed.

O devoted Ananda, her blessed original vow occurred precisely in the same ancient Buddha assembly where I gratefully offered five lotus blossoms to the Tathagata Dipankara, after I attained the infinitely patient and tolerant acceptance of all structures of relativity by fully realizing that they never substantially come into being. The Tathagata Dipankara then predicted my future enlightenment, proclaiming: *O marvelous practitioner, you will in a future aeon become the Tathagata Shakyamuni, accepting out of unusually profound compassion countless suffering beings into your Buddha field.*

O blissful Ananda, when she heard the ancient Tathagata's prophetic proclamation, this feminine being of great spiritual beauty was deeply inspired and formed an adamantine intention, resolving: *In some future time may I, too, receive such prediction to full enlightenment from a living Buddha, just as this noble practitioner has received — not for any personal benefit but for the benefit of all sentient beings.* Thus, in the presence of the Tathagata Dipankara, she planted the supreme seed of goodness and fervently wished for its flowering. Now at last she has received the precise prediction to full enlightenment which for aeons she has so ardently desired.

ANANDA: O Lord, this blessed Gangamata is one who has undergone unimaginably profound preparation. Now she is assured of her ultimate destiny as the Tathagata Golden Flower. How wonderful!

LORD BUDDHA: It is just as you say, Ananda. This is the wonderful way of Buddhahood.

TRUE HUMAN EXCELLENCE

*L*ORD BUDDHA: Consider carefully, noble-minded Subhuti, the case of a truly excellent man, perfectly parallel to a truly excellent woman. He is heroic in moral stature, energetic in commitment, among the leaders and teachers of his society, inspiring and beautiful to look upon because permeated by the highest concerns and virtues, learned in scripture and philosophy, well-practiced in the universal spiritual way. This person is sage and eloquent, possessing great gifts of language and powers of reasoning, as well as quiet inner wisdom. His timing is sensitive and he moves in harmony with everyone and with every situation. His expertise in archery is unsurpassable, as it is in other martial arts. He is also a refined artist and a superb crafts-man. His memory is prodigious, his intelligence scintillating, yet he remains steady and grounded, being well-versed in all the various wisdom teachings and their methods of contemplation. He makes friends with everyone. His body is strong, well-proportioned and well-coordinated. Never patronizing or proud, he is generous to all with his substantial wealth in a way that elevates and endears. Whatever task he undertakes, he is able to complete. He speaks with words that are entirely consonant with his actions. He honors whatever is honorable, reveres whatever is worthy of reverence and devoutly wor-ships whatever is worthy of worship. O Subhuti, would not such a person experience intense joy in his ever-expanding commitment to the well-being of all?

SUBHUTI: He would indeed, O compassionate Lord.

LORD BUDDHA: Now imagine, Subhuti, that this excellent man, whose humanity is so accomplished and so realized, takes family and friends with him on a long journey. Wandering through a trackless wilderness, they become lost. The younger members of the party begin to feel fear and even desperation. This person of supreme good will and excellence of character responds with confidence and calm: *Have no fear. I have taken responsibility to lead you out of this wilderness, to liberate you from this suffering.*

If hostile beings and treacherous conditions multiply during their arduous trek, would this person abandon his vow of responsibility to family and friends and run away, relying on his superior strength to liberate himself from these conditions? Could such a person act in this despicably selfish manner who has never in his life made any cowardly retreat, who is constantly filled with the spirit of forcefulness and commitment, who is permeated with tender compassion, who is well-versed in the wisdom which instinctively sacrifices self-interest for the benefit of others, who is a courageous and skilled warrior?

SUBHUTI: Never, Lord Buddha. The person who has developed such consummate physical, intellectual, moral and spiritual strength could not abandon those he cherishes, those for whom he has taken responsibility. His superlative efforts will attract various protective forces in the universe to come into play, compensating for whatever weakness may exist in his body or his capabilities. This excellent man is competent to deal with any situation and will certainly be able to lead his party from dangerous wilderness into civilized land.

LORD BUDDHA: Precisely the same, Subhuti, is the case of the bodhisattvas, the noble sons and daughters of the Buddha family. These heroic human beings, who are connected by most intense vows to the well-being and eventual enlightenment of all, possess hearts that melt in sympathy and love for every living being. These bodhisattvas move entirely within the four exalted spiritual stations: universal friendliness, universal compassion, universal joy and universal equanimity. These diamond beings possess no separate, divisive will but operate solely by the power of Prajnaparamita and its skillful application through boundless compassion, transforming with the principle of universal selflessness every good thought and action into abundant meritorious energy for evolving beings, precisely as the Buddhas have demonstrated.

Although bodhisattvas certainly can enter elevated states of meditative equipoise by passing through the three mystic doors to liberation—wishlessness, desirelessness and the signlessness which is the radiant emptiness of all apparent self-existence—they never abandon living beings by crossing over entirely into formlessness, by negating, rejecting or even ignoring the suffering realms of relativity. Bodhisattvas do not become liberated from life, nor do they pursue separate self-realization. They accept the union of Perfect Wisdom and liberative skill as their sole recourse, their sole protection, their sole aspiration, as they struggle ceaselessly for the cause of all conscious beings, demonstrating complete universality of both insight and sympathy. They direct an ecstatic flood of love and friendliness toward all, connecting their mind streams as intimately with all beings as with their most cherished family members and beloved friends. This astonishing spiritual feat—experiencing equal solidarity with all lives—frees the bodhisattvas from every impure intention of harming, denigrating, abandoning or even merely ignoring others.

Liberated from Mara, the powerful, attractive force of self-cherishing and self-deception, such practitioners can no longer regard their own personal liberation as a significant concern but abide calmly and evenhandedly in universal friendliness, tender compassion and sympathetic joy. They never sever or separate themselves, even subtly, from the struggles of suffering beings, nor do their intense feelings of love and concern ever dry up or burn out.

Bodhisattvas attain much greater spiritual freedom than that conceived by practitioners of ascetic detachment, for bodhisattvas clearly and blissfully perceive the emptiness, insubstantiality and transparency of all apparent self-existence, while continuing to abide in the very depth of loving concern. Of the three mystic doors to liberation, bodhisattvas concentrate on radiant signlessness, or emptiness. They neither detach from nor purge themselves of the passions and the careers of conscious beings, nor do they abandon universal love, friendship and concern by passing through the doors of wishlessness or desirelessness.

The Mahayana master of meditation on radiant emptiness, or universal selflessness, is like a great bird flying swiftly and powerfully through the open sky. This bird does not fall, like the proud nihilist who denies functional relativity, nor does it remain nervously clinging to a limb, like the naive realist who reifies the structures of relativity. This bird, soaring on wings of Perfect Wisdom and liberative skill, moves joyously and freely through ontological transparency, without any need for objective support or fundamental basis. In this way, the bodhisattvas attain a much more radical spiritual emancipation than ascetic renunciates can conceive. Never abandoning the destiny of other beings, they realize the Buddhahood which enlightens all beings.

The bodhisattva who at every moment recognizes the fusion of radiant emptiness and coherent relativity is like a consummate master of archery, graceful and steady, so perfect in aim that he or she can release an arrow high into the sky and keep it aloft indefinitely by shooting other arrows into it. Such bodhisattvas do not wish to disappear into pure presence until their roots of goodness have flowered into the vast tree of universal conscious enlightenment. Only then do they vanish into Reality, having attained and unveiled omniscience, offering true refuge to all beings and opening the way for their full enlightenment.

Bodhisattvas abide most sensitively with vulnerable, suffering beings throughout all the seductive spheres of manifestation, continuously contemplating the unthinkable depth of Reality, without disappearing into those infinite deeps, remaining active instead in the evolution of all that lives. These diamond beings master the bowmanship of Perfect Wisdom, constantly releasing arrows of liberative skill, which are selfless, transparent and transforming thought beams and blessing waves of Great Compassion, directed accurately toward every living being in its own unique situation.

INTERPRETATION OF DREAMS

*L*ORD BUDDHA: The bodhisattva unwaveringly established in the principle of Mahayana—commitment to the eventual enlightenment of all conscious beings—directly perceives the entire range of manifestation to be like a dream. Though they function harmoniously and meaningfully, phenomenal structures possess no substantial, independent self-existence. But the awakened bodhisattva does not dwell upon this characteristic of dreamlike insubstantiality, even for a moment, remaining intently focused instead on the desperate physical and spiritual plight of living beings. Even in their dreams, bodhisattvas feel no attraction to individual liberation or solitary self-realization—solutions which seek to extinguish manifestation or to become separate from manifestation. Instead, they remain sensitively engaged with the physical and spiritual careers of all conscious beings. Bodhisattvas do not wish to escape from manifestation, for they do not perceive manifestation as a substantial, independent realm. Neither do these Mahayana hearts of universal empathy and radical altruism feel the slightest attraction to possess or dwell in any particular state of bliss or region of ease within the range of manifestation.

A sure indication that bodhisattvas have attained irreversibility of commitment is dreaming themselves to be Tathagatas—surrounded by radiant Buddha assemblies of thousands of millions of dedicated practitioners, seated in deep meditation within a circular Dharma hall beneath a high peaked roof. The aspirants and adepts in this auspicious dream-gathering consist of a vast monastic community, monks and nuns wearing golden robes, and a vast community of lay bodhisattvas, men and women wearing robes of many colors. Both groups miraculously and eloquently demonstrate truth by every activity of body, speech and mind. Other spiritual dreams or waking visions which signal irreversibility portray the practitioner floating effortlessly in the air, while discoursing on truth to sincere aspirants.

In some auspicious dreams of irreversibility, a multicolored aura surrounds the noble head of a fully Awakened One. In other such dreams, the enlightened dreamer emanates holy teachers like rays of light from his or her own body and sends them into countless world systems to demonstrate truth, displaying the universal awakening function of Mother Prajnaparamita. Other dreams that signal irreversibility depict the bodhisattva remaining calm and unafraid while compassionately witnessing a town, a city or even an entire kingdom sacked by savage barbarians. Or remaining peaceful and confident while compassionately witnessing a terrible conflagration spreading over a vast, populated world. Or remaining friendly and even-minded while encountering ferocious earthly carnivores and bloodthirsty demons from subtle planes. Or remaining poised and generous while submitting to decapitation or even more ghastly tortures perpetrated by religious or political fanatics upon the dreamer or upon other cherished beings. In none of these mystical dreams does the practitioner lose concentration on Perfect Wisdom and Great Compassion, through either fear, anger or delusion. Immediately upon awaking or even while still dreaming, the dreamer reflects in meditative equipoise: *Similar to a dream in possessing neither independent nor substantial self-existence is the entire range of manifestation. May I clearly and flawlessly demonstrate this healing truth to all suffering beings without exception when I have awakened into the boundless power of full enlightenment.*

Another archetypical dream of irreversibility portrays in stark detail beings who have created hellish conditions of consciousness for themselves, either within the planetary realm or on various subtle planes of existence. Witnessing this intense, self-generated suffering, the bodhisattva vows immediately upon awakening or even while still dreaming: *When I have awakened into the boundless power of full enlightenment, I will establish a Buddha field where beings evolve and are spiritually trained and matured without the need for experiencing hellish consciousness.* This instinctive compassion, even for hell beings, shows that irreversible bodhisattvas have so purified their mind streams from violence and hatred that they can never again be involuntarily swept into the conditions of hellish consciousness during any future lifetime, though they may visit or even voluntarily incarnate into such excruciating dimensions of experience as an act of compassion.

Other such indicative dreams and visions are prophetic in nature, accurately predicting events that are occurring simultaneously with the dream or that later come to pass. The irreversible bodhisattva may dream that a certain village, town or city is being consumed by fire. Instantly upon awaking or even while still dreaming, the dreamer vows: *If the auspicious signs of irreversibility that I have perceived in visions and dreams are valid, because of this truth and because of my recognition and utterance of this truth, may this fire which is now actually raging burn itself out immediately or in some other way be extinguished.* If a conflagration has indeed broken out in the exact location indicated by the dream, and if those flames inexplicably die down or are extinguished at the moment of the bodhisattva's invocation of truth, that blessed practitioner is confirmed as irreversibly established, as predicted to the attainment of full enlightenment by Tathagatas of previous aeons.

If the conflagration is not extinguished, or has not objectively occurred in the first place, then the bodhisattva has not attained irreversibility. However, if the fire, although objectively occurring as indicated in the dream, vastly intensifies and rages through many dwellings, this indicates that the dreamer, far from being a bodhisattva, is a misguided adept who has collected dangerous levels of negative habitual energy through obvious or subtle rejection of true teaching. Or it indicates that the dreamer is one in whom transcendent insight, though once strong, has become seriously debilitated. Although this particular dreamer is now or has been a contemplative practitioner during previous lifetimes, thereby generating the power of prophetic dreaming, his or her spiritual practice and formation has become distorted or misguided, producing almost insurmountable obstacles to establishing irreversible commitment to universal conscious enlightenment.

MARA THE TEMPTER

*L*ORD BUDDHA: O Subhuti, we will continue to examine the genuine signs of spiritual irreversibility as well as their counterfeits, generated by Mara the Counterfeiter.

Suppose some man, woman, boy or girl is possessed and tortured by a wandering spirit. Moved by compassion, the irreversible bodhisattva—rather than relying for help on primitive ceremonies of exorcism, involving the counterinvocation of various other subtle beings—simply performs a demonstration of truth. The diamond being generates invincible truth force with the following powerful words: *If it is true that Buddhas from past aeons have predicted and empowered this mind stream to attain full enlightenment; if it is true that my commitment to universal conscious enlightenment is completely purified from the motives of both self-grasping and self-liberation and is therefore irreversible—then let this intruding ghost or demon instantly depart! If it is my most profound vow and highest human responsibility to awaken to full enlightenment for the sake of all conscious beings; if I am certain about the inevitability of this future awakening; if there is no phenomenon of which the Buddhas who reside in countless world systems are unaware and no phenomenon which their wisdom eye has not recognized to be empty of substantial self-existence; if these Buddhas recognize even the sublime intention to awaken all beings as itself transparent or empty of self-existence; if these very words embody truth*

166

and therefore generate the power of truth—then let this intruding ghost or demon instantly depart!

If these affirmations carry such palpable truth force that the demonic possession ceases instantly upon their utterance, it is a genuine sign of irreversibility. If suffering and struggle continue, then the bodhisattva has not yet attained the healing and illuminating power of an irreversible commitment.

However, in this process of direct spiritual demonstration, there are subtle dangers for persons who are just beginning their bodhisattva training. When inexperienced practitioners, whose vows do not as yet contain sufficient truth force, utter the command, *If these very words embody truth, let this intruding ghost or demon instantly depart,* Mara the Impostor, the active principle of negativity, may use its tempting lures and wiles to induce the possessing spirit to leave the victim temporarily, so that it will be the magical power of Mara which has effected a delusive exorcism. Naive practitioners may then believe that they have attained the power of truth and may slacken their own sincere efforts, becoming complacent in obvious or subtle ways. They may even develop virulent spiritual pride. Falsely assuming because of this apparent victory over demonic forces that they have become irreversible bodhisattvas, they may begin to look down on other practitioners, treat them ironically or even openly deprecate them. This malignant condition of prideful consciousness feeds on itself until it becomes deeply rooted, manifesting every shade of arrogant thought and behavior and creating countless obstacles to the attainment of omniscience, the total awakeness which is Buddhahood.

When such inflated persons happen to meet an authentic bodhisattva—good friend and loyal guide of humanity, impeccable in character, oriented solely to what is sublime, moved only by the adamantine vow to awaken all beings, skilled in liberative art, truly irreversible in the way of Mahayana—in their blind conceit, these deluded practitioners cannot recognize such authenticity and therefore fail to honor, love, question and learn from the true bodhisattva. This poisonous pride gradually intensifies the atmosphere of negativity surrounding these unfortunate practitioners, deluded by Mara, who

gradually regress from the longing for universal conscious enlightenment to the subtly self-centered struggle for personal liberation or
even to blatant forms of self-aggrandizement.

Therefore, even though the practice of affirming truth is a powerful method for transforming negative situations, the arrogance of Mara
can infect inexperienced or misguided practitioners, causing subtle
yet almost impenetrable obstacles to attaining enlightenment for the
sake of all conscious beings. This danger is particularly strong for
those who are just beginning on the Bodhisattva Way, whose faith
is not fully developed, whose understanding of the holy scriptures
is not yet profound, who may lack teachers with sublimely compassionate hearts, whose mind streams are not fully purified by Perfect
Wisdom and who have not yet developed a mastery of liberative
methods which can benefit beings under all possible circumstances.
Such beginners are especially vulnerable to the pervasive poison of
Mara's arrogance.

The polluting influence of Mara can also manifest through some
heavenly sounding voice which purports to announce the secret Buddha name of naive practitioners, predicting the details of their glorious
spiritual career and future enlightenment. The polymorphous Mara
approaches such practitioners in various guises—during meditative
trance, dream or even in the waking state—tempting them with these
words: *You have received prediction to full enlightenment from Buddhas of previous aeons. Here is the exalted Sanskrit name that has secretly
been conferred upon you. As confirmation and verification, here are
the family names of your ancestors, parents, siblings, relatives and close
friends.*

The psychic energy of Mara then effortlessly names the relatives
of its victims through seven generations, in order to make the temptation completely convincing. Reading the mind of these practitioners
and speaking through some hypnotically projected human or heavenly
form, this negative force tells its astonished victims where they were
born—not just the general region but the precise city, town or even
small village, including the very location of the birth. Mara also offers
deceptive readings of past lifetimes, attributing present characteristics

of the personality to specific previous life experiences and flattering these practitioners by saying that the qualities of their mind streams derive from high contemplative attainments in former incarnations.

In the case of adepts along the way of self-liberation, Mara the Tempter will praise their narrowly focused, ascetic mode of life—dwelling in desert or forest wilderness, begging food from door to door and never accepting invitations to feasts, wearing robes sewn together from discarded rags, never eating anything after midday, sleeping at night wherever one happens to be, possessing no more than three wearing cloths, meditating or residing full time in cemeteries or cremation grounds, sleeping upright with the back against a tree, living without shelter, wearing roughly woven fabric, exercising the minimum number of desires, remaining mentally and emotionally detached from the life struggle of conscious beings, speaking neutrally and only when necessary.

Mara will intensify the spiritual pride of such rigid practitioners by suggesting that they have persevered many lifetimes these ascetic practices, implying that austerity of life and external disciplines qualify someone to be called irreversible—predicted and empowered as such by Buddhas of past aeons. Contemplatives who idolize this austere, self-liberating and subtly self-involved attitude are easily filled with conceit through the guile of Mara. Mere fantasies about past lives of heroic austerity and imaginary predictions from ancient Buddhas will gradually become an obsessive and fixed viewpoint for these deluded practitioners.

The power of Mara can magically or hypnotically project various earthly or heavenly forms. Yet Mara can also act through unsuspecting human beings—be they monk or nun, lay practitioner, religious scholar, wandering sage, mother or father, sister or brother, respected relative or cherished friend. Through the medium of these attractive and trustworthy forms, the disintegrative psychic energy of Mara can tempt the aspiring bodhisattva with various imaginings which, in general, substitute the notion of rigorous renunciation, personal detachment and subtle self-elevation for the Mahayana principles of loving compassion and transparent, selfless wisdom. Such practitioners, guided by disguised forms of Mara the Tempter, cannot manifest the beautiful omens which are characteristic of an irreversible bodhisattva.

For contemplatives ensnared in religious fantasy, conceit increases geometrically, until those who are deceived by Mara ultimately come to despise and reject genuine bodhisattvas. One should take care to recognize and assiduously avoid the patterns of this entrapment by negativity. Mara may come to unwary practitioners in the guise of an adept who claims to possess supernatural powers of vision and who predicts the noble Sanskrit name that they will bear upon reaching full enlightenment. With rudimentary psychic ability, Mara will read the mind of these practitioners and will suggest some name which they may have cherished when casually pondering their own eventual enlightenment. If the victims of this power of suggestion are weak in transcendent insight and without experience in liberative art, they may assume that they have guessed correctly their own future Buddha name. They may imagine that the apparently holy adept is now bringing a confirmation or verification of their own foreknowledge. This delusive messenger can even be an actual monk who, through conceit, has become a channel for negativity. Or the messenger can be merely an apparitional projection, born from Mara's impressive hypnotic power.

Practitioners who are thus tempted and deceived should honestly recognize that they do not possess the sublime characteristics nor manifest the miraculous signs of an irreversible bodhisattva. However, they are blinded instead by the pride they feel from this spurious prediction of their future Buddha name and from other ploys of primordial arrogance. They begin to regard themselves as superior to devoted aspirants who do not claim to have reached the advanced station of irreversibility. This negativity gradually reaches such terrible proportions that the deluded ones even begin to despise the humility of authentic practitioners, generating almost insurmountable mental, emotional and spiritual obstacles to true awakening.

No longer protected by the selflessness of Perfect Wisdom; divested of the spiritual skill which can experience and express this selflessness in every imaginable situation; alienated from the true friends and guides of humanity, who are the genuinely selfless servants of all; caught up in the glamorous company of self-centered teachers, who make outrageous claims for themselves and for their followers—these distorted and misguided practitioners fall away from the ideal of universal awakening into subtly or obviously self-serving notions, both conscious and unconscious.

After fruitless wandering through realms of erroneous, egocentric thought and perception, if these practitioners wish to vow once again to awaken all living beings into full enlightenment, they must longingly take refuge in Mother Prajnaparamita, humbly visiting the practitioners of Perfect Wisdom and vomiting the poison of false ideas by clearly and vividly perceiving and declaring their falseness.

It will be extremely difficult for such persons to readjust their sensibilities to the bodhisattva ideal of humble, invisible, selfless compassion, which always acts in union with transcendent insight. Why? Because of long-term effects from this lethal dose of pride, administered by Mara. This disease of arrogance and negativity is more fatal than the four prime offenses which invalidate the precious monastic vows. The illness of self-adulation, which seeks personal glory in becoming a bodhisattva or a Buddha, is more terrible even than the five destructive forms of behavior. Therefore, both subtle and obvious temptations of Mara to cherish the self, to hold self-serving opinions and motivations, should be clearly recognized and carefully avoided.

The most common form of this deception is transmitted through an actual monk or adept already infected by pride, who approaches naive practitioners and eloquently attracts them to a life of detachment from the needs of others, to feats of personal austerity, to fantasies of self-elevation. This emissary of Mara claims that the Buddha teaches essentially the way of detachment, exhorting everyone to dwell in deserted places, such as mountains, jungles or cremation grounds, alienating themselves from the spiritual and physical concerns of precious human beings, living proudly and conspicuously on a heap of old straw. This is simply not what Awakened Enlightenment teaches.

SUBHUTI: O Lord, what is the authentic teaching of detachment?

LORD BUDDHA: The beings who are committed to universal conscious enlightenment become perfectly detached from all notions of their own separate personal liberation or individual elevation. The bodhisattvas are absorbed only in Prajnaparamita and the brilliant liberative art which it spontaneously displays. Dwelling intimately, day and night, with all conscious beings in intense friendship and experiencing ceaseless tender compassion, bodhisattvas remain perfectly detached from any notion of personal self-interest or even separate self-existence. It is immaterial whether these diamond beings live in village or palace, in the remoteness and solitude of the wilderness, in the ghastly atmosphere of a cremation ground or in the comfortable surroundings of home or monastery. Self-mortifying and self-satisfying forms of austerity and proud aloofness from other conscious beings belong to the temptations of Mara, which are the pollution of the mind stream by self-oriented and self-serving thought and behavior. Such subtly or obviously self-involved contemplatives generate an impure spiritual atmosphere around themselves. They dwell constantly in this impurity of subtle selfishness, wherever they may wander or establish their hermitage, however intensively they may meditate and study the scriptures.

The usual pattern of negativity and pride gradually arises within such unfortunate persons. They begin to despise sincere practitioners, who may be immersed in the dynamic existence of village or city, family or monastery, but who are actually living in ceaseless detachment from every notion of independent or substantial self-existence. These humble servants of all are surrounded by the unthinkable purity of Prajnaparamita—every single thought, perception and action oriented toward omniscience, permeated by compassion and supremely effective in the liberation of beings from the false limits of egocentricity and substantiality.

The practitioners who have succumbed to Mara's temptation of spiritual pride make a great show of aloofness, ascetic discipline and contemplative advancement. They express disdain for pure bodhisattvas who are compassionately immersed in the lives and concerns of all conscious beings—ignorant of the fact that these bodhisattvas express only spontaneous selflessness and altruism in whatever they think, say or do. Such distorted practitioners are merely dwelling in the defilement of self-involvement. Although their hermitages may be established in the most remote mountains, they are not abiding in true spiritual freedom. Such somber practitioners disdain the joyous bodhisattvas who live in the midst of worldly activity but who are actually abiding only in Perfect Wisdom—spontaneously expressing purity through all actions of body, speech and mind, because they are not involved in any subtly self-centered form of perception, thought or contemplative practice. The cross and cramped practitioners guided by Mara are undermined by indulging in proud disdain and gradually lose their various meditative attainments—including crystal clear concentration, peaceful and blissful trance states and paranormal abilities. Such high contemplative attainments, when they are distorted by Mara to serve as ends in themselves, gradually dissipate rather than mature, as they should, into the fullness of Perfect Wisdom and the richness of liberative art.

Even if these self-involved meditators retreat hundreds of miles into a jungle, with no other companionship than carnivorous animals and flesh-consuming demons—even though their retreat may last for one hundred years, or for thousands of millions of years—if they cannot comprehend what has been taught here by Awakened Enlightenment about the perfect freedom of the bodhisattva, the loving and selfless earnestness and engagement of the bodhisattva, then this wilderness retreat will fail to gladden the tender hearts of the Tathagatas. If such meditators, brilliant and austere as they may be, do not experience this perfect freedom from self-involvement, if they are not consummately skillful in liberating all sentient beings from self-involvement, if they indulge even slightly in relying upon ascetic or psychic feats or if they elevate themselves to a high spiritual station, they will fail to gladden the universally loving hearts of all Buddhas.

The effortless freedom from self-involvement so beautifully manifested by the fully engaged bodhisattva is absent from the wilderness hermitage of the disdainful practitioners who strive to remain aloof from the careers of other conscious beings. But the force of negativity whispers into the minds of these proud ascetics that their detachment and disdain are precisely the teaching of the Tathagatas, that they should persist in their course, regardless of any coherent arguments to the contrary, and that their stubborn perseverance is about to exalt them permanently above all other beings by granting them enlightenment. When such misguided practitioners return to civilization from prolonged and concentrated exposure to their own self-centeredness, they despise the bodhisattvas there — both monastic and lay persons, whose lives are graceful and chaste, inspiring in moral character, affectionate and loving in every gesture, breath and thought, free from the error of perceiving independent self-existence and uncontaminated by the subtle pollutants of self-centered contemplative practice.

These proud ascetics lecture the bodhisattvas insufferably about their lack of detachment, renunciation and elevation, characterizing their selfless compassion for humanity as an impure obsession with crowds, branding their selfless spiritual practice as a rudimentary form of meditation. These arrogant adepts claim to be guided by supernatural beings, when all they have experienced is the inner whisper of Mara, the archetype of arrogance and deceit. They demand special respect and even reverence from everyone for their rigid and myopic way of life. They argue heatedly: *How can you dwellers in the noise of civilization ever benefit from the supernatural voices which we hear in the undistracted quietude of our forest hermitage?* Plagued by such absurd misconceptions, these practitioners become blind to the subtlety of the bodhisattva ideal. Their spirituality is counterfeit, grotesque and extremely negative in its influence on immature or naive aspirants. These pseudopractitioners are really bandits disguised as holy sages. They attempt to plunder the wealth and even destroy the lives of those who are just setting forth on the way of universal sympathy. These false practitioners must not be humored, attended on or honored in any way, streaming as they are with the dangerous poison of conceit.

Even when precautions are taken, however, such persons will succeed in corrupting certain others, who already contain these very tendencies in subtle form, as well as harming some innocent hearts who are undeveloped in spiritual discernment. These bombastic, self-appointed teachers are themselves the only really impure beings, having rebelled against selfless guides from authentic wisdom lineages. These doctrinaire and power-hungry teachers are devoid of even the basic human quality of sympathetic love. The bodhisattvas do not pay the slightest heed to such persons, but remain serenely dedicated to the spiritual and physical well-being of all lives, irreversibly committed to universal awakening.

Bodhisattvas have been elevated to the panoramic awareness and altruism called Mahayana, and therefore always remain free from individuality and thoroughly engaged in the needs and aspirations of other beings. They unerringly penetrate any deceptions generated by Mara and always maintain a motherly mind, consecrated to the constant protection, education and maturing of living beings, inviting and guiding them along the path of all-embracing love. This Mahayana mind never succumbs to fear, anxiety or depression and is never overwhelmed by the strange adventures of consciousness in the three realms of relativity—mundane form, sublime form and formlessness.

This motherly mind cherishes an attitude of total friendliness and spontaneously self-sacrificing compassion. This mind generates astonishing blessing waves of Great Compassion which stream forth continuously from the bodhisattva, with inconceivable tenderness and transcendent insight, to an infinite expanse of suffering beings. This Mahayana mind that sensitively bears the burdens of all conscious beings also experiences constant sympathetic delight in every virtuous, kind and affectionate action undertaken by any being who aspires, who has aspired or who will aspire. This marvelous mind abides in equanimity and impartiality, because it clearly recognizes that the existential status of all phenomena is transparent, insubstantial, inconceivable.

The supremely precious, jewel-like Prajnaparamita mind, which is the perfect fusion of transcendent insight and compassionate method, is composed of this single adamantine commitment: *I will engage in such universally significant motivation and action that the deceptions of Mara, or primal arrogance, will find no place to take root in any conscious being, or if such temptations do take root, that they will immediately be uprooted again by the power of truth. I will train selflessly and live vigorously and tirelessly for the enlightenment of all beings.*

This is the sublime vow by which bodhisattvas ever advance courageously toward their own true mind.

CONNECTIONLESS AND RELATIONLESS

S UBHUTI: O omniscient Lord, how is the Perfection of Wisdom to be clearly distinguished and thus recognized?

LORD BUDDHA: Its unique distinction is to be without connections or relations of any kind.

SUBHUTI: Is the same connectionless and relationless nature which distinguishes Perfect Wisdom demonstrated as well by all possible structures?

LORD BUDDHA: Of course, Subhuti! All structures and processes of relativity are empty of substantial self-existence, isolated from any conceptual description and therefore possess no connections. The connectionless and relationless nature which distinguishes the noble Prajnaparamita also distinguishes every manifest phenomenon without exception.

SUBHUTI: If all phenomena are free from limiting connections and substantial relations, how can we conceive that various mind streams are polluted and need to be purified? What has no connections cannot be either defiled or purified. What is without substantial relations cannot be either bound or freed. Nor can what is unrelated to any notion of separate identity manifest enlightenment at some particular place or time. Where in sheer connectionlessness can there substantially exist any structure of awareness which has become related to enlightenment or which will someday become related to enlighten-

177

ment? How are we to understand, in the light of Prajnaparamita, the gradual purification, liberation and full awakening of any particular being, much less of all beings? Only you can illumine and clarify this paradox for us, O one who has so beautifully disappeared into truth, O Sugata.

LORD BUDDHA: Consider carefully, Subhuti. Is it not true that conscious beings have indulged from beginningless time in the constant generation and projection of the conventional experiential constructs, *me* and *mine?*

SUBHUTI: Without doubt, O Lord.

LORD BUDDHA: Is it not also true that the pervasive notions *I am me* and *this is mine* are entirely empty of substantial and independent self-existence?

SUBHUTI: Absolutely true, O Lord.

LORD BUDDHA: Finally, Subhuti, is it not precisely because of this fantastic projection of *me-ness* and *my-ness* that conscious beings wander in circles and thus falsely experience Reality as the cyclical realm of birth and death?

SUBHUTI: Precisely, O Lord.

LORD BUDDHA: Only in this context of the conventional projection of selfhood and the delusive sense of personal power and possession are the provisional teachings about defilement and purification relevant. The level of defilement depends upon the level of intensity with which conscious beings project themselves and others as independent entities, as mere things, and upon the intensity with which they attempt to grasp and manipulate selfishly these and other conventionally constructed conceptual and perceptual entities. But there are obviously no separate or substantial entities which arise in the first place and then become defiled by this imaginary process. As the habitual energy of projecting, crystallizing, grasping, routinizing and manipulating is released, consciousness can cease its constant and feverish fabrication of this allegedly substantial and independent *me* and *mine*. Only in this habitual and abstract context of *me-ness* and *my-ness,* both individual and collective, are the teachings of purification relevant. But obviously no separate persons emerge in the first place, who are then gradually purified through awakening to the merely conventional nature of their own constructions. When the mind stream of the aspirant totally accepts and clearly envisions this primal ontological transparency, then this mind stream simply flows as Perfect Wisdom, without any process of purification.

Only in a sharply restricted sense can one propound any teaching about the defilement and purification of conscious beings. The final truth remains that all appearing structures of relativity, including conscious beings, are empty of the slightest substantial self-existence and therefore cannot be contained or even touched by any conventional conceptions or perceptions.

SUBHUTI: Wonderful, O Lord, absolutely wonderful! The bodhisattva who lives and breathes as this all-embracing transparency is the living, breathing Prajnaparamita—no longer just a narrowly focused conscious being but an omnipresent compassionate awareness, fully awake to universal enlightenment, no longer attending to personal form, feeling and consciousness as the essential reality. This diamond being cannot be destroyed, overwhelmed or even slightly distracted from Perfect Wisdom by the entire range of manifestation, including all its high heavenly beings, earthly beings and beings on the subtle planes. Why? Because all manifestation is simply the expression of Perfect Wisdom. This enlightened awareness transcends entirely the mode of existence experienced by naive persons or by immature practitioners, who remain confined within the illusory projections of self-perpetuation, self-control or self-elimination.

Radical is the wayless way of the bodhisattva called Perfect Wisdom. Radical is the subjectless, objectless way of omniscience which resolves instantly the suffering of all living beings. Radical is the unencounterable way of the Tathagatas who disappear into pure presence, who awaken into total awakeness. The bodhisattva who day and night embraces and is embraced by Goddess Prajnaparamita is awake as the all-encompassing wakefulness of Buddhahood.

AWARENESS FULL OF FRIENDLINESS

*L*ORD BUDDHA: O wise Subhuti, visualize now with your powerful mental eye. Billions of conscious beings in the central region of this particular world system suddenly acquire a human mind stream and, even more miraculous, elevate their thought to the longing for universal conscious enlightenment. They sustain this selfless longing for their entire life span, constantly cherishing and serving all lives and fervently revering the Awakened Ones. Contemplate this entire realm of bodhisattvas, O Subhuti, as they express generosity and love toward every living being in existence, dedicating every drop of transferable meritorious energy to universal awakening. How vast a reservoir of merit would be generated?

SUBHUTI: Unimaginably vast, O Lord.

LORD BUDDHA: Surprisingly, Subhuti, a single son or daughter of the Buddha family can generate an even greater reservoir of meritorious energy by spending just one day selflessly studying, copying, chanting, venerating, contemplating, expanding upon or teaching the *Prajnaparamita Sutra*. Remaining immersed—day and night, waking and sleeping—in the active expression of Prajnaparamita, the bodhisattva becomes worthy of the reverence and love of all. Such universal devotion is attracted spontaneously, for this bodhisattva develops an awareness more full of friendliness toward all beings than any other awareness except Buddha awareness. A Buddha's mind has ceased to be a distinct stream of consciousness and, infinite in every sense, cannot be compared to any finite mind in existence, no matter how sublime.

How does the son or daughter of the Buddha family begin to approach the practice of Prajnaparamita? By perceiving with uncompromising insight that living beings are like sacrificial animals being led to slaughter. The intense compassion that arises from such a shocking vision permeates one's entire awareness. With this same uncompromising clarity, the bodhisattva not only envisions the plight of the visible life forms on this planet but also surveys in an instant the implacable existential situation of all conscious beings on all planes of being within all world systems. This act of insightful vision fills the sensitive bodhisattva with unbearable longing for the solace and freedom of all these beloved beings.

The bodhisattva not only accurately visualizes the present situation but also penetrates the future situation, perceiving with crystal clear accuracy how conscious beings develop the negative habitual energy which veils their mind streams from truth, eliminating even the possibility of honestly considering the radical teachings of Prajnaparamita. The bodhisattva perceives vividly as well how beings create or have already created conditions of hellish consciousness on the earthly plane or on subtle planes and how other beings, including even conscious beings in the heavenly spheres, inexorably entangle themselves in nets of false viewpoints.

With unbearable compassion, the bodhisattva observes how even those fortunate beings who have the aspiration and opportunity to seek truth fail to find an authentic guide and how those rare persons who have actually encountered and even entered the spiritual path recklessly or inadvertently wander away from it again. With every fibre of spiritual, moral, mental and physical energy, the bodhisattva concentrates on this terrible spectacle, vowing: *I shall prepare myself to become the liberator of all these beloved beings. Without a single exception, they must be freed from their unbearable suffering and established irreversibly on the way of universal conscious enlightenment.*

But the diamond being who embraces Prajnaparamita does not

substantialize or objectify either this panorama of suffering or this adamantine vow — not attributing independent or substantial self-existence to any phenomenon whatsoever. This attitude springs from the great illumination of Perfect Wisdom, leading the bodhisattva, who is inseparable from all conscious beings, to complete and unspeakable enlightenment. Committed to universal awakening, abiding solely in the light of Perfect Wisdom as they survey sensitively the suffering of all beings, these bodhisattvas become worthy of reverence and love from the entire universe. They are not distracted by even the most lavish outpouring of recognition and praise, nor by rejection or abuse. They purify with the principle of selflessness whatever anyone may offer them, whether humble gifts for daily sustenance or priceless treasures, for they live, think and move only by Perfect Wisdom, and their entire being is focused only upon the supreme evolutionary goal, universal conscious enlightenment.

The bodhisattvas, immersed in the active, daily expression of Prajnaparamita, never receive gifts from devoted friends without blessing all beings by pointing out, verbally or silently, the Perfection of Generosity, which is free from any false notion of separate donor, receiver, gift or process of giving. The presence of the bodhisattvas shines with the light of Perfect Wisdom, illuminating all beings by setting them free from the delusive sense of being born, living and dying as independent, substantial, self-existing entities, by awakening their supreme organ of vision, the eye of transcendent insight. These diamond beings, focusing every strand of their attention through Prajnaparamita alone, work constantly for both the relative and the supreme happiness of all consciousness. They experience no conceptual or perceptual functions which are not infused by the principle of Perfect Wisdom. Day and night they engage in the contemplation, expression and transmission of Prajnaparamita.

O noble Subhuti, suppose a knowledgeable collector acquires a rare gemstone. He will be gratified and elated. If he misplaces this stone, he will become even more distressed than he was previously delighted. He will not, nor can he, cease from thinking about this unique gemstone and deeply regretting its loss until he has recovered it. Just so is the bodhisattva who hears the compassionate teaching of Mother Prajnaparamita but allows this priceless knowledge to become dormant through forgetfulness. Inspired by expert evaluation of how rare and precious the transcendent jewel of Perfect Wisdom really is and inwardly certain that direct access to it is indeed possible, the bodhisattva will vigorously explore, examine and contemplate, tirelessly searching until he or she has directly experienced the teaching and transmission of omniscience constantly emanating from all Buddhas. During the course of this intense search, the bodhisattva will not for a single instant neglect the line of thought conducive to discovering this healing and illuminating gem—the diamond of omniscience, the Perfection of Wisdom.

SUBHUTI: O Lord Buddha who simply is omniscience, you have clearly demonstrated that all structures of relativity, including all possible thought forms, are empty of independent self-existence. How, then, can some bodhisattva become engaged in some line of thought conducive to discovering some object called Perfect Wisdom?

LORD BUDDHA: If the ontologically transparent mind stream of the bodhisattva constantly explores, examines, contemplates and demonstrates this very fact—that all structures, including all forms of thinking and perceiving, are empty of independent self-existence and are removed from any possible characterization or description, because without delineating boundaries—then this bodhisattva is authentically engaged in the line of thought conducive to discovering the omniscient Perfection of Wisdom. This bodhisattva will experience the diamond of Prajnaparamita to be like brilliant open space which never decreases or increases, which is never lost and never found.

YOUR PRAYERFUL REQUEST IS GRANTED

SHAKRA: Most revered Lord Buddha, courageous indeed must be those who gratefully receive your revolutionary teaching, longing only to awaken the entire universe into enlightenment. Why? Because you uncompromisingly reveal that no separate teacher exists in the unthinkable depth of Prajnaparamita and that no separate practitioner listens to the teaching or attains any separate state of enlightenment as a result. These daring aspirants are not shocked or even faintly disturbed by the total absence of any substantial self-existence, nor do they experience the slightest sense of hesitation as they advance along the subjectless, objectless way of Perfect Wisdom.

SUBHUTI: O heavenly king, you praise aspirants who feel no shock or hesitation when presented with the indescribability and unthinkability of Prajnaparamita, but since no structure ever exists independently, who is there to feel shock or hesitation in the first place? And who is there to give or to receive praise?

SHAKRA: The formidable Subhuti always refers unerringly to the emptiness of self-existence and thus never becomes confined by any finite line of reasoning or by any limited sentiment. The magnificent Subhuti moves through the insubstantial veils of conceptions and perceptions like an arrow through the clear blue sky.

O Lord Buddha, under the illuminating guidance of this realized master of Perfect Wisdom, the Elder Subhuti, may I become one who authentically transmits the truth of pure presence, coherently unfolding for countless aspirants the irrefutable and all-transcending logic of your most radical teaching?

LORD BUDDHA: Your prayerful request is granted, noble sovereign. You will realize and transmit Buddha nature precisely as the Elder Subhuti. You will become an authentic guide who can unfold coherently the beautiful, healing and illuminating logic of Prajnaparamita.

Whatever Subhuti says always provides sudden clarification of the inconceivable openness, freedom and bliss that radiate from the absence of substantial self-existence, called *emptiness, pure presence, Buddha nature, omniscience.* Subhuti's insight is so penetrating that he does not apprehend even the principle of Prajnaparamita as separately existing, much less any supposedly separate person who contemplates this principle. Subhuti does not isolate or objectify even the state of enlightenment, much less some independent being who will eventually awaken the entire universe into the glory of full enlightenment. Subhuti does not project even some notion of omniscience, much less the image of an individual person who is somehow approaching the total awakeness of omniscience. Subhuti does not pay attention even to pure presence, much less to some particular Tathagata who has mysteriously disappeared into pure presence. The holy Elder neither holds nor proposes any limited conceptual doctrine whatsoever about Reality, much less does he conceive the independent existence of a practitioner who is employing such doctrine to understand the nature of Reality or to refute limited views of limitless Reality.

Subhuti pays no heed to the paranormal abilities developed by advanced meditators, much less to any supposedly separate person who possesses such abilities. He does not isolate or objectify the marvelous spiritual experiences which are called the grounds for confident certainty, much less any supposedly separate person who possesses such certainty. Subhuti does not thematically represent even Buddha nature, much less various Awakened Ones, who embody and demonstrate Buddha nature. The unthinkably deep realization of

Subhuti is to abide without abode, to dwell where no objective or subjective structures can dwell, without any underlying physical or metaphysical foundation, totally isolated from conventional conceptions, perceptions and descriptions.

This spontaneous and foundationless dwelling in isolation from every abstract world view is of infinitely greater value than any religious teaching or any contemplative experience. Except for the universal enlightenment of the fully Awakened Ones—the Tathagatas, who disappear utterly into pure presence—this dwellingless dwelling of the bodhisattva, whose mind stream flows as Perfect Wisdom alone, surpasses all possible modes of realization. This abodeless abiding is incomparable and transcendent, excellent and sublime. Dwelling as Prajnaparamita far surpasses the calm dwelling of those who practice self-liberation or any form of aloofness from universal suffering. Therefore, O Shakra, the sons and daughters of the Buddha family who long to manifest the complete perfection of their humanity, who long to express the ultimate degree of compassion and insight possible for any conscious being, should dwell in the transparent dwelling of the bodhisattvas who flow as Perfect Wisdom alone.

WHEN LORD BUDDHA SMILES

O NE of the exalted beings from the Thirty-Three Heaven gathers paradise flowers and comes to make an offering to Lord Buddha, the visible embodiment of truth. At this moment, six thousand monks and nuns, assembled for the teaching of Perfect Wisdom in the sublime presence of Awakened Enlightenment, arise from their meditation cushions and wrap their upper robes of saffron so as humbly to bare their right shoulders. Placing right knees upon the sanctified ground, heads slightly inclined, they offer the traditional salute of respect, palms almost together, fingertips lightly touching. Through the concentration power of Lord Buddha, their graceful hands, held at heart level, suddenly fill with the flowers brought by the heavenly visitor. With surprise and jubilation, the practitioners reverently scatter brilliant and fragrant blossoms over the golden body of the Awakened One, repeating this sacred vow: *We will ever practice the astonishing Perfection of Wisdom. We will ever abide in the unsurpassable and abodeless abode of Prajnaparamita.*

Now a rare and precious event occurs. Lord Buddha smiles a total smile. Such is the mystic power of the ones who have fully awakened, that when they manifest a total smile in response to the vows of those who commit themselves to the enlightenment of all beings, variously colored rays of light sparkle like rainbows from the parted Buddha lips and pearl-like Buddha teeth, assuming delicate and harmonious shades of blue, yellow, red, white, crimson, crystal, silver and gold. These rainbows of delight spread swiftly in concentric waves, illuminating the boundless expanse of world systems on the plane of physical being and the Thirty-Three Heaven as well. This smile of light ascends to the highest paradise realm, returns again across vast distances to the shining body of the Buddha, swirls thrice around it and vanishes, just as the beautifully formed lips meet once more.

In response to this display of Buddha delight, the venerable Ananda—the very heart of love—rises from his meditation cushion, wraps upper robe so as humbly to bare his right shoulder, places his blessed right knee upon the ground, gracefully inclines his joined hands toward the embodiment of enlightenment and softly inquires: *O Lord, it is never without an illuminating reason that the Tathagatas manifest their cosmic smile.*

LORD BUDDHA: Beloved Ananda, these six thousand consecrated servants of truth, in a distant future to be known as the New Constellation Aeon, will awaken to full enlightenment and will fruitfully demonstrate truth to countless beings through the root principle of Prajnaparamita. Each one incarnating in a different billion-world system, they will bear the same name, Buddha Avakirnakusuma. They will each accept an equal number of advanced disciples who will receive fully the transmission of Perfect Wisdom. These six thousand Buddhas will manifest subtly in the center of their respective Buddha fields for precisely the same unimaginable period, twenty thousand aeons. During their visible lifetimes, each will unfold extensive scriptures, containing the complete array of eighty-four thousand Dharma teachings. These holy sutras will be carefully studied and consistently practiced by earthly, subtle and heavenly beings in each world system. After these six thousand Buddhas have entered Final Nirvana, the powerful spiritual lineages streaming from each will remain vigorous, transmitting truth for yet another unimaginable period of twenty thousand aeons.

During their archetypal eighty-year span of earthly existence, a fragrant rain of five-colored flower petals will descend, both at the point when they leave their archetypal royal homes to demonstrate the attaining of enlightenment and again at the point when they first turn the wheel of Dharma, demonstrating the Four Noble Truths, the open door to Mother Prajnaparamita. After their archetypal forty years of earthly teaching begins, this brilliant flower rain, which they have just now showered over the figure of Buddha, will accompany them as a miraculous sign wherever they dwell and wherever they instruct and inspire the seekers of truth.

GREAT DISCIPLE
RECEIVES TRANSMISSION

*L*ORD BUDDHA: O blessed Ananda, most blissful disciple of Awakened Enlightenment, I now totally entrust and thoroughly transmit to you the scriptural form and the spiritual energy of Mother Prajnaparamita. This teaching, beyond any expression or explanation, has been clothed in Sanskrit letters, so that over millennia it may be carefully investigated, profoundly contemplated and openly proclaimed to the whole world and not disappear or be neglected for many thousands of years.

Most beloved Ananda, if you who devotedly know my eighty-four thousand teachings by heart should experience the disaster of forgetting some of these voluminous instructions, received directly from Buddha mind, with the exception of the *Prajnaparamita Sutra* — even if the impossible occurred and you discarded all scriptural teachings other than Prajnaparamita, allowing them to become forgotten by humanity — that would not constitute a fundamental offense or disservice to truth. But Ananda, were you to forget, discard or even inadvertently allow humanity to forget or discard a single verse of the *Prajnaparamita Sutra,* or even the smallest part of a verse, that would constitute a fundamental offense against truth and would be displeasing to all Buddhas of the past, present and future.

After assimilating the letters, penetrating the sublime meaning and imbibing the nectar of this scriptural transmission and empowerment, if you or anyone in the Buddha lineage forgets it again, consciously neglects it or even inadvertently allows humanity at large to forget or neglect it, this will amount to a serious break in the intense respect, reverence, devotion and veneration which must flow to Awakened Enlightenment in order to assure the continuity of the wisdom teaching. The Tathagatas, those who have gone entirely beyond conventional views and are awake as pure presence, perennially proclaim and acknowledge Prajnaparamita as mother, creator, native ground and tender wet nurse in omniscience for every past, present and future Awakened One.

With this call for unwavering commitment, I now formally entrust to you, Ananda, this entire body of esoteric lore and its limitless energy, so that the Perfection of Wisdom will not disappear for thousands of years, until the sun of this Buddha's wisdom teaching finally sets.

The *Prajnaparamita Sutra* should be venerated ceremonially, contemplated profoundly, studied intensively, chanted melodiously, written beautifully by hand and expanded liberally by commentary. Pay closest attention, devoted Ananda, to the transcendent meaning of Perfect Wisdom, bearing it constantly in heart and mind, studying it with a sensitive spirit and spreading it with a generous spirit. Whenever any sincere practitioner becomes conversant with Prajnaparamita, this lover of Perfect Wisdom should then begin a painstaking scrutiny of the sacred text—word by word, letter by letter. Why? Because this magnificent Dharma teaching is none other than the truth body of all past, present and future Buddhas and is therefore supremely authoritative.

O sublimely consecrated Ananda, just as you behave toward the one now before you who manifests the principle of Buddhahood—that is, with utmost solicitude, tender affection, inspired respect and total commitment of body, speech and mind—just so should you behave towards the *Prajnaparamita Sutra*, venerating it, contemplating it, studying, chanting, copying by hand and commenting upon it, holding it in the highest respect, reverence and awe. This is the unequivocal way to honor and meditate upon Awakened Enlightenment. To adore

Mother Prajnaparamita is the infallible way to show love, faith, confidence and gratitude to past, present and future Buddhas, all of whom are undifferentiable in essence. Beloved Ananda, as you cherish and never abandon even for a moment this present Buddha, precisely so should you cherish and never abandon even for a moment the *Prajnaparamita Sutra*, not forgetting or neglecting to meditate on every single word of it. With all your devotion, courage and commitment, guard this text and its pristine teaching from distortion and oblivion.

How long could this present Buddha continue to speak to you, Ananda, about the transmission and trust you are now receiving? For one entire cycle of history could this discourse extend—for one hundred such ages, all the way to millions of them. But the essence of this endlessly rich discourse will always be the same. Precisely the way this Buddha is your beloved teacher, friend and guide—precisely the way past, present and future Buddhas are beloved teachers, friends and guides of countless beings in countless universes, including heavenly beings, human beings and beings on intermediary planes—just so is Mother Prajnaparamita the universal teacher, friend and guide.

Therefore, blessed Ananda, with the full energy of a spiritual transmission inconceivable in scope and intensity, the present Buddha now entrusts you with this Perfection of Wisdom, this depth of unthinkability, for the sole purpose and altruistic aim of generating happiness and spiritual fulfillment for the entire range of consciousness. If one longs never to abandon for a moment, even inadvertently, the Buddha who is truth, the Dharma which is the teaching of truth and the Sangha who are the practitioners of truth—if one longs never to abandon the authentic enlightenment of all past, present and future Buddhas—one must never abandon Prajnaparamita. She is the Mother of the Buddhas.

Those who venerate, contemplate, study, chant, copy by hand and expand upon the *Prajnaparamita Sutra*, particularly during an era when the Perfection of Wisdom is neglected, are actually participating in and transmitting the enlightenment of all past, present and future Buddhas. This is because the total awakeness which constitutes Buddhahood shines forth solely from Prajnaparamita and as Prajna-paramita. The infinitely diverse teachings of truth which the humble Lords of Enlightenment dialectically demonstrate and tenderly transmit to all living beings in this beginningless realm of apparent birth and death—all these subtle teachings flow and shine forth solely from the inexhaustible reservoir, treasury and womb of truth energy, Mother Prajnaparamita.

Cherished Ananda, were you to demonstrate the teachings of truth on the narrowly focused level of those who are committed solely to their own escape from ignorance and suffering, and if as a result of your efforts, all the conscious beings in this billion-world system were to attain personal liberation, you would not have fulfilled your sacred responsibility as the direct disciple of a Buddha. You would not have truly turned the wheel of Dharma or demonstrated the universally compassionate and radically insightful way of life. By contrast, if you transmit the spiritual energy of a single verse of *Prajnaparamita* to even one sincere aspirant, who then becomes committed to the enlightenment of all conscious beings, then the Buddhas experience delight, the wheel of Dharma turns and the true life of compassion and wisdom is revealed.

Inconceivably vast is the transferable meritorious energy generated by one bodhisattva who clarifies to just one receptive being a single verse of the *Prajnaparamita Sutra,* expounding Perfect Wisdom intensely during the period from sunrise to sunset, during the morning only, for just an hour or even half an hour, for a minute, a second or even a split second. This luminous gift of Prajnaparamita from one who is consecrated to universal conscious enlightenment surpasses in value and fruitfulness all the good intentions and actions generated throughout beginningless time by every saint or sage who belongs to the way of personal liberation or solitary self-realization.

It is absolutely impossible, Ananda, that the adamantine awareness who bears this unspeakably precious gift of Prajnaparamita, and who at every moment remains profoundly conscious of its value, could ever turn away or become even slightly distracted from the goal of awakening all beloved living beings.

PALACE OF TATHAGATA AKSHOBYA

O N this auspicious occasion, the Awakened One unexpectedly unveils, before the astonished gaze of his entire assembly, the miraculous truth power that streams through him secretly and continuously. In the radiant Buddha assembly are arrayed monks and nuns, lay practitioners, high heavenly beings and many others, including subtle beings of sublime musical skill. Through Buddha power, which is truly miraculous because it relies upon nothing at all, these assembled practitioners suddenly perceive directly and tangibly before them the immeasurable, transmundane Buddha field of Tathagata Akshobya.

This experience is like suddenly perceiving the worlds of a distant constellation in living detail right before one's eyes. The glorious Akshobya is seated with profound dignity in a central palace of dark blue sapphire, surrounded on all sides by intense practitioners in monastic robes, immersed in silent meditation, and by dynamic waves of single and married bodhisattvas who wear an unimaginable diversity of garments, demonstrating truth with eloquent words or simply with the beautiful gesture of their being. This magnificent assembly is vast as an ocean extending to all horizons and as profoundly peaceful as an ocean at its uttermost depths.

194

The diamond beings who surround Tathagata Akshobya are gifted with inconceivable spiritual attributes. All have been victorious over primordial ignorance. With objectivizing tendencies evaporated, their awareness is pristine, not subject to inner impulses or external pressures. Hearts emancipated and infinitely wise, these beings are like spiritual thoroughbreds or like the great wisdom serpents who guard the *Prajnaparamita Sutra* at the bottom of the ocean of knowledge. Their subtle task of selfless purification has been completed. Their burden of apparent self-existence has been laid down forever. Their blissful freedom is accomplished and assured. The conceptual bonds that held them in conventional temporality have been dissolved. Their compassionate minds, illumined by true understanding, have been brought into delicate harmony.

Just as suddenly and unexpectedly, Lord Buddha withdraws this manifestation of his truth power. The dark blue Akshobya Buddha and his brilliant realm, consisting solely of the living jewels of victorious spiritual practitioners, no longer appear before the conscious beings in Shakyamuni Buddha's assembly.

ANANDA: O one who is spontaneously adored by all conscious beings, what is the meaning of this most elusive event?

LORD BUDDHA: Consider carefully, beloved Ananda, what you have just witnessed. Precisely as the structures of Tathagata Akshobya's pure Buddha field do not substantially come within the range of your perception, so it is with all possible structures of relativity—they do not substantially come within the range of any perception or cognition. Their coherent functioning is the miraculous manifestation which relies on nothing. Transparent phenomenal structures cannot approach, perceive or know other transparent phenomenal structures. Why? Because all manifestation is free from any independent self-existence which could be approached, perceived or known. These non-self-existing structures and processes can never substantially act upon or grasp another, because they are by nature neither active nor passive, just as the principle of space cannot be designated as active or passive. The true nature of all beings and events is unthinkable and unformulatable, but they can be likened to imaginary characters in a theatrical drama. Although they appear vividly and act in certain consistent dramatic roles, one cannot actually encounter these characters anywhere. Why? Because they possess no independent self-existence.

By understanding this delicate situation clearly, the person lovingly committed to universal conscious enlightenment naturally and in every moment practices Perfect Wisdom—without reifying, objectifying, classifying or even representing any structures whatsoever. Through this radically simple contemplative awareness alone, the bodhisattva receives intimate training from Mother Prajnaparamita and overflows with the motherly tenderness of Prajnaparamita toward all beings. Those who aspire to the great enlightenment beyond all levels of practice and attainment should train vigorously and merge effortlessly in Perfect Wisdom.

Prajnaparamita has been universally recognized as more advanced than all contemplative practices—as the supreme practice, the most beautiful, delicate, refined, rarefied and exalted practice. Unequaled by any other wisdom teaching, Prajnaparamita is known to bring extensive external benefits and immeasurable inward joy to the whole universe. The Perfection of Wisdom has proved to be a vigilant and powerful mother and protector for helpless beings who are at the mercy of countless delusive forms of awareness. The indescribable practice of Perfect Wisdom has been undertaken and praised by all Buddhas. Goddess Prajnaparamita alone has empowered all Buddhas to manifest and embody Buddha nature.

The Tathagatas, who as a result of the guidance of Perfect Wisdom have disappeared and awakened as pure presence, can lift up and balance a billion-world system on their big toe, without any process of expansion or contraction, and then replace it again, totally undisturbed. But even while nonchalantly demonstrating this miraculous Buddha power which extends beyond any imaginable miracle, since they are masters of Prajnaparamita, it would never occur to these Tathagatas that any independently self-existent world system is lifted up and balanced upon any substantially self-existing big toe or returned to any describably self-existing location.

Thus is the Perfection of Wisdom endowed with impeccability of insight, as well as with countless other inconceivable powers and qualities. Simply because they vigorously train and joyfully play in Perfect Wisdom, have the Buddhas, the humble Lords of Enlightenment, awakened into total freedom from the conventional conceptions of past, future and present. Among all possible modes of contemplation from the beginningless past, the open future and the boundlessly extending present, this radical practice of Prajnaparamita is most beautiful, delicate, refined, rarefied and exalted.

INEXHAUSTIBLE ABUNDANCE

*L*ORD BUDDHA: Prajnaparamita is not limited in any conceivable way and is, by its very nature, absolutely inexhaustible in transforming power and illuminating vision. Prajnaparamita is subject to no restrictions and is confined within no boundaries, final or provisional. Nor can there be any draining away, or even minute diminution over time, of its fecundity and universal applicability. To attribute any circumscribed nature or merely finite energy to Prajnaparamita would be like describing space as being inherently partitioned or as subject to some intrinsic process of diminution or degeneration. Prajnaparamita is limitlessly open, empty of any categorical divisions and inexhaustibly rich in its power to awaken, heal, liberate and enlighten. No Buddha has ever indicated Prajnaparamita to be limited in power or partial in implication, to be confined to a certain period of history or dimension of manifestation. Nor is Perfect Wisdom to be defined by conceptualizations such as *relative* or *absolute*. The number of words contained in this scriptural expression is finite, but Prajnaparamita as a principle is formless, wordless and infinite, generating an astounding variety of sutras, from the length of one hundred thousand verses to the length of the single letter *A*. The Perfection of Wisdom is never limited to any of its verbal or nonverbal expressions. Prajnaparamita is sheer limitlessness.

ANANDA: O most eloquent Lord, why do all the Awakened Ones teach Perfect Wisdom as limitless in this radical way?

LORD BUDDHA: Prajnaparamita is always taught radically, in its limitlessness, because it is impossible to divide or diminish. Perfect Wisdom can never be transmitted as a partial, provisional or conventional doctrine. It is utterly isolated from any conceptual or experiential convention whatsoever. In precisely the same way, every single structure and process of relativity is isolated from any personal interpretation or from any collective definition, no matter how adequate or widely accepted these may be. Nor can this isolatedness itself become subject to any mental or perceptual fixation, to any general or particular definition.

Prajnaparamita is free from every possible circumscription or measurement, precisely because Perfect Wisdom is unthinkability, ungraspability, immeasurability. Awakened Ones from the beginningless past have found their inexhaustible source of strength and illumination in Perfect Wisdom alone. It is a sacred, healing spring that can never run dry. Perfect Wisdom can never cease to be immediately and abundantly available, any more than open space can cease to be spacious. This inherent spaciousness, openness and emptiness of limitation is the inexhaustible abundance of Prajnaparamita, which is not drawn from anywhere and does not flow or collect anywhere.

SHARIPUTRA: O miraculous embodiment of Perfect Wisdom, inspired by the unthinkable depth of your teaching and in order to receive the illuminating power of your response, we cry out again and again: *Inexhaustibly abundant, O Lord, is the Perfection of Wisdom!*

LORD BUDDHA: Prajnaparamita is sheer Reality. It can never be diminished or extinguished, just as empty space can never be collapsed or even slightly compressed. Perfect Wisdom clearly recognizes that no self-existing structures, no manifestations of any kind, have ever been or will ever be substantially generated. Where there is no generation, there is no exhaustion. There is only transparent, harmonious and effortless functioning.

SHARIPUTRA: How can the bodhisattva, committed to the eventual enlightenment of all conscious beings, awaken as the intimate and complete expression of Prajnaparamita?

LORD BUDDHA: This most subtle awakening occurs through remaining at every moment attentive and attuned to the inherent openness and transparency of the various principles of manifestation, such as form and consciousness. The bodhisattva awakens as Prajnaparamita by becoming blissfully free from any obsession with battling or obliterating root ignorance, habitual formations, conventional names, sense experiences, personal consciousness, taking birth or physically degenerating and dying and the pain, grieving and despair commonly associated with them.

Free from regarding as in any way substantial the apparent arising of transparent manifestation and interdependent functioning, the bodhisattva avoids two fundamental misconceptions—that the structures of relativity represent or are rooted in any solid foundation, and the opposite misconception that these manifesting structures are mere illusions, without serious physical and moral implications for every mind stream.

Thus the diamond being clearly envisions and existentially experiences, moment by moment, the entire range of possible manifestation as coherently functional yet ontologically transparent—without substantial generation and therefore without substantial cessation—without original source, present position or final goal. To contemplate interdependent functioning compassionately is precisely what constitutes the bodhisattva, who is joyously seated on the high terrace of enlightenment, surveying the boundless panorama of universal enlightenment. This panorama is the omniscience, or total awakeness, of all the Buddhas.

As adamantine awareness flows onward—inseparable from Perfect Wisdom, free from any sense of generation or extinction—it is impossible for even the most subtle egocentric motive to take root, including concern for self-liberation or any other form of aloofness, retreat or escape from the excruciating suffering of conscious beings. The bodhisattva's only ground of motivation is total awakeness and tender compassion.

Some aspirants may turn from the way of radical spontaneity presented by Mother Prajnaparamita, because they remain obsessed with controlling, battling, repressing or extinguishing the principles of manifestation. They fail to comprehend the sublime ease with which the bodhisattva becomes a blissful expression of Prajnaparamita— simply by regarding all manifestation, in the light of Perfect Wisdom, as absolutely free from substantial generation or extinction. Without developing the consummate contemplative art of the bodhisattva— skillful nonchalance and ceaseless concern—no aspirant can remain authentically and passionately dedicated to the boundless task of universal awakening. The Perfection of Wisdom alone can keep selflessness and love pure and steady under all conditions.

Such is the realization of Perfect Wisdom through the entire body, speech and mind of the bodhisattva, who is free from controlling, battling, repressing or extinguishing any form of manifestation. Such is complete intimacy with Mother Prajnaparamita, which does not thematize, represent or imagine any independently existing structure—either as illusory appearance, as provisional construct or as final reality.

The bodhisattva intimate with Prajnaparamita does not perceive any structure as spatially located or as temporally or eternally fixed. Nor does the bodhisattva crystallize any structure into independent agent or isolated subject. This intimacy and fluid ease is the consummation of Perfect Wisdom, which never anxiously seeks the suppression or extinction of any structure, regarding the entire range of interdependent functioning as ontologically transparent, free from the opacity and conflict inevitable in the conventional experience of separate, independent and substantial entities.

Such is the blissful consummation of realization, which never reifies, objectifies or reviews in any way the principles of manifestation called root ignorance, habitual formations, conventional names, sense experiences, personal consciousness, taking birth or physically degenerating and dying, and the pain, grieving and despair commonly associated with them.

The Awakened Ones do not even consider their magnificent Buddha fields, containing countless beings that shine forth spontaneously as the radiance of the truth body, to be independent, substantial existences. They would never frame an assertion such as *this is my Buddha field* or *that is another Buddha field*. Since Prajnaparamita, Mother of the Buddhas, perceives no independently existing structures of relativity, how could she perceive separately existing Buddhas or Buddha fields? O Shariputra, empty of here or there, this or other, the principle of inseparability constitutes the true universality of Perfect Wisdom.

ASTONISHING LION'S ROAR

*L*ORD BUDDHA: Listen, O noble Shariputra, to how bodhisattvas, tenderly committed to the enlightenment of all, approach their glorious Mother Prajnaparamita. These sons and daughters of the Buddha family approach Perfect Wisdom through noninvolvement in the apparently separate self-existence of any structure whatsoever. They approach by the avenue which enables them to recognize that no functioning structures are essentially separate or separable from one another. They approach through acknowledging and contemplating the most fundamental of all facts: that appearing structures, which are totally interrelational and harmoniously functional, could never possibly arise in the first place as independently or substantially self-existing entities.

These diamond beings, who live and breathe only through commitment to universal conscious enlightenment, approach the Perfection of Wisdom with the existential conviction that every structure which may appear is alike in being essentially unaffected by flux or change, because it is totally without any separate self-existence which could either change or not change. No structure or process, once understood to be spontaneously selfless, gives any hint or offers any trace of the slightest substantiality.

Bodhisattvas joyously approach Prajnaparamita with the clear realization that all talk or investigation concerning principles, laws, states of consciousness or material forms consists only of interaction between various conventional verbal and perceptual systems. These systems function coherently but do not refer to any substantial entities independent from their own grammatical or routinized structuring processes. These verbal and perceptual systems are not derived from any independent, underlying basis, nor do they themselves constitute some form of independent existence.

Bodhisattvas approach Prajnaparamita through the experiential understanding that even the mundane structures which daily language and routinized perception purport to describe or reflect cannot be truly described or reflected, for there are absolutely no independently self-existing entities to be found, even in the sphere of conventional discourse and habitual expectation.

Bodhisattvas approach Prajnaparamita through recognizing that all appearing structures are intrinsically boundless, unframable and uncircumscribable, be they material forms or mental states. Adamantine awareness approaches Perfect Wisdom through acknowledging and contemplating the startling fact that no structures actually manifest any sign of solid self-existence, nor can they be essentially pointed out by any conventional sign. This constant recognition of radiant emptiness is true penetration into the nature of every possible manifestation which may be experienced by any possible living being. Such is the approach to Perfect Wisdom through contemplating the fact that all manifestations are perfectly pure in their intrinsic nature, untouched and untouchable by any verbal descriptions or perceptual constructions.

The various spiritual paths or contemplative methods that purport to control, escape from, renounce or destroy limiting structures are ultimately useless, because no structure has ever been or could ever be substantially encountered, much less stopped or dismantled. The utter and direct simplicity of What Is remains the same everywhere, regardless of whatever structures may appear, for these apparent structures have all, as it were, attained Nirvana—the total illumination, peace and bliss of selflessness.

Those who uphold the radical understanding of universal enlightenment as already present approach Prajnaparamita through the unwavering conviction that the complex structures which appear to be physically or metaphysically substantial never actually come from anywhere, abide anywhere or go anywhere when they disappear. There is nothing substantial to generate these structures, which can therefore be called *birthless* or *creationless*. This characteristic of never having substantiality or independently been brought into being is not merely a metaphor for relativity or relationality. All structures are without any birth, createdness or substantial coming into being. Similarly, relative structures and processes are without any death, destruction or plunging out of being. Thus bodhisattvas never conceptually reify any world or even casually observe themselves or others as independent, self-existing beings.

Prajnaparamita is approached by bodhisattvas with the wonderful conviction that all structures of relativity are, as it were, illumined sages who have fully realized their intrinsic purity and freedom. This conviction envisions phenomena to be like enlightened beings who have put down absolutely all their burdens simply by realizing that no burdens were ever put upon them in the first place.

Prajnaparamita is approached through contemplating the basic fact that appearing structures have no actual localization in space or time, because space, time and locality are just other appearing structures. Thus material forms and mental states, along with all the possible modes of awareness by which they may be perceived and arranged, are without any particular specifiable location, because their essential nature is neither locatable nor isolatable.

Bodhisattvas are continuously exhilarated by the fact that no structures ever actually begin or cease, even though relativity or relationality continues to function harmoniously. This peaceful exhilaration is the cessation of considering structures of any kind to be substantially self-existent. Interdependent manifestation continues to appear as suffering beings, awakening increasingly intense compassion in the wise, loving hearts of the bodhisattvas. In this unique exhilaration, the bodhisattva experiences neither discontent nor complacent contentment. Diamond beings are neither obsessively involved in the play of structures nor dispassionately distant from the evolutionary careers of living beings. In fact, no modes of consciousness ever essentially become either obsessive or dispassionate, because they possess no independent self-existence. This is the adamantine refuge of the bodhisattva—the subjectless, objectless knowing that recognizes the original and present nature of all structures of relativity as unthinkably pure, free from both attachment and nonattachment, untouched by conflict, transparently selfless, blissful and already at peace.

Those who clearly recognize the present fact of universal enlightenment approach Prajnaparamita with the marvelous conviction that all structures, simply as structures, are themselves essentially enlightenment, remaining perfectly transparent to the ineffable, all-embracing and all-transcending insight known as Buddhahood. Bodhisattvas approach the Perfection of Wisdom fearlessly by recognizing that all structures are radiant, empty of opaque self-existence and untouched by extrinsic verbal or perceptual signs, as well as generating no intrinsic signs of their own. All structures are primordially and perpetually free from any self-centered dynamic of obsession or desire.

Bodhisattvas are ceaselessly inspired by the rare conviction that the infinitely diverse structures of relativity, far from being some dangerous disease, are actually a healing medicine. Why? Because in their intrinsically selfless nature, interdependent structures perfectly express the mystery and transmit the spiritual energy of universal friendliness. Not just illumined sages but all structures of relativity are dwellers in the boundlessness which brings about all-embracing love, in the boundlessness which constitutes selfless compassion, in the boundlessness which blossoms as sympathetic rejoicing, in the boundlessness which opens the treasure of blissful equanimity.

Bodhisattvas ceaselessly radiate to all conscious beings the powerful and healing conviction that functioning structures themselves constitute universal enlightenment. Why? Because in the free and open nature of these structures, no substantial faults of any kind can ever possibly arise. This illuminating conviction also recognizes that no structure whatsoever can be intrinsically harmful or discouraging.

One may contemplate the Perfection of Wisdom through the visionary metaphor of an ocean of milk without shores or the brilliant white peak of the mystical Mount Meru, the axis of existence, miraculously streaming with rainbows. One may approach the boundlessness of Perfect Wisdom by contemplating the essential freedom from formal boundaries evinced by any and every form, that is, by contemplating the intrinsic formlessness of forms, the patternlessness of patterns. One may envision the world of mental states and material forms as the ever-expanding field of the sun's rays, composed simply of intense radiance, without internal or external separation or differentiation.

One may meditate on the world of material forms and mental states as pure sound, whose expanding and dispersing resonance has no fixed borders. One may contemplate most radically the apparently limited world of forms as the ultimate expression of Buddhahood—every facet and every function streaming with the excellence and goodness of Buddha's positive energy and transcendent insight. The basic elements termed earth, water, fire, air, space and consciousness can be directly experienced, not as solid limits but as distinct currents in a transparent, indivisible and boundless ocean.

One may contemplate the limitless nature of Perfect Wisdom by envisioning, without any division, the infinitely extensive field of whatever physical and metaphysical structures can appear under all possible conditions. One may approach and assimilate the limitless nature of Perfect Wisdom through boundless, transparent meditation on the boundless, transparent field of all possible structures.

One may also approach Prajnaparamita through contemplating the boundlessness of the marvelous qualities of an enlightened Buddha, the Buddha energy that instantly pervades all universes, which are themselves already simply Buddha nature. Or one may contemplate the innate boundlessness of apparently limited structures themselves— the total emptiness of any substantial or independent self-existence, even in the most mundane context or miniscule detail.

One may approach Prajnaparamita through recognizing the boundlessness of the thinking process as it considers boundlessness. Or one may approach through envisioning the inexhaustibility of compassionate action which such transcendent thoughts inspire.

One may contemplate the measurelessness, unthinkability and indescribability of Perfect Wisdom by considering the measurelessness, unthinkability and indescribability of the entire range of possible structures, planes and dimensions, including even the smallest natural event. Or one may awaken to the presence of Mother Prajnaparamita simply by experiencing these resounding declarations themselves, here and now, as the astonishing lion's roar of a fully awakened Buddha.

One should contemplate the amazing yet simple fact that the all-encompassing Perfection of Wisdom cannot be shaken by counterclaims or by any evidence from outside or beyond itself, for it has no claims or boundaries. One should consider the parallel fact that no structures whatsoever can be subject to internal or external pressures, to claims or counterclaims, for internality and externality are simply non-self-existing structures. Physical and metaphysical structures are like an ocean without shores. What could possibly impinge upon such an ocean from the outside, and what could possibly threaten to divide it from within?

Each and every being or event which can be experienced—small or great, particular or general—is boundaryless like the clear blue sky, like the dazzling rainbow colors of Mount Meru, like interpenetrating rays of light from the sun, like sounds which have no sharp edges, like the frontierless expanse of living worlds and conscious beings, like the supreme wakefulness of the Buddha, like the cumulative kindness and insight of all aspiring beings everywhere, like earth, water, fire, air, space and consciousness manifest as transparent currents in a single ocean.

Material forms and mental states are none other than perpetual awakening into Buddhahood. The intrinsic nature of every appearing form and every mode of consciousness is already and always perfect Buddha nature—the simplicity, directness and totality of universal enlightenment. The bodhisattva vow is simply that all beings become conscious of universal enlightenment, which is the fact that the intrinsic nature of awareness, or life itself, is just Buddha nature—simple, direct, total. Each particular or general structure expresses the boundless freedom of all structures, radiantly empty of circumscribing or confining self-existence. Each structure is inseparable from the intrinsic clarity of the entire process of consciousness, which spontaneously displays the limitless panorama of intentions and actions, beings and events. Not only these transcendent declarations of Goddess Prajnaparamita, but every single mundane structure as well is the lion's roar of Perfect Wisdom—adamantine, courageous, imperturbable.

In all these ways, bodhisattvas are continuously approaching the Perfection of Wisdom—faithfully and fully comprehending it, enthusiastically entering into it, penetrating it with illumined intellect, reflecting upon it with each breath, examining and investigating it through each perception, developing it with ever greater intensity, precision and fullness, pursuing it with the prayerful commitment of the entire body, speech and mind in a manner which is free from the slightest self-deception and free from any attempt to deceive or manipulate others.

Bodhisattvas are therefore free from all conceit which, obviously or subtly, exalts oneself and depreciates others. They are free from even the slightest mental or physical laziness, in every instant actively expressing the illumined energy of compassion by avoiding the false implications of self-existence—including such notions as gain, fame, honor, respect, self-satisfaction or complacency of any kind. Bodhisattvas divest completely from habitual, self-concretizing patterns such as envy, pettiness and vacillation. How? Simply by divesting from the very notion of being a separate individual or even being a bodhisattva.

Approaching the Mother of the Buddhas along any of these avenues with great reverence and delight, it will not be difficult to experience the spontaneous and supreme flowering of goodness, which displays all actual and possible structures of relativity as a harmonious and transparent Buddha field, as a natural expression of the astonishingly beautiful Buddha qualities, foremost among which is tender and loving compassion for all lives.

SUBLIME SAGA OF
SADAPRARUDITA

*L*ORD BUDDHA: A certain practitioner who belongs completely to the quest for enlightenment, Sadaprarudita by name, has persevered in study and practice to such an intense degree that he feels no concern for the beauty, health or even the existence of his own body. He is not instinctively connected with maintaining his life force, much less is he preoccupied with material gain or with the joys of personal honor and good reputation. This aspirant is now led on his contemplative quest into a remote forest, where he remains in solitude, incessantly studying, chanting and prayerfully bearing in mind and heart the glorious *Prajnaparamita Sutra*. Suddenly, a miraculous voice resounds from the empty space around and within Sadaprarudita.

BUDDHA NATURE: Travel toward the eastern dawn of wisdom, O son of the family of Awakened Enlightenment. There you will observe and absorb the consummate demonstration of Prajnaparamita. Pay no attention to bodily weariness during this arduous pilgrimage, nor should you succumb to any sense of mental, emotional or spiritual fatigue. Do not plan how to obtain food or drink, nor discriminate between night and day, nor dress with any attention to heat or cold. Entertain no expectations whatsoever, either concerning outward conditions or inward experiences. Do not glance left or right, nor orient yourself in any of the four geographical directions, nor travel in any spatial or mental direction whatsoever. Renounce even the conceptual and perceptual sensibility of upward and downward, inward and outward.

Do not permit your awareness to be focused through the faintest residual sense of being an independent, substantial self. Do not entertain even a general concept of individuality. Nor should your awareness become enthralled with viewing existence through analytic contemplation as composed of various material forms and modes of consciousness. Anyone whose awareness is fixated or fascinated on this metaphysical level is turned away from the nonperspectival perceiving and modeless knowing of the Awakened Ones, the humble Lords of Enlightenment. When turned away from Buddha perception and Buddha knowledge, awareness wanders in the grossly limited mode of apparent birth and death or in the subtly limited mode of apparent escape from birth and death. Such obviously or subtly constricted awareness cannot flow with the natural freedom of Perfect Wisdom, spontaneously realizing Prajnaparamita to be the very nature of awareness.

SADAPRARUDITA: I shall act precisely as the voice of truth has counseled, because I desire nothing other than to awaken all conscious beings into the light of Perfect Wisdom. Since only a Buddha can do this, I long to awaken into the subjectless, objectless knowing which is Buddhahood.

BUDDHA NATURE: Beautifully spoken, son of the Buddha family. Yet it is possible to approach truth right now. How? Simply by establishing the existential conviction that material and mental structures, even as they continue to appear and function, are empty of the slightest independent self-existence. Guided by this adamantine conviction, observe that no structures generate signs which indicate separateness or substantiality; thus no structures can be connected in any way with limited desires, including even the desire for personal spiritual advancement or self-liberation.

In this manner you should penetrate through any appearances of independent self-existence, as they are simply products of habitual conceptualization. Benignly ignore those religious persons who uphold subtle presuppositions of substantial self-existence; they are simply not good spiritual friends. But it will be fruitful to pay loving and careful attention to good spiritual friends—those adepts who demonstrate truth in every moment and with every movement, teaching both intellectually and intuitively with their body, speech and mind that all manifestations are blissfully and radiantly empty of self-existence, essentially without characteristic marks and free from wishful or fearful projections of every kind. Such good friends demonstrate that structures or processes which have never been produced in the first place never need to be escaped from, suppressed, dismantled or destroyed.

When you embrace this illumined knowing, O Sadaprarudita, you will pass beyond the stage of studying Prajnaparamita from books or listening to Perfect Wisdom expounded by excellent scholars. You will be able to experience the teaching that emanates through diverse human and divine forms directly from the supreme teacher, Prajnaparamita, Mother of the Buddhas. Your gratitude for the scriptures and thankfulness toward your preceptors will become infinite, because at last your devotion will be fully directed to the infinity of Perfect Wisdom. You will then be able to affirm: *This particular spiritual friend now demonstrating truth is none other than Mother Prajnaparamita. My commitment to universal conscious enlightenment is irreversible because no longer based upon any limited human teacher or personal opinion. I am now intimate with all those who have disappeared into Reality, the Tathagatas who have listened directly to the delicate voice of Prajnaparamita. I am now ranging through Buddha fields filled with living Tathagatas and can be reborn only in such Buddha fields.*

With this blessed perception and knowledge, you will experience whoever is authentically expounding the Perfection of Wisdom to be none other than the blissful wisdom teacher, Goddess Prajnaparamita. What greater spiritual opportunity can there be than this? From this point on, you can no longer follow any teacher from the slightest motive of gain—either wealth, honor or religious stature—but only from longing for truth and with an overwhelming respect for truth. Why? Because the teacher is now clearly perceived as none other than living truth.

Sadaprarudita, you must first penetrate, disclose, unmask and release the thoughts and actions of Mara, the force of negation and limitation which may otherwise generate false judgments concerning the teacher you are destined to encounter. Mara will claim that the great bodhisattva is still engaged in honoring and savoring objects of the senses and mind, whereas, in spiritual fact, he will be none other than the voice and energy of Prajnaparamita, using the human form as skillful means of liberative art.

At the ultimate level of contemplative development, when you directly experience the Wisdom Goddess, you will never lose confidence in the human teacher, but will simply reflect: *I cannot fathom the unthinkable depth of liberative skill that flows from Mother Prajnaparamita through the blessed form of my teacher. He concerns himself intensely with finite situations in order to awaken the disciplines of compassion and carefulness in his disciples—in order to encourage them to establish wholesome roots of extensive goodness for the benefit of all future practitioners. Regardless of his ceaseless Buddha activity, while relating freely with every dimension of manifestation, there is no recognition of even an atom of self-existence exists within his expansive heart of Perfect Wisdom.*

Immediately upon receiving this powerful initiatory guidance from Buddha nature, Sadaprarudita faces the mysterious dawn of wisdom, without orienting in any of the four geographical directions. He clearly remembers that the strong feminine voice instructed him not to travel with conventional perception of space or location, nor to indulge in any conceptuality of path or approach. Therefore, Sadaprarudita simply remains standing where he is for seven symbolic days, weeping with uncontainable longing, waiting for truth to reveal precisely where and how to experience the direct, timeless demonstration of the supremely precious Prajnaparamita. Tears stream ceaselessly from his eyes. He pays no attention to any circumscribed phenomenon, thinking neither about food, drink nor even breath. His entire being

is focused in homage to Perfect Wisdom. Just as a father who has
become separated from his beloved child in a deep forest can think
only of the lost child, can search only for it and can taste only the
excruciating sorrow of loss, so Sadaprarudita can now experience
nothing but the most intense longing to encounter Prajnaparamita
directly.

The miraculously emanating golden form of a Tathagata suddenly
appears before the wisdom eye of Sadaprarudita, approving the intensity of his longing with these words.

BUDDHA NATURE: Well done, O noble son of the Buddha family.
The Awakened Ones of the past, while they were still in quest of
enlightenment, approached Prajnaparamita with exactly the same
radical spirit. With this indomitable vigor and determination, commitment and longing, go forward into the mystic east, realm of the
perpetually rising sun of wisdom.

After traveling five hundred miles, you will discover the exalted
city of Gandhavati, which is constructed from the seven precious
substances. The city is a circular mandala containing a mystic square,
twelve miles on each side, surrounded by seven walls, seven moats
and seven rows of royal palms. This brilliant mandala city is dynamic
in nature, manifests complete abundance and remains secure against
any attack from the forces of negation. Gandhavati is the abode of
illumined human beings as well as countless other living beings, both
earthly and subtle. Five hundred shops, containing every kind of
precious creation, are arranged geometrically around this twelve-mile
square as in a richly colored sand painting. These beautiful places of
display and offering are joined internally by transparent, symmetrical
passages, some designed for animal-drawn vehicles, others for palan-
quins and still others for pedestrians; thus the transactional flow of
the city remains balanced and harmonious.

The seven surrounding walls are constructed artfully from the seven
precious substances. Their powerful foundations slope into the golden
river that encircles the sanctuary. Enclosed by these jewel walls grow

miraculous palm trees, also composed of the seven precious substances
—including jade, turquoise, gold and coral. These jewel trees bear
brilliant fruit of living gems. Each tree is joined to the others by an
ornamental rope, interwoven with the seven precious substances, from
which a tapestry of small silver bells is hanging. When moved by the
wind, the seven rows of bells that surround the city produce the
sweetest, most enchanting music, comparable to the sound which
emanates from the miraculous instruments played in the dimension
of the Gandharvas, those subtle beings supremely skilled in melody
and ecstatic song. These waves of heavenly sound cause the citizens
of this mandala city to walk and dance in constant spiritual delight.
The boats on the golden river are brilliant in sunlight or moonlight,
since they are constructed as well from the seven precious substances.
These sailing ships bear to Gandhavati the treasures of joy generated
by the extensive deeds of goodness performed in their previous
lifetimes by its inhabitants.

Seven encircling moats, contained within the seven walls and seven
rows of palms, are filled with clear, flowing water. Some are the
appropriate temperature for bathing, others refreshingly cold for
drinking. The cold water moats brim with blue, pink and white lotus
blossoms. Their banks are luxuriant with countless varieties of fragrant
flowers. There is no beneficent floral species in the billion-world
universe that is not represented in this blessed city of enlightenment,
flourishing somewhere among the five hundred parks contained
within the twelve-mile square center of the mandala. Each park
manifests five hundred lotus ponds, their surrounding gardens filled
with medicinal plants and rare herbs. The lotuses which blossom in
these reflecting pools are the size of cart wheels. More fragrant than
the finest incense, they radiate mystic lights of blue, yellow, red and
white.

The musical calls of geese, cranes and countless species of singing
birds fill the sky above these ornamental parks, which the citizens
do not regard as their personal property but simply as the spontaneous
blessings that flow inevitably from previous thoughts and acts of
radical generosity, selfless compassion and transcendent insight. For

the secret of the manifestation of this miraculous city is that its blissful inhabitants have practiced the Perfection of Wisdom over long periods of incarnation. Their hearts and minds are devoted unwaveringly to Prajnaparamita, guide and matrix of all Buddhas and bodhisattvas. They are concentrated totally on listening to her and truly understanding her, their attention fully and perpetually consecrated with every breath and heartbeat to her most profound teaching.

O noble vessel, Sadaprarudita, listen carefully. Near the center of Gandhavati, where the four principal thoroughfares meet, you will discover the palatial residence of the royal teacher of Perfect Wisdom, the awakened bodhisattva Dharmodgata. A full mile in circumference, utterly resplendent because composed only of the seven precious substances, his beautiful palace, surrounded by walls, palms and moats, is a mirror image of the whole city. Within the inner precincts are four parks for contemplative enjoyment and blissful interaction among the intimate companions of truth, who are inseparable from their radiant teacher.

Each of these inner gardens manifests eight lotus ponds with unique spiritual names and functions. One bank of each pond is gold, the second silver, the third emerald and the fourth diamond. The beds of these transparent pools are composed of natural crystals and covered with sand of pure gold. Each pond has eight entrances, whose steps are constructed with various jewels. These bright blue pools, each of which is an eye of mystic vision, are surrounded by rich green plantain trees. Their shallows blossom with water lilies. The sky above them is filled with singing birds, constantly on the wing. Groves of flowering trees of every beneficent variety grow in the ceremonial gardens which enclose these ponds, and when blown by the wind, brilliant petals of many colors float down to the smooth surface of the water, which emanates the scent of sandalwood.

In the central palace of Perfect Wisdom, the bodhisattva Dharmodgata dwells with great delight among his mystical companions, including sixty-eight thousand wisdom women, fully consecrated to Goddess Prajnaparamita. He dances and plays gracefully through the six dimensions of pure sense pleasure, as do all the inhabitants of this blessed city, both women and men, who live in complete equality and harmony.

The sole responsibility of Dharmodgata is to demonstrate the Perfection of Wisdom. The denizens of this secret earthly Pure Land have built a teaching throne in the absolute center of the mandala city. Its unshakable base is gold, over which is spread a simple cotton mat covered with a fine white woolen blanket, upon which is placed silk brocade and a silk-covered meditation cushion. High above this royal Dharma seat for Mother Prajnaparamita, a white parasol, brilliantly embroidered with pearls, floats gracefully in the bright sunlight. About this sacred throne, where Perfect Wisdom manifests through and as the bodhisattva Dharmodgata, flowers of the five symbolic colors are scattered freely. This Dharma throne of Goddess Prajnaparamita is scented with rare perfumes.

Here, the unthinkably deep purity of heart and diamond clear intention of both teacher and listeners are spontaneously revealed. Every single conscious being who lives in Gandhavati listens to the teaching of Perfect Wisdom with infinite respect for truth, with total confidence in truth, with radiant faith in what alone is worthy of faith, with mind and heart exalted by this supreme faith. Hundreds of thousands of fully attentive beings, not only human but also subtle and heavenly, gather here at the center of the mandala to receive empowerment from the Mother of the Buddhas. Some aspirants receive the initiatory gift of explaining Perfect Wisdom; others are able to repeat the teaching from memory. Some record these eloquent teachings in illuminated manuscripts; others simply focus entirely on listening, understanding and assimilating. None of these beings blessed with full attention to Prajnaparamita can fall into states of depression or limitation, during this life or in any future lifetime. They can only grow in wisdom and swiftly approach the ultimate goal, conscious Buddhahood.

O noble son of the family of enlightenment, now travel east to that sublime teacher, Dharmodgata. Through his transparent body, speech and mind, you will experience Prajnaparamita directly. For a vast period of time, during innumerable incarnations, Dharmodgata has inwardly and secretly been your spiritual friend. He has called you, encouraged you and driven you to seek full enlightenment. He himself, in the distant past, searched with his entire being for the direct encounter with Mother Prajnaparamita, just as you are doing now. Go joyously to him, beloved one. Travel day and night with every breath, placing every strand of your awareness and every heartbeat at the service of this sacred task. Sooner than you can imagine, you will meet the Perfection of Wisdom.

When Sadaprarudita hears these exhilarating words of truth from the Buddha emanation, he becomes indescribably peaceful and at the same time profoundly ecstatic. An experienced warrior, struck by a poison arrow, can only think: *Where will I find the skilled physician to remove this arrow and to prescribe the proper antidote for its poison?* Just so, this bodhisattva, this warrior of truth, can form absolutely no thought other than the ardent longing: *When will I encounter Prajnaparamita through that blessed diamond being who resides in the subtle city of enlightenment? The moment I directly encounter the Mother of the Buddhas, all clinging to the notion of any substantially self-existing base, foundation or limit will instantly disappear.*

Without moving through space, through time or along any conceptual avenue of approach, Sadaprarudita suddenly meets his beloved teacher and ancient friend, Dharmodgata, established on the Dharma throne in the center of the mandala city, clearly and tenderly offering the empowerment of Goddess Prajnaparamita.

TATHAGATAS NEITHER COME NOR GO

*D*HARMODGATA: O worthy vessel, Sadaprarudita, consider carefully. Tathagatas, who disappear into pure presence, cannot be described as coming from anywhere nor as going anywhere. Pure presence, called suchness, does not emigrate, migrate, transmigrate or emanate, and the Tathagatas are simply suchness — utterly wonderful and unimaginable. Universal ontological transparency, although functioning harmoniously, never generates any independent self-existence. It does not come from anywhere nor go anywhere. The Tathagatas are simply this universal transparency, this depth of unthinkability. The coming or going of limitlessness is obviously not possible, and the Tathagatas are the limitlessness of Prajnaparamita. The absence of self-existence, which can be likened to open space, never takes birth or rebirth, and the Tathagatas are simply the absence of self-existence, simply the radiant open space of total awakeness.

Nevertheless, the Awakened Ones are not outside or beyond any appearing structures of relativity. The suchness of all possible structures and the suchness of the Awakened Ones is sheer, inconceivable presence. There is no division within pure presence. There is no multiplication of pure presence. Suchness cannot be enumerated, even with the numeral one.

Travelers in a dry wasteland, overcome by the summer heat at noon, might perceive a mirage floating in the distance and run toward it, imagining: *We shall quench our thirst with that water.* O son of the Buddha family, does such water come from any spring or rainfall? Does it flow into any of the great rivers or oceans of the planet?

SADAPRARUDITA: Beloved teacher, although the mirage is objectively manifest to various observers in interdependence with various conditions, no water exists substantially or independently in that desert. Therefore, how could it have come from somewhere or be flowing anywhere? The thirsty travelers are foolish to construct and project the notion of substantial water from the shimmering appearance of the mirage.

DHARMODGATA: Equally foolish are those practitioners who construct and project the notion of the Awakened Ones as beautiful bodily forms, as tender tones of speech or as substantial self-existences which can arrive and leave, be born and die, appear and disappear. The Tathagatas cannot be identified with any body of mundane or transmundane form. They are the universal body of truth, which is already the true nature of all possible structures of relativity and which never arrives or leaves, is never born and never dies, never appears or disappears.

There is no substantial coming or going of an elephant, horse, chariot or warrior vividly projected by the hypnotic powers of a magician for the entertainment of his audience. Similarly, there is no substantial coming or going of the various beautiful or terrifying forms which the Tathagatas skillfully and compassionately project for the instruction and illumination of all conscious beings. In dream or vision, a practitioner might perceive one Tathagata, three Tathagatas or even the thousand Tathagatas whose successive manifestation constitutes a single aeon. Returning to normal waking awareness, the contemplative would no longer perceive those intensely animated golden bodies of sublime form. O dedicated son of the Buddha family, does this mean that those Tathagatas came from somewhere else or have now gone somewhere else?

SADAPRARUDITA: Revered teacher, the structures which manifest in dream or vision simply do not possess independent, substantial self-existence. They are sourceless and goalless, pathless and abodeless.

DHARMODGATA: Precisely so do the Buddhas teach that all relative experience whatsoever, common or sublime, is like a dream or vision. Mind streams which lack the transcendent insight that clearly perceives the dreamlike nature of all structures imagine the Awakened Ones to be physically and culturally conditioned bodies of mundane form which come and go through birth and death. To presuppose the substantial coming and going of the Tathagatas, who are simply pure presence, is to indulge in the most limited viewpoint. Such persons confine themselves within the delusive six realms of birth and death and alienate themselves from the total awakeness which is Buddhahood. By contrast, those who exercise the transcendent insight that clearly perceives the dreamlike nature of all beings and events are living and breathing as the teaching of the Tathagatas. They do not construct from the shimmering appearance of conventional experience any notion of the coming or going of any structure of relativity, for no such structures are substantially generated, and therefore none are substantially distanced or terminated.

Practitioners of transcendent insight, therefore, clearly know and revere the true nature of the Tathagatas as pure presence, as the play of sheer openness and harmonious functioning. These mature practitioners of Perfect Wisdom are humble disciples of Buddha nature and loving servants of all conscious beings. They are worthy of whatever wealth or honor may be conferred upon them, because they transform every gift and every event into wisdom energy for universal awakening. They are incomparable living gems in the fathomless ocean of Prajnaparamita. They have not originated from the east nor from the west, nor from any of the ten directions, but are miraculously generated within this boundless ocean of Reality by the collective aspiration of conscious beings. These gemlike disciples of Buddha nature manifest within the interdependent suffering of all living beings, formed through the great pressure and intensity of spiritual intention. Nonetheless, these diamond beings cannot be imagined as emerging from a dark mine somewhere or arriving at a bright palace somewhere else.

The manifestation of a Tathagata is never outside the transparent network of causality. Awakened Enlightenment is displayed only through the most subtle cooperation of contemplative practices and their energies, extending over vast expanses of temporality. Yet the universal truth body of pure presence does not exist substantially at some independent location within the ten directions of physical and mental space. Whenever the appropriate contemplative conditions manifest, the universal truth body is unveiled as a graceful Buddha emanation. Without these fruitful conditions, which include clear awareness of pervasive suffering as well as rigorous training in Prajnaparamita, to perceive the truth body intuitively as a Tathagata remains impossible.

When the harp is played skillfully, its tones are not brought into the world from somewhere else; nor when the music finishes, do they go forth from the world to somewhere else; nor while they are resounding, do they exist substantially or independently. Their exquisite beauty is the unveiling of a musical sensibility, which has been carefully trained and which depends as well on complex factors concerning the quality of the instrument and the organ of hearing. Similarly, the beautiful music of Perfect Wisdom depends for its manifestation on the authenticity of its spiritual transmission and the purity of the mind stream which receives the transmission. However, Prajnaparamita does not substantially come forth from the body of mundane or transmundane form, any more than the harp music substantially comes forth from the harp frame or from the fingers of the musician. The total interdependent manifestation and inspired unveiling is the music. Just so, the magnificent wisdom music of all Buddhas manifests through rich and ancient spiritual aspirations and their delicate balance of interdependent conditions. But Perfect Wisdom does not substantially come from somewhere, abide somewhere or go somewhere. Nor do Tathagatas independently come, abide or go. Nor does any structure of relativity come, abide or go. Precisely this transcendent insight opens suddenly into full enlightenment and spontaneously generates the intricacies of liberative art. This music eventually attracts the hearts and awakens the minds of all conscious beings.

When Dharmodgata presents this sublime teaching to Sadaprarudita, clearly demonstrating that Tathagatas neither come, stay nor go, the living planet and the surrounding billion-world universe tremble in all six dimensions with a thunderous resonance of joy. The subtle realms of negativity are exposed to the cleansing radiance of truth. Green grasses and branching trees on all worlds bend and bow miraculously in the direction of the great bodhisattva Dharmodgata. Flowers from every season spring up and blossom simultaneously. From the empty blue sky above the Dharma throne, a vast rain of brilliantly-colored petals descends spontaneously.

Shakra, sovereign of the Thirty-Three Heaven, along with the powerful protector kings of the four spiritual directions, scatters intensely fragrant sandalwood powder and paradise blossoms over Dharmodgata, as they cry out with a single voice, resonant as thunder.

HEAVENLY REALM: Truly spoken, revered master of Prajna-paramita. We have heard clearly, streaming through you, a teaching presented directly and only by Reality – a most radical teaching which runs completely counter to worldly convention, a teaching that gives not even the slightest credence to any presupposition of substantiality or independent individuality, a teaching which has not even subtly capitulated to any sense of separate self-existence or underlying basis.

SADAPRARUDITA: Revered and beloved teacher, what is the meaning of this dramatic and thunderous cosmic demonstration?

DHARMODGATA: Because of your noble quest, which has drawn forth these words of truth, eight thousand aspirants in this assembly have opened the infinitely patient sense that no structures are ever substantially produced. Eighty million aspirants have elevated their hearts and minds into the infinitely loving commitment to universal conscious enlightenment. And sixty-four thousand practitioners have opened the pure eye of transcendent insight, which instantaneously penetrates and clarifies all structures of relativity without exception.

MYSTERIOUS DOORS OF OMNIPERCEPTION

*L*ORD BUDDHA: Directly encountering and assimilating this effortless presentation and perfect demonstration of Prajnaparamita, Sadaprarudita responds with the bodhisattva's omniperception, which does not base itself upon any structure nor which, even in the slightest degree, reflects any structure. The intense quest of this noble human being now blossoms into universal enlightenment, manifesting as various mystic doors. The following are some of the vast, mysterious doors which swing open wide at the mere touch of the bodhisattva's spontaneous, baseless and relationless omniperception.

There is the door which opens as the clear vista of the essenceless essence, the true nature of all possible structures of manifestation. There is the door of liberation from any partial or perspectival perception of this true nature. And there is the door which enters directly into the authentic knowing of this true nature.

There is the door to the indivisible expanse of all structures in their interdependent, transparent and harmonious functioning. And the door for clearly witnessing the intrinsically unchanging and indivisible expanse of all dynamically functioning structures. And the door which opens as the primal illumination that alone permits any perception or cognition in the first place.

There is the door of omniperception which removes obscurity and opacity of every kind from all structures in all their detail. And the door which, when opening, explodes and obliterates any false perception or cognition of material or metaphysical structures as independently self-existing entities. There is the door which, simply by opening, causes all phenomena, beings and events to tremble and to lose the false sense of their own separate, individual groundedness. And the door which opens into the total absence of the apprehension of any structure as substantially self-existing.

There is the mystic door of omniperception which opens into intense fragrances and colors, revealing the expanse of relative structures, or manifestations, as an infinite profusion of flowers. There is the mystic door which opens into the sublimely awakened human body, experienced as the culmination and consummation of all possible manifestation.

There is the door of truth, by passing through which the persistent illusion of substantial self-existence is forever abandoned. The door to experiencing appearing structures as mirror images—crystal clear and coherent, yet without the slightest independent substance. The door to experiencing appearing structures as pure resonance, without any intrinsic location or boundary. The door of total purity, upon passing through which no dirt, stain or pollution of any kind is perceived. The door of total joy, by passing through which the selfless and sympathetic rejoicing among countless conscious beings is ceaselessly experienced. And the door of comprehending and speaking the languages of all living beings as the supreme mastery of liberative art.

There is the door to the wise balance and ease which is free from any sense of doctrinal rigidity. The door to complete immersion in the deep unthinkability and inexpressibility of Buddha nature. The door of complete awakening into the essential expanse, which is without partitions or frontiers. The door to open which is like receiving the full ceremonial visit of a glorious world emperor. And the door of the illumined analysis of the language of all structures into interdependent words and letters with no independent self-existence.

To the omniperception of the bodhisattva there manifests as well the door that opens into all-penetrating insight. And the door which opens beyond all notions of regions, dimensions, levels or spheres. Then the door swings open to limitlessness itself and to the total absence of even the slightest obstacle or obstruction. There is the door of awakening through which one gazes with awe into the limitless expanse of all structures of relativity as into the starry night sky. And the door which opens like a flash of lightning. There is the door into the intimate private chamber of a glorious world emperor. And the mystic door whose very nature is that of a world emperor, free from any possible challenge or rivalry.

There is the door of supreme victory. And the door after passing through which one cannot look away from truth, even for an instant. There is the door which leads to flawless concentration on the true nature of What Is. And the door which is composed simply from intense concentration on this true nature. There is the mystic door of awakening which opens into the sweetest sense of solace and tender consolation. And the door which opens with the magnificent sound of the lion's roar of a fully enlightened Buddha. There is the door which opens to the essential expanse where no circumscribed worlds exist and into which no circumscribed beings could ever be born or reborn. And the door to the undefiled, unprofaned, unsullied expanse which is like an array of lotus blossoms or like a single infinite blossom.

There is the door to the enlightened mood in which hesitation and vacillation of every kind disappears into universal love, generosity and compassion. And the door to the contemplative mood which is attracted only to the quality of supreme excellence. There is the door to the enlightened mood of sublime elevation, never burdened by any notion of substantially self-existing structures. And the door to the spontaneous flowering of all miraculous modes of superknowledge and superaction.

There is the door which opens by instantaneously piercing through all possible structures, or ontologically transparent manifestations, with the pure light of insight. There is the door which, as it opens, places the final seal on the cessation of the notion that structures evolve, devolve or intrinsically transform in any possible manner. There is the door opening into the ocean of wisdom, in which all structures are submerged, losing their false appearance as solid, separate, independently evolving self-existences.

To the omniperception of the bodhisattva swings open the door to the clear witnessing, without the slightest distortion or coloration, of every single phenomenon, being or event which may appear. Then the door swings open which leads beyond the tangled, dangerous jungle of partial perceptions and the selfish actions they generate. Then the door which leads beyond the very notion of darkness or obscuration. Then the door to the emancipation from every limited signal, sign, definition, doctrine or description. There is the door to the awakened mood in which even the slightest trace of laziness or reliance on limits has disappeared. And the door which, simply by opening, shines brilliant light upon the deepest spiritual teaching. The door vast and beautiful as the sacred and luminous Mount Meru. The door whose attraction is absolutely irresistible. And the door which, simply by opening, routes the armies of negativity, in whatever subtle or obvious forms they may appear.

There is the door to the exquisite enlightened mood that experiences not even the slightest inclination to possess treasures in the world of material form, nor to acquire spiritual wealth in the realm of sublime form, nor even to attain any exalted station in the formless realm.

There is the mystic door of omniperception which leads into the brilliance of infinite rays of light. And the door which opens onto the ever-expanding vista of all the Awakened Ones. And, finally, there is the door which opens as the very seeing and knowing of the Awakened Ones themselves.

PART III

PRACTICE

INTRODUCTION

*P*RESENTED here, freely paraphrased, are several short texts of great importance from various Buddhist practice traditions. Such inspired texts are condensations of vast numbers of Sutras and their complex commentarial literature. Designed as sparks to kindle the fire of sub-jectless, objectless knowing, they have remained extremely effective for practitioners throughout history, to this present day.

The first selection is the famous Heart Sutra, which contains in mantra form the essential teaching of the entire Prajnaparamita transmission. The Heart Sutra has been chanted with great loyalty, intensity and transformative power by some fifteen centuries of Bud-dhist practitioners, both in its original Sanskrit as well as in Tibetan, Mongolian, Chinese, Korean, Japanese, Vietnamese and now in English and other Western languages. The chanted text must be linguistically spare. The contemplative expansion of the Heart Sutra presented here attempts to make its deep meaning more clear.

The second selection is a poem of the genre called *mind training*, composed by the Tibetan Lama Tsongkhapa at the beginning of the fifteenth century. This text has also been contemplatively expanded here to bring out its significance in more dramatic form. Tsongkhapa's poem is designed as a memory key, which can open the treasure-house

to the many hours of oral commentary which are traditionally offered
to practitioners on the intensification of universal compassion in the
light of Perfect Wisdom.

The third selection is the ancient poem on Mahamudra sung five
hundred years before Lama Tsongkhapa by the Indian *mahasiddha*
Tilopa to his student Naropa, former headscholar at the Buddhist
university of Nalanda. Mahamudra is the most direct assimilation
of Prajnaparamita. The power of this radical *whispered teaching* later
entered Tibet through the master Marpa and became established
through the yogi Milarepa, whose Songs of Enlightenment are known
throughout the English-speaking world. There is a profound affinity
between the *Prajnaparamita Sutra*, the *whispered teaching* of Mahamudra, carefully preserved today by Tibetan tradition, and the Zen
of China, Japan and Korea. This affinity is not a doctrinal content
but an elusive flavor or fragrance.

This selection of spiritual practices concludes with a contemplation on Dharma, a Refuge Prayer, a Bodhisattva Vow, a prayer to
the spiritual guide and other prayers from Tibetan Buddhist oral tradition, based on the words of the present Dalai Lama. Thus we con-
clude our encounter with the *Prajnaparamita Sutra in 8,000 Lines*
in the mood of prayerful devotion so often invoked by the Sutra and
considered by the bodhisattvas to be essential for the process of intellectual and spiritual assimilation.

Once again, we are reminded that Mahayana Buddhism is not
primarily metaphysical or critical philosophy, nor introspective or
contemplative science, but a revolutionary stream of revealed religion.
Mahayana releases the transformative powers of Mother Prajnaparamita—selfless love and objectless, subjectless knowing—in order to
enlighten even the most instinctive experience of all beloved conscious
beings. Joyfully, moment by moment, may we practice together this
art of liberation!

HEART SUTRA

*T*HE HUMBLE Lord of Enlightenment is seated at the center of his radiant assembly of monks, nuns, single and married practitioners of Perfect Wisdom and celestial beings. Suddenly, Lord Buddha enters the astonishingly profound concentration on Prajnaparamita in which every single structure of relativity shines clearly and distinctly. This particular concentration is known as the Samadhi of Deep Light.

To the right of the golden Buddha, the sublime form of Avalokiteshvara—embodiment of enlightened compassion—now manifests, like a brilliant white cloud shining in the sunlight. Avalokiteshvara is also spontaneously engaged in the profound practice of Prajnaparamita, clearly experiencing the insubstantiality and transparency of the five constituents of personal and communal awareness, including material forms and conscious states.

SHARIPUTRA: O sublime Avalokiteshvara, as I inquire only through the power of Buddha nature, so may you reply through the same transcendent power. How should a son or daughter of the Buddha family proceed in order to study truly and to practice powerfully the unthinkable depth of Perfect Wisdom?

AVALOKITESHVARA: O noble Shariputra, a beloved son or daughter of the wisdom lineage who longs to awaken to the depth of unthinkability should proceed this way. All material forms and all conscious states are to be known as absolutely selfless, without separate identity, luminously pure. The processes of personal awareness do not need to be purified. They are ontologically transparent, or perfectly pure, by their very nature. All the apparently complex forms of functional interdependence remain utterly simple, indivisible, pristine, open and free. Universal transparency is what manifests as both form and consciousness. Material forms are empty of the slightest substantial self-existence, and luminous emptiness of self-existence is precisely what is manifest as material forms. In the same way, conscious states are empty of the slightest independent self-existence, and luminous emptiness of self-existence is precisely what is manifest as conscious states.

O Shariputra, all structures of relativity without exception are empty of inherent self-existence, free from characteristic marks or limits, never created and therefore never destroyed, transparently pure, untouched by any conventional notion of imperfection, never increasing or diminishing.

O Shariputra, in the light of Prajnaparamita, ontological transparency alone reigns, free from substantial material forms and from independently existing conscious states. Interdependency functions harmoniously and unerringly without any need for self-existing form, perception, conception or separate awareness of whatever description—without substantial eyes, ears, nose, tongue, nervous system or mind. The profoundly significant karmic careers of all beloved conscious beings unfold coherently without any need for separate subject or object—without subjective or objective sound, smell, taste or touch and without any substantial subjective or objective structures, either particular or general.

O Shariputra, Reality is never veiled or crystallized by primordial ignorance, and so there is no moment of illumination when veils or constructs are removed and ignorance ceases. There is no time at which total awakeness grows old or dies, and so there is no moment of liberation when the function of aging and dying is overcome. There is no substantial need for the drive to attain liberation, for there is no substantial bondage.

O Shariputra, in precisely this sense, there can be no independent self-existence of what conscious beings conceptually and perceptually project as pervasive suffering. Even the notions developed by contemplative science about the inevitable arising of universal suffering, its ultimate cessation and the spiritual disciplines conducive to its cessation—even these venerable teachings are relative, or conventional. Since there is no separate moment of attaining wisdom, there is no time when Perfect Wisdom has not been attained. The uncompromising light of Prajnaparamita even reveals that there is never any independently existing Perfect Wisdom in the first place.

O Shariputra, bodhisattvas never generate any awareness of intermediate attainment or of reaching some supreme spiritual goal. They abide in abodelessness, standing their ground within the groundlessness of Perfect Wisdom. Their entire sensibility, or mind stream, is free from the slightest obscuration, free from the faintest trace of separate subjects or objects and free as well from the root anxiety that arises inevitably from the instinctive notions of objectivity and subjectivity. These fantastic notions and other false assumptions upon which the conventional world claims to be founded simply evaporate in the blazing light of Prajnaparamita. The entire complex of cyclical sorrow becomes transparent.

O Shariputra, the fully awakened Buddhas of the beginningless past, the open future and the limitless dimensions of the present can manifest the total awakeness of Buddha nature only by birthless birth from Mother Prajnaparamita, womb of Perfect Wisdom.

O Shariputra, listen carefully to these syllabic sounds which contain the entire Perfection of Wisdom, as a vast tree is miraculously contained within a small seed. This is the mantra which awakens every conscious stream into pure presence. This is the mantra of all mantras, the mantra which transmits the principles of incomparability and inconceivability, the mantra which instantly dissipates the apparent darkness of egocentric misery, the mantra which invokes only truth and does not acknowledge the separate self-existence of any falsehood:

> *tadyatha gaté gaté paragaté parasamgaté bodhi swaha* Pure presence is transcending, ever transcending, transcending transcendence, transcending even the transcendence of transcendence. It is total awakeness. It is suchness.

During the pregnant silence which follows this amazing discourse and miraculous mantric transmission of the full power of Perfect Wisdom, Lord Buddha comes forth from his blissful absorption and addresses Avalokiteshvara.

LORD BUDDHA: Beautifully expressed and impeccably transmitted, O sublime celestial bodhisattva. A son or daughter of the Buddha family should enter the unthinkable depth of Prajnaparamita in precisely the way you have indicated.

The voice of Awakened Enlightenment rings out with such perfect clarity that members of this and every other Buddha assembly, as well as conscious beings in all world systems, are plunged immediately into the peace of universal transparency and the ecstasy of universal praise.

TWENTY-SEVEN VERSES ON MIND TRAINING

from Je Tsongkhapa, Great Dharma King of the Three Realms

1. With body, speech and mind fully aligned,
   I prostrate fervently before those rare beings,
   who are victorious over all notions of limitation,
   and before their spiritual daughters and sons.
   May a cosmic celebration of pure poetry,
   perfectly expressing the most subtle teaching
   of these victorious sages and the inheritors of their wisdom,
   now burst forth like an infinite garden in perpetual spring.

2. Gaze calmly with the clear eye of Prajnaparamita
   upon universal manifestation, this beginningless tapestry
   woven from vibrant karmic threads of conscious beings,
   and listen to the harmonious symphony of interdependence.
   Purify entirely from the slightest shadow of negativity
   this boundless expanse of apparent struggle and conflict.
   With diamond-clear intention, instill faith everywhere.
   With mirrorlike wisdom, stabilize all chaotic minds.

3. If shadows of negativity are not dispelled immediately,
   these strange, insubstantial absences of light

gain immense potency with every new action,
until even those who understand the dangers of negation
will not have enough power to choose the way of Clear Light.
Even those who study philosophy and speak eloquently
are unable to release themselves from illusory darkness.

4. The full spectrum of struggling and aspiring humanity,
from immature persons to advanced contemplatives,
suffers the painful delusion of clinging
to these empty shadows, as they become filled
with affective power by egocentric action and intention.

5. This apparent bondage, this clinging to shadows,
is constituted by reactions of pleasure and pain,
obviously or subtly rooted in self-serving motivation.
By those rare beings who have gone beyond,
who throughout all time abide in bliss as Buddhas,
the true nature of reactions and their results
is clearly known to be insubstantial.
But the boundless expanse of self-oriented beings
who bind themselves inexorably to selfish motivation,
therefore cannot liberate or even distance
themselves slightly from egocentricity.

6. We should meditate carefully and thoroughly
upon the inevitably binding nature of negativity,
learning to discriminate sensitively and unerringly
between actions which negate the preciousness of others
and actions which affirm and judiciously care for others.
From this clear viewpoint, renounce all negation
and strive with the total commitment of your being
to become entirely affirmative of all life everywhere.

7. The seeds of action are positive and negative intentions.
Any intention consciously rooted in selfless motivation,

desiring only sheer goodness for all conscious life,
will establish the stable ground of goodness
and will universally generate rich results of goodness.
Any intention even slightly weakened by selfish motivation
undermines both the ground of our life and its fruits.
Intention is the sole creative force of existence.

8. To cling to the intention of triumphing over another,
the desire to prosper at the expense of any being
or to indulge in the slightest bias against any being
because of personal feelings of attraction or repulsion,
these alone are the causes for whatever suffering exists
in personal lives and in the universe as a whole.
We should meditate ceaselessly on this revolutionary truth,
remaining conscious of it during every moment of existence.

9. Those who attempt to deceive with words of advice
that in any way exalt selfishness and depreciate selflessness
become hopelessly lost in narrow-mindedness,
obsessed with their own selfish interests.
Such persons create the only error in the universe,
diverting our precious care and concern for others to ourselves.
This deception not only expresses hatred for Buddha's wisdom
but is the absurd attempt to destroy universal Buddha nature.

10. To avoid decisively this disastrous way of hatred,
bring to birth within your stream of awareness
the maternal mind of totally positive intentions
toward all beings as toward cherished children.
This mind of kindness, supremely skillful in loving care,
unveils the infinite value of every single life,
demonstrating compassion as the meaning of existence.
But the clumsy negative mind, operating blindly
without concern for the preciousness of others,
drains the nectar of meaning from human life.

Cultivate assiduously the selfless love
that transforms every thought and action
into tangible help for conscious beings.

11. The method taught by awakened sages
to develop this skillful mind of kindness
is to cut the root of all selfish projections
by repeatedly and intensively studying Perfect Wisdom,
meditating single pointedly on its essence
in a state of contemplative stillness and stability.
With the clarity and honesty of such concentration,
projected worlds of self-serving desire will melt
in the sunlight of meditation, like structures of ice,
revealing the magnificent secret of our existence,
its total significance and absolute justification,
which is active compassion for all conscious life.

12. Such meditative practice brings to light
the mind which envisions only the well-being of others,
which is constantly grateful to all beloved beings
for the immeasurable kindness they have poured forth
through beginningless time as mothers, fathers,
children, friends, benefactors and teachers.
This mind of goodness knows only the ceaseless longing
to benefit all these blessed beings without exception
in whatever manner and on whatever level imaginable.

13. To remember vividly during every moment
the kindness that has been expressed by all beings,
and to cultivate an intense and constant longing
to return even a small portion of this kindness,
unveils the true significance of life in all worlds.
The person who fails to respond wholeheartedly
to this call for universal kindness and concern
is on a lower plane of development than animals,
who are capable of experiencing immense gratitude.

14. Those who unhesitatingly embrace and tenderly serve
    all suffering creatures during this degenerate age,
    just as a loving mother painstakingly cares
    for even the most wayward of her children,
    they alone are the teachers of the holy life
    who authentically walk the Buddha Way.

15. The mind which faithfully and tirelessly
    serves and elevates conscious beings
    is sheer goodness, constantly giving the gift of itself,
    its faith in ever-expanding goodness, to all other minds,
    thereby benefitting them in the most direct way.
    Of all possible forms of benefit on any level,
    the highest is to teach this practice of love,
    this indomitable faith in universal goodness,
    by the direct transmission of selfless awareness
    flowing transparently from mind to mind
    in accordance with the need and capacity of each mind.
    This is true teaching, tangibly transmitting
    the living energy of universal goodness
    that becomes perpetually active in the recipient,
    even during the most pressing times of crisis,
    never evaporating into mere words or concepts.

16. During this blissful practice, continually cultivating
    the wonderful, ever-expanding mind of goodness,
    even the slightest lack of sympathetic joy disappears
    and awareness becomes more concentrated and selfless,
    while the selfish emotions and conceptual projections
    which compose this narrow conventional world
    are gradually effaced, and we are completely liberated.
    The brilliant sun of Great Compassion shines unobstructed.
    The spirit of wholehearted love in every thought and action
    constitutes the spontaneously radiating sunlight,
    effortlessly melting the mist of egocentricity,
    vastly strengthening our constant efforts for all beings.

17. Beings benefit each other, consciously or unconsciously.
    Even enemies become profound benefactors in subtle ways.
    Those who clearly perceive this radical principle
    find no isolated object for hostile thought.
    They can discover and encounter only friends,
    benefactors and inseparably related beings.
    This insight avoids aggressive thinking
    and allows the mind to expand endlessly
    into wholesomeness, generosity and sympathy.

18. Never offering the slightest encouragement to hostility,
    never hesitating to embrace the concerns of others,
    pay complete attention to every altruistic impulse
    that arises in the stream of pure awareness.
    Contemplate the teaching of selfless compassion,
    calming and clarifying the turbulent flood
    of egocentric mind with the sweetest meditation.
    Renounce the meaninglessness of selfish life.
    Become devoted to the true meaning of existence,
    the spontaneous, active compassion for all lives.
    If one does not refute self-centered motivation,
    the subtle tendencies of the mind can never be free
    from the gross or subtle disposition to negation.

19. Transform the intense activity of daily life
    into the harmonious expression and teaching of truth
    by affectionately reminding and being reminded
    that the bitter dark fruits of negating others
    are poisonous, to be most carefully avoided,
    while the sweet bright fruits of affirming others
    are life-giving, to be thoroughly enjoyed.
    Authentic delight exists only in serving others
    and suffering springs only from harming others

or insensitively ignoring the needs of living beings,
all of whom are as intimately related to us
as our own precious mother and father.

20. So sensitive an ecology is the interdependence of all
    that the slightest attention and assistance to others
    creates moral elevation for ourselves and humanity,
    while the slightest indifference or neglect toward others
    creates moral harm for ourselves and our civilization.
    The faintest spark of ill will toward other beings
    can burst forth into a terrible forest fire,
    consuming vast expanses of sympathetic joy.
    Even the faintest negative reaction or malicious wish
    opens wide channels throughout our entire being
    for life-destroying poisons of negation
    and life-obscuring shadows of self-cherishing.

21. Cast far away from all precious humanity
    these lethal doses, these ominous shadows,
    by cultivating instinctive admiration and love
    for those who practice the way of selflessness.
    Adore such bodhisattvas for their irreversible vow
    to remain intimate with the struggle of living beings
    as beacons of love and as the light of panoramic vision.

22. Once identified with this luminous way of life,
    you will experience every moment as soaked in bliss,
    tasting the delight of compassionate responses
    to even the most negative actions of other beings.
    I have composed this poem of rapturous affection
    further to strengthen the diamond-sharp conviction
    of those already faithful to the path of wisdom.

23. Gazing back over these exuberant verses,
    I perceive an abundant banquet of poetry,
    easy to assimilate and to understand clearly.
    Entirely in accord with the teaching of the sutras
    and with the deep realization of awakened sages,
    these words are full of subtle nourishment.
    To contemplate their various levels of meaning
    is not only to taste the nectar of wisdom
    but is to walk the sublime path of compassion.

24. This surprising poem condenses into a few verses
    the profound and extensive teachings of my lineage.
    I have composed these melodic lines,
    like heavenly wish-fulfilling gems,
    to benefit the minds of all beloved beings.
    Those with strong capacity for meditation in action
    will deepen their insight into the nature of Reality
    by following these words into the heart of Buddha.

25. Some authors tie complex knots of philosophical terms,
    while others rave incoherently like mad persons.
    In the most beautiful hermitage, the snow mountains of Tibet,
    this poet, known as Ever-Expanding Mind of Goodness,
    has attempted to write with richness and lucidity.

26. May the bliss of the mystical fusion
    of transcendent wisdom with tender compassion
    fall like sweet summer rain from dark blue clouds,
    the motivation of goodness, skillfully and gracefully
    opened by lightning flashes of selfless awareness.
    May conscious beings in every realm and condition
    enjoy their glorious existence as the dynamic play
    of Lord Buddha's four modes of manifestation:
    transparent, universal, heavenly and earthly.

27. Having become, through the medium of this poem,
    the powerful and eloquent speech of Divine Manjushri,
    speaking directly with the harmonious and melodious
    voice of the transcendent Wisdom Deity,
    may I and all my relations and companions,
    from small insects to tenth-level bodhisattvas,
    attain the blessings of primordial Buddha nature:
    infinite bliss, infinite fulfillment, infinite perfection
    and universal conscious enlightenment.

TILOPA'S SONG TO NAROPA

Mahamudra, the royal way, is free
from every word and sacred symbol.
For you alone, beloved Naropa,
this wonderful song springs forth from Tilopa
as spontaneous friendship that never ends.

The completely open nature
of all dimensions and events
is a rainbow always occurring
yet never grasped.
The way of Mahamudra
creates no closure.
No strenuous mental effort
can encounter this wide open way.
The effortless freedom of awareness
moves naturally along it.

As space is always freshly appearing
and never filled,
so the mind is without limits
and ever aware.
Gazing with sheer awareness

into sheer awareness,
habitual, abstract structures melt
into the fruitful springtime of Buddhahood.

White clouds that drift through blue sky,
changing shape constantly,
have no root, no foundation, no dwelling;
nor do changing patterns of thought
that float through the sky of mind.
When the formless expanse of awareness
comes clearly into view,
obsession with thought forms
ceases easily and naturally.

As within the openness of universal space
shapes and colors are spontaneously forming,
although space has no color or form,
so within the expanse of awareness
realms, relations and values are arising,
although awareness possesses
no positive or negative characteristics.

As the darkness of night,
even were it to last a thousand years,
could not conceal the rising sun,
so countless ages of conflict and suffering
cannot conceal the innate radiance of Mind.

Although philosophers explain
the transparent openness of appearances
as empty of permanent characteristics
and completely indeterminable,
this universal indeterminacy
can itself never be determined.

Although sages report
the nature of awareness to be luminosity,
this limitless radiance cannot be contained
within any language or sacramental system.
Although the very essence of Mind
is to be void of either subjects or objects,
it tenderly embraces all life within its womb.

To realize this inexpressible truth,
do not manipulate mind or body
but simply open into transparency
with relaxed, natural grace—
intellect at ease in silence,
limbs at rest in stillness
like hollow bamboos.
Neither breathing in nor breathing out
with the breath of habitual thinking,
allow the mind to be at peace
in brilliant wakefulness.

This is the royal wealth of Mahamudra,
no common coin of any realm.
Beloved Naropa, this treasure of Buddhahood
belongs to you and to all beings.

Obsessive use of meditative disciplines
or perennial study of scripture and philosophy
will never bring forth this wonderful realization,
this truth which is natural to awareness,
because the mind that desperately desires
to reach another realm or level of experience
inadvertently ignores the basic light
that constitutes all experience.

The one who fabricates
any division in consciousness
betrays the friendship of Mahamudra.
Cease all activity that separates,
abandon even the desire to be free from desires
and allow the thinking process to rise and fall
smoothly as waves on a shoreless ocean.

The one who never dwells in abstraction
and whose only principle
is never to divide or separate
upholds the trust of Mahamudra.

The one who abandons
craving for authority and definition,
and never becomes one-sided
in argument or understanding,
alone perceives the authentic meaning
hidden in the ancient scriptures.

In the blissful embrace of Mahamudra,
negative viewpoints and their instincts
are burned without remainder, like camphor.
Through the open door of Mahamudra,
the deluded state of self-imprisonment
is easily left behind forever.
Mahamudra is the torch of supreme liberty
shining forth through all conscious beings.

Those beings constituted by awareness
who try to ignore, reject or grasp awareness
inflict sorrow and confusion upon themselves
like those who are insane.

To be awakened from this madness,
cultivate the gracious friendship
of a sublime sage of Mahamudra,
who may appear to the world as mad.
When the limited mind
enters blessed companionship
with limitless Mind,
indescribable freedom dawns.

Selfish or limited motivations
create the illusory sense of imprisonment
and scatter seeds of further delusion.
Even genuine religious teaching
can generate narrowness of vision.
Trust only the approach
that is utterly vast and profound.

The noble way of Mahamudra
never engages in the drama
of imprisonment and release.
The sage of Mahamudra
has absolutely no distractions,
because no war against distractions
has ever been declared.
This nobility and gentleness alone,
this nonviolence of thought and action,
is the traceless path of all Buddhas.
To walk this all-embracing way
is the bliss of Buddhahood.

Phenomena on every plane of being
are constantly arising and disappearing.
Thus they are forever fresh,
always new and inexhaustible.

Like dreams without solid substance,
they can never become rigid or binding.
The universe exists in a deep, elusive way
that can never be grasped or frozen.
Why feel obsessive desire or hatred for it,
thereby creating illusory bonds?

Renounce arbitrary, habitual views.
Go forth courageously to meditate
in the real mountain wilderness,
the wide open Mahamudra.
Transcend boundaries of kinship
by embracing all living beings
as one family of consciousness.
Remain without any compulsion
in the landscape of natural freedom:
spontaneous, generous, joyful.
When you receive the crown of Mahamudra,
all sense of rank or attainment
will quietly disappear.

Cut the root of the vine that chokes the tree,
and its clinging tendrils wither away entirely.
Sever the conventionally grasping mind,
and all bondage and desperation dissolve.

The illumination from an oil lamp
lights the room instantly,
even if it has been dark for aeons.
Mind is boundless radiance.
How can the slightest darkness remain
in the room of daily perception?
But one who clings to mental processes
cannot awaken to the radiance of Mind.

Strenuously seeking truth
by investigation and concentration,
one will never appreciate
the unthinkable simplicity and bliss
that abide at the core.
To uncover this fertile ground,
cut through the roots of complexity
with the sharp gaze of naked awareness,
remaining entirely at peace,
transparent and content.

You need not expend great effort
nor store up extensive spiritual power.
Remain in the flow of sheer awareness.
Mahamudra neither accepts nor rejects
any current of energy, internal or external.

Since the ground consciousness
is never born into any realm of being,
nothing can add to or subtract from it.
Nothing can obstruct or stain it.
When awareness rests here,
the appearance of division and conflict
disappears into original reality.
The twin emotions of anxiety and arrogance
vanish into the void from which they came.

Supreme knowing knows
no separate subject or object.
Supreme action acts resourcefully
without any array of instruments.
Supreme attainment attains the goal
without past, future or present.

The dedicated practitioner
experiences the spiritual way
as a turbulent mountain stream,
tumbling dangerously among boulders.
When maturity is reached,
the river flows smoothly and patiently
with the powerful sweep of the Ganges.
Emptying into the ocean of Mahamudra,
the water becomes ever-expanding light
that pours into great Clear Light —
without direction, destination,
division, distinction or description.

CONTEMPLATION ON DHARMA

PROFOUND salutations to the glorious primordial Buddha, the supremely subtle fundamental innate Mind of Clear Light.

Not identifying with any of the marvels which may appear during this or future lifetimes, as if such were the essence, and surrounded by the countless conscious beings of the six transmigratory patterns sympathetically visualized in human form, foremost among them my parents of this lifetime, I completely renounce any motivation to seek relief, pleasure, peace, happiness, fulfillment, liberation or enlightenment for myself alone but seek it for all these beloved beings.

I contemplate with uncompromising clarity the impermanence of conventional existence, the inevitability and unpredictability of physical death, and the nature of *samsara* which is the intense suffering, both obvious and subtle, of limited forms of consciousness on the six planes and within the three worlds. I gratefully acknowledge that all these conscious beings, throughout beginningless time, have showered great kindness upon me like mothers.

I contemplate the healing, liberating and enlightening power of taking refuge in truth as Buddha, Dharma and Sangha—as total awakeness, as the Sutra of Perfect Wisdom and as the limitless community of bodhisattvas.

I contemplate the transparent functioning of the universal principle of moral cause and effect that generates karmic balance throughout every detail of existence.

I contemplate the extreme rarity of attaining this precious human incarnation, as well as the amazing good fortune to have received authentic initiation into Dharma and the even greater fortune to have the capability and the leisure to practice sincerely the disciplines of Dharma.

I now generate, with as much intensity as possible, the vast motivation to be liberated entirely from conventional consciousness, from false self-existence, because of a deep sense of personal responsibility to free all mother sentient beings from suffering and to awaken them into the great bliss which is the essential nature of awareness.

REFUGE PRAYER AND
BODHISATTVA VOW

*T*HROUGH this sublimely transformed Buddha body, Buddha speech, Buddha mind, Buddha pristine consciousness and Buddha bliss, I go for refuge again and again to all the glorious Guru-Lamas, Tantric Deities, Buddhas, enlightened Teachings, enlightened Spiritual Communities and fierce Dharma Protectors with wisdom-eye open, all of them undifferentiable in essence, so that through living beings everywhere, the supremely subtle fundamental innate Mind of Clear Light as universal conscious Buddhahood may shine.

I now fervently renew the Bodhisattva Vow, equalizing and exchanging myself with all other conscious beings, vowing to become fully enlightened, solely in order to offer the supremely powerful help to others. Abandoning all obvious and subtle assumptions of independently or substantially existing *I-ness* and *my-ness,* I will liberate all those not yet liberated from conceptual obstructions to attaining the total awakeness of Buddhahood. I will release all those not yet released from the afflictive emotions of cyclic existence. I will relieve all those not yet relieved from the three terrible lower transmigrations. I will tenderly care for all the needs of all mother beings on all planes of being. I will strive ceaselessly to establish all living beings consciously in the Final Nirvana of Buddha nature.

CULTIVATING UNIVERSAL LOVE AND SYMPATHETIC JOY

I NOW intensely cultivate universal love, wishing for all conscious beings only true happiness, fulfillment, peace and freedom from suffering. I experience great ecstatic joy at the very thought of conscious beings abiding forever in equanimity and bliss, free from every obvious fear and subtle anxiety. As universal love increases in this mind stream, harmful forces cannot affect me, and I become a protector of living beings.

I sympathetically rejoice in the inconceivably vast oceans of good actions performed by conscious beings since beginningless time, particularly those actions generating the life-giving rain of Theravada, Mahayana and Vajrayana—manifested skillfully in accord with the varying capacities of conscious beings. I deeply rejoice in all authentic religious and moral teachings which have elevated any person into selfless love. I rejoice as well in all kind actions performed by or for even the least evolved sentient being. I remember constantly that all societies and relationships, in order to be fruitful, can be based upon and sustained by loving-kindness alone.

PRAYER TO THE GURU-LAMA

*P*PROSTRATE repeatedly, with as many bodies as there are cells in my body, at the lotus feet of the Guru-Lama, perceived as the principle of three Buddha bodies: the formless truth body of Great Bliss, primordially free from the slightest dualistic elaboration; the subtle form body, manifesting in various Pure Lands above the heavenly realms; and the vast dance of emanation bodies, taking various forms, mundane and supramundane, in the countless oceans of realms where transmigrators travel and evolve. I clearly know these three Buddha bodies to be undifferentiable in essence.

The Guru-Lama consciously embodies all glorious Guru-Lamas, all meditation deities, all Buddhas with their teachings and their communities, all Dharma Protectors. I now offer to my precious Guru-Lama the entire universe, purified and transformed into sanctity, as a jeweled mandala. This mandala of selfless offering includes the body, speech, mind, pristine consciousness and bliss of myself and all other living beings. This mandala includes all the merit from compassionate action and from the wisdom of discerning selflessness that has been accumulated since beginningless time and that will be accumulated in the open future.

Perceiving this entire mandala to be your own resplendent play as the one fundamental innate Mind of Clear Light, O beloved Guru-Lama, please accept my offering through your great compassion. Please bless and transform me, along with all sentient beings, into the conscious state of glory and magnificence.

You are Divine Avalokiteshvara,
infinite treasure of compassion
not touched by any sense of self-existence.
You are Divine Manjushri,
master of flawless, mirror-like wisdom.
You are Divine Vajrapani,
diamond transformer of all negative energy.
All-holy Guru-Lama Tsongkhapa,
crown jewel of the sages of the Land of Snow,
all-kind Lobsang Dragpa,
Ever-Expanding Mind of Goodness,
we place our spiritual aspirations
and those of all mother beings
at your lotus feet.

CLOSING PRAYER

*T*HE SUPREMELY subtle fundamental innate Mind of Clear Light is all goodness. It has no beginning or end. It constantly emanates the dance of compassion and wisdom, performed by oceans of Awakened Ones and their daughters and sons who pervade innumerable dimensions. May I ripen limitless numbers of transmigrators in this profound realization.

Abiding in the primordial peace of the natural purity of all phenomena, a fortunate one am I who seeks Great Bliss. May I be a vessel for the nectar of Secret Mantra—to help all beings, in all worlds, in all ways.

INDEX

Quest Books
encourages open-minded inquiry into
world religions, philosophy, science, and the arts
in order to understand the wisdom of the ages,
respect the unity of all life, and help people explore
individual spiritual self-transformation.

Its publications are generously supported by
The Kern Foundation,
a trust committed to Theosophical education.

Quest Books is the imprint of
the Theosophical Publishing House,
a division of the Theosophical Society in America.
For information about programs, literature,
on-line study, membership benefits, and international centers,
see www.theosophical.org
or call 800-669-1571 or (outside the U.S.) 630-668-1571.

Related Quest Titles

The Lost Teachings of Lama Govinda,
edited by Richard Powers

Mother of the Universe, by Lex Hixon

The Opening of the Wisdom-Eye,
by the Fourteenth Dalai Lama

To order books or a complete Quest catalog,
call 800-669-9425 or (outside the U.S.) 630-665-0130.